Soul Work

Participants

Dianne E. Arakawa

Wayne Arnason

José Ballester

George Kimmich Beach

Marjorie Bowens-Wheatley

Susan Suchocki Brown

John Buehrens

James Cone

Danielle Di Bona

Robette Dias

Elizabeth Ellis

Anita Farber-Robertson

William Gardiner

Melvin Hoover

Patricia Jimenez

Nancy Palmer Jones

William R. Jones

Susan Leslie

Victor Lee Lewis

Rosemary Bray McNatt

Peter Morales

Fred Muir

Kenneth Olliff

Rebecca Parker

Paul Rasor

Tracey Robinson-Harris

Thomas R. Schade

Gary E. Smith

Leon E. Spencer

Thandeka

George Tinker

JoEllen Willis

Soul Work

Anti-racist Theologies in Dialogue

EDITED BY
Marjorie Bowens-Wheatley
AND
Nancy Palmer Jones

Skinner House Books
Boston

Printed in Canada.

Cover design by Kathryn Sky-Peck
Text design by WordCrafters

ISBN 1-55896-445-2

Library of Congress Cataloging-in-Publication Data

Soul work : anti-racist theologies in dialogue / edited by Marjorie Bowens-Wheatley and Nancy Palmer Jones.
    p. cm.
    Includes bibliographical references.
    ISBN 1-55896-445-2 (alk. paper)
    1. Racism—Religious aspects—Unitarian Universalist Association—Congresses. 2. Multiculturalism—Religious aspects—Unitarian Universalist Association—Congresses. 3. Unitarian Universalist Association—Doctrines—Congresses. I. Bowens-Wheatley, Marjorie. II. Jones, Nancy Palmer. III. Unitarian Universalist Association.

BX9841.3 .S68 2002
261.8'348'00973—dc21
                                                        20002040869

10 9 8 7 6 5 4 3 2 1
05 04 03 02

We gratefully acknowledge the use of the following material:

"Say Yes Quickly," ghazal 2933 in *Open Secret: Versions of Rumi* by Jelaluddin Rumi. Translated by A. J. Arberry and Coleman Barks (Threshold Books, 1984), p. 69. Reprinted by permission of Coleman Barks.

Quotation by Gloria Anzaldera on p. 49 copyright 1994. From *Barrios and Borderlands: Cultures of Latinos and Latinas in the United States,* edited by Denis L. Heyck. Reproduced by permission of Routledge, Inc., part of the Taylor & Francis Group.

"A Litany for Survival," from *The Black Unicorn* by Audre Lorde. Copyright © 1978 by Audre Lorde. Used by permission of W. W. Norton & Company, Inc.

Contents

᪣

Foreword

~

As a religious people, Unitarian Universalists in America have a mixed record in dealing with what some have called "America's original sin"—racism and slavery. The early Puritans, from whom we descend, came to America to set up a moral commonwealth as a "city on a hill," a quasi-biblical model in which Native Americans played the part of Canaanites in the Promised Land, and were therefore subject to outright genocide.

Dr. Benjamin Rush, a signer of the Declaration of Independence, may have advocated the abolition of slavery on religious grounds connected to his Universalism, and the oldest Universalist church in America (in Gloucester, Massachusetts) may have had a man of color among its charter members. But in the 1920s, at least one Universalist church, in Medford, Massachusetts, was openly allied with the Ku Klux Klan!

Early Unitarians like Abigail and John Adams considered slavery a sin that would bring judgment on the new United States. So did their friend and fellow Unitarian Thomas Jefferson, who in pondering the subject said that he "trembled" to think that God is just. Yet his trembling did not inspire him to free his own slaves—even when he died.

The early abolitionist movement found important leaders in Unitarian ministers like Samuel May and Theodore Parker. The latter kept a gun in his desk in case he had to protect any of the freed slaves in his flock from the Fugitive Slave Law. Emerson wrote of that law, "I will not obey it, by God!" The Underground Railroad had many Unitarian supporters, like Susan B. Anthony and her family. Yet when the Constitution was to be amended to give former slaves—but not yet women—the vote, Anthony opposed the step.

When the Native American tribes were assigned to various religious denominations during the Grant administration, the

Unitarians were given the Colorado Utes. Rev. Jabez Trask, a young Harvard-trained minister, was sent as their "superintendent" to set up churches and schools, teach agriculture, and establish trade. Trask had the good sense to see that the Utes were doing just fine with their traditional hunting and fishing. He left all the government money that he was provided on deposit in Denver to earn interest to pay for scholarships for those Utes who might one day want some schooling. He settled down to learn from the Utes— until he was relieved, as he put it, "for doing my job too well."

Yet official policies of cultural genocide against Native peoples were actively promoted by Unitarian leaders like American Unitarian Association President Samuel A. Eliot and AUA Moderator William Howard Taft. Before becoming U.S. President, Taft had carried "the white man's burden" as governor-general of the Philippines. And Sam Eliot had no use for a Jamaican like Rev. Ethelred Brown in the Unitarian ministry.

During the Civil Rights movement of the 1950s and 1960s, Unitarians and Universalists had some noble moments. In 1965, in Selma, Alabama, it may have been the death of a young African American, Jimmie Lee Jackson, that brought Rev. Dr. Martin Luther King Jr. to focus a campaign for voting rights on that city. But it was the beating death of the white Unitarian minister Rev. James Reeb that caught the attention of the nation and provoked President Johnson to say "We *shall* overcome" to the Congress and to the whole nation in pushing forward the Voting Rights Act of that year.

Yet by 1968 and 1969 the Unitarian Universalist General Assemblies were full of rancorous division between advocates of integration (Black and White Action or BAWA) and advocates of black empowerment (Black Affairs Council or BAC). The latter had persuaded the Assembly to give it a million dollars for "empowerment" projects. In retrospect, I sometimes see these as competing strategies for maintaining a sense of white liberal innocence— one involved pretending to be color-blind, the other involved paying reparations. Similar things were happening throughout the culture.

So it was in the twenty years that followed. During the 1970s—which pundits in white America dubbed the "Me Decade"—and during the Reagan years, there were only scattered efforts in Unitarian Universalism to re-engage with issues of racial justice. A network of urban church activists helped.

Finally, during his second term, UUA President William Schulz (1989–1993), along with staff and volunteers, began to seriously consider issues of racial diversity in the Association. A broad task force soon came to the sound conclusion that only through real work for racial justice on the part of its white and privileged members could Unitarian Universalism regain the trust of people of color.

During my own tenure as UUA president (1993–2001), several further steps were taken on what became known as the Unitarian Universalist "Journey Toward Wholeness." First, the journey came to be seen as not just an institutional or political process, but as one of spiritual transformation. Second, it came to be seen as more than just a black-white issue. Third, despite periodic murmurings in the ranks, the leadership of the Association became broadly and deeply committed to this Journey—to this process of transformation toward becoming a more consciously anti-racist, multicultural religious movement. Fourth, it became clear that deeper theological reflection would be essential to continued progress on the journey.

The present volume emerges from a consultation I chaired and its editor convened, in late January of 2001. A number of people who were invited were not able to be present, as inevitably happens, but the participants included a broad range of Unitarian Universalist theologians, ministers, educators, and activists as well as two distinguished guests, Professor Cone and Professor Tinker.

In June of 2001, the UUA held its General Assembly in Cleveland, Ohio, the same city where the General Assembly of 1968 had been so rancorous on matters of race. This time, what seemed to emerge, as the Association marked its fortieth birthday, was a more mature sense of calling—to be what Rev. Dr. James Forbes, in his Ware Lecture, called "human race activists." At the same General Assembly, the Unitarian Universalist Association also overwhelmingly elected an African American, Rev. William G. Sinkford, as its new president.

These papers and responses are offered as spiritual resources for the next steps on the "Journey Toward Wholeness." May they be received with clear communication and mutual forbearance, with honesty and with courage.

John Buehrens

Introduction

∽

Individual Unitarian Universalists and some Unitarian Universalist congregations have been engaged in *racial justice* work for decades, but only since the 1992 General Assembly resolution entitled "Racial and Cultural Diversity in Unitarian Universalism" has the Unitarian Universalist Association (UUA) made a sustained effort to address racism as a systemic issue. Racism was raised as a theological issue in the 1996 report to the General Assembly entitled *Journey Toward Wholeness—The Next Step: From Racial and Cultural Diversity to Anti-Oppression and Anti-Racist Multiculturalism.* Following the 1997 General Assembly's adoption of the resolution, "Toward an Anti-Racist Unitarian Universalist Association," the Association began to play a decisive role in work that was intentionally focused on *anti-racism*—not only as an institutional and structural issue, but also as a spiritual issue. In the ensuing years, as leaders and participants continued ever-deeper engagement in the work, it became clear that the spiritual dimension of anti-racism is of critical importance.

So why theology? Because, as part of the spiritual quest, theological reflection helps us to test our beliefs, assumptions, and religious values in relation to the experiences and viewpoints of others. Are racism and violence, for example, social constructions or aspects of human nature? What is our epistemology? In other words, how can we respond with certainty or proclaim "the truth" about racism when we live in a pluralistic world? How do we know what we know (or think we know) about racism, about social systems, about injustice in the world when our social location may not mirror the worldview or experience of one whose social context is quite different? How can we respond with certainty or proclaim "the truth" about racism when we live in a pluralistic world where racism manifests itself in radically different ways? These are cutting edge theological questions that participants begin to engage. Through theological reflection, social engagement, and discourse with others, our perspectives deepen, and sometimes change how we respond. Our spiritual yearnings are not fully coherent without such theological engagement and subsequent integration into our lives. This is part of what faith development means—in light of new information, we are called to reconsider everything we "know," everything we have put our faith and trust in.

Seeking to continue deepening our work, and to include a broader range of voices in its theological reflections on racism, in January 2001, the Unitarian Universalist Association convened a three-day invitational consultation on theology and anti-racism at UUA headquarters in Boston. This book represents the proceeds of that event. In the following pages, the authors and their dialogue partners—approximately thirty scholars, ministers, theologians, seminarians, teachers, and activists—address some of the most pressing issues of our time.

The authors and participants address a complex dynamic of critical issues and concepts that have often not been part of the lexicon of Unitarian Universalists in the struggle against racism. Thus, it would be an oversimplification to say that this volume focuses entirely on racism. The consultation took place eight months before the events of September 11, 2001, and the tragedy of those events and their aftermath have made this volume all the more current.

While neither the consultation nor this volume was designed specifically to comment on or critique the Association's past or current anti-racism efforts, the participants brought a wide range of experiences and suggestions to the table that inform the Association's ongoing engagement with and commitment to combating racism.

Highlights and Themes

This volume addresses such broad questions as:

- What theological or philosophical beliefs bind us together in the struggle against racism, even across—perhaps *especially* across—our differences?

- What are the costs of racism, both to those whom racism oppresses and to those who benefit from it?

- What are the tensions and the interconnections between "our common humanity," as invoked by James Cone and others, and affirming our particular identities in the struggle against racism, as José Ballester, Patricia Jimenez, and Marjorie Bowens-Wheatley urge?

- Rosemary Bray McNatt, Tracey Robinson-Harris, and Rebecca Parker ask readers to consider the extent to which "white folks" ask African Americans, Asian Americans, Latinos and Latinas, and Native Americans to do their "spiritual domestic work" for them. In other words, are white anti-racists implicitly asking people of color to forgive, affirm, teach, and bless them in this work? On the other hand, how might the "spiritual labor of accountability" (an idea echoed by Tracey Robinson-Harris, John Buehrens, and Wayne Arnason) lead to spiritual wholeness? And Gary Smith asks: How can we companion each other in this work? Fred Muir questions whether "a condition of companioning can be to walk down a new path."

- How do we name the multiple forms of violence that have sustained racism historically, and how do we take responsibility for the ongoing daily violence to which our society seems "addicted," as George Tinker suggests?

- What does it mean to be a citizen of this country and of the world? Patricia Jimenez urges us to examine public perceptions of "true citizenship," while Rebecca Parker suggests that if we are to be intentional in becoming responsible citizens, there is a need for committed people to engage in the work of anti-racism as the work of the soul, which requires both "engaged presence" and action.

- How can we take into account the inseparable linkages of oppression, such as those related to race, class, language, culture, gender, sexual orientation, age, ability, and more? How can we *not* take these into account?

As participants wrestled with these issues, themes began to emerge. Silence was a major theme—beginning with James Cone's opening essay, which focuses on the silence of white theologians in dismantling institutionalized racism. Patricia Jimenez highlights the importance of self-naming as an act of liberation and the silence of "pluralism" with respect to "inequity and power relations." Anita Farber-Robertson identifies the silence of denial or "designed blindness" within dominant groups with respect to their complicity with racism. Danielle Di Bona speaks of the silence of "being *made* invisible," while Rebecca Parker and Mel Hoover address the silence of socially constructed identities that sometimes lead people to *render themselves* invisible. These silences reinforce a *culture of invisibility*, which we add to the panoply of systemic injustices. Participants contend that giving voice to these silences is a part of the religious work of anti-racism.

Another recurring theme was *language*—as a conceptual framework and as an issue of power, and thus as a theological issue, in the work of anti-racism. Indeed, the editors of this volume were not immune from wrestling with the complexities of language as a tool of social and theological discourse. George Tinker and Rebecca Parker open up a conversation about the importance of history and the delicate issue of how we have been shaped by particular interpretations of history, language, and social discourse. For example, how does language function to embrace or to exclude? How do we name others and ourselves, and who has the power to name? Who is left out or made invisible by the names and categories that have become standard in the language of race in America? Just as language is an important part of the symbol system of communication, George Tinker would have us recognize that the *symbolic* language of our culture is equally significant. He invites us to take stock of Columbus Day as a federal holiday that sanctions "state-supported hate speech" and celebrates the "quintessential white American hero."

George Tinker further observes that the European American concept of the "self" as an autonomous individual disconnected from the whole has no meaning among American Indians. Similarly, José Ballester points out that in Latino and Latina culture, the "self in community" subsumes the individual. How can religious liberals who are of European American ancestry deepen their understanding of these differences and broaden their view?

Some participants considered social discourse or *talk* about racism—whether acknowledging that racism has been caught in the grip of silence or speaking out against it—as a necessary but insufficient action in the struggle to overcome structural and institutional oppression. Indeed, some expressed impatience with being "talked to death" around issues of race—and feared that over time, such talk would limit effective action for systemic change.

Over and over, the dangers of oversimplification rang forth. Participants maintained—indeed, they demonstrated—that all of us engaged in the struggle against racism and other forms of oppression—no longer need to fear or avoid conflict, for out of such tensions may come our most creative, collaborative, and productive efforts. Indeed, such tensions may be part of "doing the work" of anti-racism.

There are inherent difficulties in "doing theology" within a religious movement that embraces and affirms theological diversity. It is not surprising, therefore, that these essays take as their starting point radically different theological premises. Academicians and theologians—both Unitarian Universalist and non-Unitarian Universalist—ministers, activists, social analysts, and staff members of the UUA sat side by side at the table to thresh out the relationships between theology and ethics, belief and action, and the personal and the pastoral. The resulting conversations were intellectual and emotional, philosophical and spiritual. From the early Universalists, the Radical Reformation, and the Unitarians in Transylvania (Ken Olliff) to modern heroes such as Martin Luther King Jr. and César Chávez (Rosemary Bray McNatt and José Ballester); from black religious humanism to liberation theologies in the United States and elsewhere (William R. Jones), the sources of inspiration are many. Rosemary Bray McNatt and others suggest that Unitarian Universalist congregations need to be more hospitable to and more welcoming of the theologies that speak deeply to people who have historically been oppressed. For some, this means re-examining and reclaiming the biblical stories that have shaped our culture (Rebecca Parker), while for others it means finding new ways to embrace the Jesus story (Elizabeth Ellis and Gary Smith).

Theological concepts not often discussed among Unitarian Universalists—from sin and evil to the idolatry of capitalist "commodification of everything," including human beings (Paul Rasor)—were subjects of great debate among participants. And there was no agreement on whether categories of identity are "idols" that diminish human complexity (Peter Morales) or whether "the beloved community" becomes an idol if religious liberals do not embrace transcendence (Thomas Schade) or some understanding of the holy (Kim Beach).

Such complexity—and a deeper, heart-based motivation for anti-racism work—may be better reflected in stories than in facts and figures, urge JoEllen Willis and Dianne Arakawa. Yet, without social analysis and some understanding of the "startling statistics" that document racist institutional structures, Bill Jones asks, how can racism be accurately diagnosed or an effective therapy found to cure the disease of racism? The drives to heal our individual psyches, restructure cultural institutions, and address the relationship between racism and classism sparked tensions among the participants.

Methodology, which has theological, psychological, and sociological implications, sparked considerable discussion as well, and further illustrated the complexity of racism. Instead of the announced format of the consultation, prepared essays followed by prepared responses and open dialogue, Bill Jones would have preferred that each participant advocate for a particular methodology, followed by a "cuss and discuss" session, which he felt might yield a more constructive approach to the work. Similarly, Fredric Muir and other participants struggled with the centrality of our woundedness, whether personal or social, in the work of eliminating systemic racism. Thandeka spoke of "violent shaming experiences that create white identity," while Mel Hoover said that "the loss of wholeness within ourselves is disorienting." Tom Schade, a self-identified ex-Communist, expressed skepticism and was "very alert to the ways in which the worldview of historical materialism creeps into the Unitarian Universalist movement." Is healing our woundedness, then, a *personal* issue to be addressed separately, or is it a *social* issue that emanates from racism or other systems of domination, and thus an integral part of anti-racism work?

Thandeka, Dianne Arakawa, Rebecca Parker, Paul Rasor, and other contributors to this volume remind us that systemic racial oppression cannot be viewed narrowly—only as institutional or structural racism. Recovering from psychological and spiritual damage, they caution, is a major undertaking. It is *soul work* for both victim and perpetrator that requires theological engagement.

While it is easy to focus anti-racism work on victims, the participants ask us to remember that perpetrators who were taught to
split body from mind and soul are *also* victims. But compassion is
not enough. Contributors ask readers to not only engage in dismantling institutional and structural change to eradicate racism,
but to also engage in *soul work*, which Rebecca Parker defines "an
internal struggle to recover from the ways in which [oppression]
has led to the loss of aspects of [the] self." This, says Parker, is the
work of a lifetime.

The Process

Following a deeply considered consultative process, nine individuals were invited to present major essays reflecting on any aspect
of theology and anti-racism. Sixteen respondents were each asked
to write a reflection on one essay. Thus there were two respondents for each essay with the exception of the opening essay. In
preparation for an informed and critical discussion, the nine
essays were distributed to all participants (essayists, respondents,
and three participant-observers) prior to the consultation.

On a late wintry Sunday evening in January, participants gathered at Pickett and Elliot House at UUA headquarters in Boston for
dinner and a worshipful in-gathering. The opening paper was presented by James Cone, to which John Buehrens offered a solo
response, followed by dialogue. Monday morning's session began
with a centering, followed by the second presentation. Because participants read these essays beforehand, and in order to conserve
time, essayists were allotted only five minutes each to introduce
their essays. Each of the two respondents was then given ten minutes to present a prepared response, copies of which were distributed prior to the session. Following each set of papers (one essay
and two responses), all participants were asked to reflect on the
presentations in silence and through journaling. This process
proved fertile ground for many of the issues that emerged in the
dialogue, which lasted approximately forty minutes for each paper.
Each essayist was then given an opportunity to offer "the last
word," a two-minute reflection on the responses and dialogue.

A little over one hour was dedicated to each chapter presented
here, far less time than would have been desirable for discussion of

such a complex topic. Rebecca Parker presented the final essay on Tuesday morning, which was followed by two respondents and dialogue about her paper. This was followed by a two hour open dialogue in which participants were free to raise any issue related to the topic. Following the open dialogue, participant-observers were invited to offer their observations, and all participants were invited to make recommendations for what we can do as the "next steps" in focusing our anti-racism work following the consultation. These observations and recommendations are summarized in the Conclusions chapter.

The essays and responses at the consultation were not offered in the same sequence as they are presented in this book.

In organizing this volume, we arranged the essays in a sequence that, in our view, lent support to the themes that emerged. While each of the nine essays is presented here in its totality, we included only highlights of the seventeen responses and an edited summary of major points of the dialogue. Our goal was to capture as much of the richness and texture of the consultation as possible—the liveliness and sincerity, the humor and emotion, the tension and the thoughtfulness, all of which reflect the very nature of anti-racism work.[1] Thus, this volume is not a transcript of the consultation, but instead an abridgment of a wide-ranging conversation that was both joyous and difficult. Each chapter ends with study questions for personal or group reflection. The final article in this volume, written by Susan Leslie (who was also a participant-observer) offers suggestions for anti-racist structural change as well as a variety of resources.

Ways to Use This Book

Edward T. Hall[2] argues that communication is culture. Like every culture, liberal religion—and Unitarian Universalism in particular—comes with its own trappings of culture and communication. It is not surprising then that language was a major theme throughout the consultation. But language is not an independent variable; it must be placed in a context to have meaning. The participants in the consultation each had the courage to acknowledge their particular cultural context—whether geographic, religious, or otherwise. Our task begins with recognizing that overcoming racism is more than a sociological or political task. It is a *theological* task that involves struggling with difficult questions, among them: How can we be human together in the face of suffering and oppression? Further, it involves translating religious language and interpreting different cultural contexts.

We hope that this volume inspires readers to become more fully engaged in anti-racism work as part of the task of justice making—from reconsidering their most dearly held beliefs to becoming more fully engaged in ever-deepening theological reflection and action. Readers may wish to use this book in any of the following ways:

- For individual reflection and study, including journaling as a spiritual task.

- As a text (perhaps a chapter at a time) for book discussion groups.

- As a resource for church leadership discussions regarding your congregation's vision, mission, and engagement in the wider community.

- Youth, young adult groups, or other affinity groups, to stimulate ideas on how to connect values with the kind of world they hope to create.

- Social Justice/Social Action, Anti-Racism, or Journey Toward Wholeness committees.

- Adult enrichment/education classes.

- Theological schools classes and libraries.

- Minister's study groups or retreat.

- Sunday programs, including inspiration for sermons.

- Inspiration for congregants sharing their own stories connecting anti-racism as a spiritual task.

- To create or supplement anti-racism workshops.

- As a source for beginning the task of remedial education (see Rebecca Parker essay).

As a movement, Unitarian Universalism has not explored either of the two major themes of this book—racism and theology—in any depth in recent years. Because religious language employs myth, symbol, story, and metaphor, this may be difficult for those who are theological literalists—unless readers set aside whatever anger, hurt, and preconceived ideas they may have. A respectful reading of the writers presented in this volume requires empathic "listening" to more than their exact words. This too is part of the theological task, the *soul work* of anti-racism. If you find some of the theological language difficult or the cultural context of a particular essay unfamiliar, it may be helpful to engage in reflective activity with others in a small group

A luta continua! The struggle continues!

Keeping the faith,

Marjorie Bowens-Wheatley
and Nancy Palmer Jones

Theology's Great Sin: Silence in the Face of White Supremacy

James Cone

Silence in the face of evil is itself evil: God will not hold us guiltless. Not to speak is to speak. Not to act is to act.
— Dietrich Bonhoeffer

We will have to repent . . . not merely for the vitriolic words and actions of the bad people but for the appalling silence of the good people.
— Martin Luther King Jr.

Dietrich Bonhoeffer and Martin Luther King Jr. were two of the most outspoken Christian theologians against injustice and suffering in the twentieth century. Bonhoeffer, a German Lutheran, was hanged in a Nazi prison at Flossenburg in Bavaria on April 9, 1945. King, an African American Baptist, was assassinated while fighting for sanitation workers in Memphis, Tennessee, on April 4, 1968. Both were thirty-nine years old at the time of their deaths. What distinguished Bonhoeffer and King from most theologians was their refusal to keep silent about the great moral issues of their time and their ability to use the injustices in their societies to challenge religious meaning. They opposed Nazi and American racism fiercely—knowing that it would probably lead to their death. "When Christ calls a man," Bonhoeffer said, "he bids him come

1

and die."[1] King was just as prophetic and courageous: "If physical death is the price I must pay to free my white brothers and sisters from the permanent death of the spirit, then nothing could be more redemptive."[2] The lives and writings of Bonhoeffer and King tell us far more about what it means to be a Christian and a theologian than all the great tomes in the history of theology. Their martyrdom placed Christian identity at the foot of the cross of Jesus and in the midst of oppressed people fighting for justice and freedom.

We need more Christians and theologians like Bonhoeffer and King—more people with the courage to speak out against wrong, especially the evil of white supremacy. No one can deny that racism is a major killer in the modern world. Yet there has been considerable resistance to seeing it as a profound problem for Christianity. During the course of five centuries, Europeans and white North Americans systematically confiscated lands and committed genocide against untold numbers of indigenous people around the world. When whites "discovered" something they wanted, whether land or labor, they took it—with very little thought as to the consequences for the lives of the people already there.

"Can any nation . . . discover what belonged to someone else?" asked the Dutch jurist Hugo Grotius (1583–1645).[3] Few Europeans asked such questions; instead, they exploited lands and peoples unhindered by philosophy, religion, or ethics. In fact, these disciplines assisted them in justifying their violence, as they viewed themselves as God's chosen people, to subdue indigenous peoples and their land. Author Eduardo Galeano claims that 150 years of Spanish and Portuguese colonization in Central and South America reduced the indigenous population from 90 million to 3.3 million.[4] During the twenty-three-year reign of terror of King Leopold II of Belgium in the Congo (1885–1908), scholarly estimates suggest that approximately 10 million Congolese met unnatural deaths—"fully half of the territory's population."[5] Then, in one brief moment, the Nazis committed an unspeakable racist crime: the industrialized mass murder of six million Jews in Europe.

Physical death is only one aspect of racism that raises serious theological questions. Spiritual death is another, and it is just as destructive, if not more so, for it destroys the soul of both the racists and their victims. Racism is hatred gone amok; it is violence against one's spiritual self. As James Baldwin put it, "It is a terrible, an inexorable, law that one cannot deny the humanity of another without diminishing one's own; in the face of one's victim, one sees oneself."[6]

Through cultural and religious imperialism, Europeans imposed their racist value system on people of color and thereby forced them to think that the only way to be human and civilized was to be white and Christian. It not only makes the oppressed want to be something other than what they are but it also makes them want to become like their oppressors. Malcolm X called it self-hate—the worst mental sickness imaginable. The poison of white supremacy is so widespread and deeply internalized by its victims that many are unaware of their illness and others who are often do not have the cultural and intellectual resources to heal their wounded spirits. In my travels around the world, I am amazed at how much people of color want to be white. They want to look like whites, talk like whites, and even pray like whites. Many are still worshipping a white God and a blond-haired, blue-eyed Jesus—still singing, "Wash me and I will be whiter than snow."

We are all bound together, inseparably linked by a common humanity. What we do to one another, we do to ourselves. That was why Martin King was absolutely committed to nonviolence. Anything less, he believed, was self-inflicted violence against one's soul. "Through violence you may murder the hater, but you do not murder hate. In fact, violence increases hate. . . . It [begets] what it seeks to destroy."[7] King struggled mightily to redeem the soul of America so that people of all colors and religious orientations could create the beloved community.

Racism is particularly alive and well in America. It is America's original sin and, as it is institutionalized at all levels of society, its most persistent and intractable evil. Though racism inflicts massive suffering, few American theologians have even bothered to address white supremacy as a moral evil and as a radical contradiction of our humanity and religious identities. White theologians and philosophers write numerous articles and books on theodicy, asking why God permits massive suffering, but they hardly ever mention the horrendous crimes whites have committed against people of color in the modern world. Why do white ministers and theologians ignore racism? This is a haunting question—especially since a few white scholars in other disciplines (such as sociology, literature, history, and anthropology) *do* engage racism. Why not theologians? Shouldn't they be the first to attack this evil?

When I began writing about racism in American theology, in the churches, and in the society more than thirty years ago, I really thought that, after being confronted with the sin of their silence, white ministers and theologians would repent and then proceed to incorporate a radical critique of racism into their theological and religious reflections. Most were sympathetic to the Civil Rights movement and some even participated in the marches led by Martin Luther King Jr. Whenever King asked for help, white ministers vacated their pulpits and a few theologians even suspended classes or cut short summer vacations and joined him in the fight for racial justice. In addition, the rise of Latin American liberation and feminist theologies and the deepening of the Jewish-Christian dialogue on the Holocaust created a liberating theological atmosphere for a serious and sustained engagement with racism. Some dialogue on race and gender did occur between white feminist and womanist and *Mujerista* theologians. There were also spirited dialogues on race and class among white Latin Americans and people of color in the Ecumenical Association of Third World Theologians. We are all familiar with the many heated exchanges in white churches as blacks created caucuses and called for Black Power and white churchpeople wondered why their black brothers and sisters felt so powerless and angry after the breakdown of segregation in God's house. It took a while for whites to realize that blacks and other people of color did not want to be integrated out of power with a few white-selected colored tokens as window dressing. Even Martin King called for a period of "temporary segregation in order to get to the integrated society."[8]

In contrast to these small but important efforts in the churches and in other contexts, white North American and European male theologians hardly ever mentioned the sin of racism in their public lectures and writings during the 1960s and 1970s. They wrote mostly about the "death of God" controversy and the secular spirit that created it. It was as if they were intellectually blind and could not see that white supremacy was America's central theological problem. They engaged Latin Americans with respect to class contradictions, talked to feminists about gender issues, and dialogued with Jews about Christianity and anti-Semitism, but when the time came to talk about theology and racism, at first they could not believe that we had the audacity to engage them in a serious intellectual discussion about theology and its task. What could blacks possibly know about theology? When we refused to be intimidated by their intellectual arrogance, they tried to convince us that race was secondary to class in importance and would be automatically eliminated when justice was achieved in the political economy. When we forcefully rejected that view as faulty and racist, they walked away as if we were too emotional and not intelligent enough to understand their sophisticated theoretical analysis. Progressive white male theologians also tried to pull that same intellectual trick with women regarding sexism. But the women rejected that outright, and through the sheer power of their numbers and the brilliance of their intellect, forced men to see patriarchy for what it was and is: man's way of exploiting half of humanity.

This consultation and a few others I've attended demonstrate some awareness among whites in the churches that all is not well on the racial front. Awareness of racism as a problem of religious identity, and not just a societal one, is the first step toward engaging it theologically. After reading about the Unitarian Universalist Association's participation in the Civil Rights movement, its struggles with Black Power in the late 1960s and early 1970s, and the present "Journey Toward Wholeness," I am impressed with your anti-racism fight in the church and the society. The journey toward wholeness is long and profoundly difficult, and that is why most UUA members and other whites become impatient with the time and money devoted to this concern. Since the UUA "uphold[s] the free search for truth" "that is distinctly antiauthoritarian," it is to be expected that many congregations will resent and resist any pressure from national headquarters trying to tell them what to think and do.[9] But we must not be deterred from the anti-racism fight because of the noise of critics. We may debate strategies for fighting white supremacy, but there can be no debate about whether the anti-racist struggle is a worthy and necessary calling for a religious institution and its theology.

But before I get into strategies, it is important to make a distinction between personal prejudice and structural racism. The distinction is found throughout your literature, which means that you have been hard at work on this issue. Dealing with people's personal prejudices should not be the major concern. It is emotionally too exhausting and achieves very little in dismantling racism. I am not very concerned about what people think about me as long as their personal prejudices are not institutionalized. The issue is always structural. While I may not get people to like me, it is important that the law prevent them from harming me on the basis of their prejudices.

Before we can get whites to confront racism, we need to know why they avoid it. Why don't whites write and speak about racism? This is a complex and difficult question, because the reasons vary among individuals and groups in different parts of the country. There are probably as many reasons as there are people. I will advance my perspective on this issue and invite whites and people of color to participate with me in an exploration of white silence on racism. We all have some insight into this problem. My reflections focus mainly on white theologians, ministers, and the churches. I hope what we say will have meaning for people in other institutions as well.

1) Most importantly, whites do not talk about racism because they do not *have* to talk about it. They have most of the power in the world—economic, political, social, cultural, intellectual, and religious. There is little that blacks and other people of color can do to change the power relationships in the churches, in seminaries, and in society. Powerful people do not talk, except on their own terms and almost never at the behest of others. All the powerless can do is disrupt—make life uncomfortable for the ruling elites. That was why Martin King called the urban riots and Black Power the "language of the unheard." The quality of white life is hardly ever affected by what blacks think or do. The reverse is not the case: Everything whites think and do has a profound impact on the lives of blacks on a daily basis. We can never escape white power and its cruelty. That is why blacks are usually open to talking to whites in the hope of relieving their pain but the latter seldom offer a like response, because they perceive little or nothing to gain.

Power corrupts, and as Lord Acton said, "absolute power corrupts absolutely." When this idea is applied to the relations between whites as a group and people of color, it is possible to get a glimpse of how deeply white supremacy is embedded in the American way of life. "The sinfulness of man," wrote Reinhold Niebuhr, "makes it inevitable that a dominant class, group, and sex [and race should be added here] should seek to define a relationship, which guarantees its dominance, as permanently normative."[10]

How can we journey toward wholeness when whites as a group hold most of the power? The UUA's experience with Black Power was similar to that of other white churches and institutions: profoundly alienating, gut-wrenching, and divisive in every segment of our communities. How do whites avoid arbitrary group power or condescending patronage? How do blacks avoid racial essentialism, talking and acting as if biology alone defines truth? Again I quote Niebuhr, but this time on the blindness of the oppressed: "Every victim of injustice makes the mistake of supposing that the sin from which he suffers is a peculiar vice of his oppressor."[11]

That the oppressed are sinners too is a very important point to make but often hard to hear, especially when it is made by the oppressor. The ever-present violence in poor communities is at least partly due to the sins of the oppressed. We must never assume that God is on the side of the oppressed because they are sinless but rather because of God's solidarity with weakness and hurt, with poor people unable to defend themselves against violent oppressors.

When black theology first appeared, the few white theologians who addressed it often quoted Niebuhr to us about the sins of the oppressed. Because I questioned their motives, I quoted Niebuhr back at them. "Socio-economic conditions," wrote Niebuhr, "actually determine to a large degree that some men are tempted to pride and injustice, while others are encouraged to humility. The biblical analysis agrees to the known facts of history. Capitalists are not greater sinners than poor laborers by any natural depravity. But it is a fact that those who hold great economic and political power are more guilty of pride against God and of injustice against the weak than those who lack power and prestige. . . . White men sin against Negroes in Africa and America more than Negroes sin against white men."[12]

2) White theologians and ministers avoid racial dialogue because talk about white supremacy arouses deep feelings of guilt.

Guilt is a heavy burden to bear. Most Americans have at least a general idea of the terrible history of white supremacy, and that alone can create a profound guilt when blacks and others tell their stories of suffering and pain. Whites know that they have reaped the material harvest of white domination in the modern world. The material wealth of Europe and North America was acquired and enhanced through the systematic exploitation of lands and peoples in Africa, Asia, and North and South America. A critical exploration of the theological meaning of slavery, colonialism, segregation, lynching, and genocide can create a terrible guilt. As Reinhold Niebuhr said: "If . . . the white man were to expiate his sins committed against the darker races, few white men would have the right to live."[13]

. Whites do not like to think of themselves as evil people or to believe that their place in the world is due to the colonization of Indians, the enslavement of blacks, and the exploitation of people of color here and around the world. Whites like to think of themselves as honorable, decent, and fair-minded people. They resent being labeled racists. There are whites who say that they do not owe blacks anything because they did not enslave anybody, did not segregate or lynch anybody, and are not white supremacists. They claim to be color-blind and thus treat everybody alike. At an individual level, there is some common-sense truth to that observation. But if you benefit from past and present injustices committed against blacks, you are partly and indirectly accountable as an American citizen and as a member of the institutions that perpetuate racism. We cannot just embrace what is good about America and ignore the bad. We must accept the responsibility to do everything we can to correct America's past and present wrongs.

3) Another reason why whites avoid race topics with African Americans is because they do not want to engage black rage. Whites do not mind talking as long as blacks don't get too emotional, too carried away with their stories of hurt. I must admit that it is hard to talk about the legacies of white supremacy and not speak with passion and anger about the long history of black suffering. It is not a pleasant thing to talk about, especially for people of color who have experienced white cruelty. I would not recommend race as a topic of conversation between blacks and whites during a relaxed social evening. Things could get a little heated and spoil a fun evening.

Whites who talk with me about white supremacy need to be informed and sensitive to the common humanity we all share. All I ask of whites is to put themselves in black people's place in this society and the world, and then ask themselves what they would say or do if they were in black people's place. Would you be angry about 246 years of slavery and 100 years of lynching and segregation? What would you say about the incarceration of one million of your people in prisons—one-half of the penal population— while your people represent only 12 percent of the U.S. census? Would you get angry if your racial group used 13 percent of the drugs but did 74 percent of the prison time for simple possession?[14] Would you caution the oppressed in *your* community to speak about their pain with calm and patience? What would you say about your sons who are shot dead by the police because their color alone makes them prime criminal suspects? What would you say about ministers and theologians who preach and teach about justice and love but ignore the sociopolitical oppression of your people? Black anger upsets only whites who choose not to identify with black suffering.

But even whites who acknowledge black suffering often insist that we talk about our pain with appropriate civility and restraint. That was why they preferred Martin King to Malcolm X. Malcolm spoke with too much rage for their social taste. He made whites feel uncomfortable because he confronted them with their terrible crimes against black humanity. Addressing the question about whether he spoke with too much emotion, Malcolm responded:

> When a man is hanging on a tree and he cries out, should he cry out unemotionally? When a man is sitting on a hot stove and he tells you how it feels to be there, is he supposed to speak without emotions? This is what you tell black people in this country when they begin to cry out against the injustices they're suffering. As long as they describe these injustices in a way that makes you believe you have another 100 years to rectify the situation, then you don't call that emotion. But when a man is on a hot stove, he says, "I'm coming up. I'm getting up. Violently or nonviolently doesn't even enter the picture—I'm coming up you understand."[15]

Malcolm called his style telling the "naked truth" about the white man. He knew whites did not like to hear blunt truth. "I love to talk about them," he proclaimed to a Harlem rally. "Talk about them like dogs. And they should be able to take it. Now they know how we feel. Why, when I was a little boy they called me nigger so much I thought that was my name."[16] Malcolm believed that whites needed to know how blacks really felt, and he did not think that civil rights leaders like King were forthcoming in this regard. They were too compromising. They sugarcoated the truth so whites would not feel so bad about what they had done. When Malcolm felt that black leaders were letting whites off the hook, he turned his anger on them and accused them of making it easy for whites because they cared more about white emotional comfort than the suffering of the black poor.

Because the spirit and language of black theology was closer to Malcolm than to Martin, white theologians were reluctant to engage us. They got nervous and made their way toward the exit every time a militant black theologian came near them. I must admit I was pretty hard on them, and that partly accounts for their silence. But I was not going to pamper privileged whites. How could our relationship be comfortable and easygoing, lovey-dovey, when black people were dying in the streets?

Blacks invoking the race card also makes whites uncomfortable. I must admit that blacks sometimes play the race card at inappropriate times and places. It is a quick conversation stopper. But whites should remember that blacks have the race card to play because America dealt it to them. It is not a card that we wanted.

When blacks play the race card, it is often a desperate attempt to get whites to listen to them and to take their suffering seriously. Racism is a highly charged subject for blacks—similar to the strong reactions anti-Semitism generates among Jews. White Americans have some empathy for Jewish suffering. That is why the United States supports Israel and built a huge Holocaust Museum in Washington, D.C. Whites do not have a similar empathy for black suffering, even though our suffering is much closer to home. That is why there is no slavery museum in Washington and no reparations forthcoming for blacks. Such thoughts are anathema to most white Americans. When America is forced to consider black suffering, whites advance all kinds of technical and legal reasons to dismiss doing anything about the crimes committed against black people.

Consider the insightful comment of Pamela A. Hairston of Washington, D.C., responding in a letter to the *Christian Century* on the issue of reparations for African Americans:

> With the Homestead Act of 1862, Congress gave away more than 270 million acres of land to more than 2 million white Americans—160 acres per person or family, free. This was enacted on January 1, 1863, the same day President Lincoln signed the Emancipation Proclamation. Another such act, the Southern Homestead Act, granted ex-slaves or freed men 40 acres, and some ex-slaves did receive a few acres, which were later given back to the Confederates. The ex-slaves were evicted. America preferred to keep the ex-slaves as sharecroppers.
>
> After 200-plus years of inhumane slavery and hard free labor they gave my ancestors nothing but 100-plus more years of hate, black codes, Jim Crow laws, the Klan, lynchings, poverty, oppression, segregation, and fear. Wouldn't black America—no, America as a whole—be a better nation if they had been given the 40 acres as promised? Right now, I'd take an acre and a chicken.[17]

With this terrible history, why is it so difficult to get white people to acknowledge what America owes to black people?

We all benefit and suffer from what happened in the past, and we owe it to ourselves to learn from the good and to correct the bad. We cannot survive as a nation with huge economic divisions between rich and poor, or deep social alienation between whites and people of color. We are one people. What happens to one happens to all. So, even if we are not directly responsible for past injustices, we are responsible for the present exploitation. It is our responsibility to create a new future for all. We need to ask, What kind of society do we want? Do we want a society that puts more blacks in prisons than in colleges? We are all responsible for this world, and as human beings, we will have to give an accounting of what we said and didn't say, what we did and didn't do, about justice for all.

Whites and people of color must learn to work together. Our future depends on it. But that can never happen creatively until whites truly believe that their humanity is at stake in the struggle for racial justice. Speaking on behalf of Jews, Rabbi Joachim Prinz, then president of the American Jewish Congress, expressed this

point eloquently at the 1963 March on Washington: "It is not merely sympathy and compassion for the black people of America that
motivates us, it is above all and beyond all such sympathies and
emotions a sense of complete identification and solidarity born of
our own painful historic experiences."[18] There are few whites who
really know how to express that sort of solidarity.

4) Whites do not say much about racial justice because they are
not prepared for a radical redistribution of wealth and power. No
group gives up power freely; power must be taken against the will
of those who have it. Fighting white supremacy means dismantling white privilege in the society, in the churches, and in theology. Progressive whites do not mind talking as long as it doesn't
cost much, as long as the structures of power remain intact. & you

I have been at Union Theological Seminary more than three
decades and have observed white power in churches, seminaries,
and theology up close. On the positive side, no theological school
has spoken out more forcefully against social injustice in America
and the world than the Union community. This is one of its great
contributions in the twentieth century. Our social justice tradition
is similar to the one in the UUA. Through our graduates and faculty, our stand on racial, economic, gender, homosexual, and environmental justice has been heard around the world. It has cost the
institution much, and we are still struggling for survival in a world
ruled by corporate power. Our doors are open to all who are concerned about using disciplined intellect to interpret the meaning of
religion for the liberation of humanity from everything that
enslaves. About 23 percent of all blacks teaching in divinity
schools graduated from Union Seminary. Nine of its twenty-four
faculty members are people of color—three men and six women.[19]
The theological atmosphere has been radically transformed, so
that Union's theological self-understanding includes the histories
and cultures of people of color. This is genuine progress. I am
proud of Union, especially the faculty of color and students of
color because they represent the best of Union's tradition of academic excellence.

Despite this positive picture of Union, we are still struggling
with race issues. Speaking about structural racism at Union creates
silence among most whites, because they do not want to acknowledge their privilege or engage black rage. When whites do
speak about race, their knowledge of the depth of the problem—

personally and intellectually—is so limited that they often offend blacks and other people of color.

Although white Christians and other religious communities acknowledge their sinful condition and know that their inordinate power as a group makes them more prone to injustice in relation to other minority groups, they find it nearly impossible to do anything to relinquish their advantage. Individuals are often self-critical, but groups are inevitably selfish and proud. No theologian has been more insightful on this point than Reinhold Niebuhr: "The group is more arrogant, hypocritical, self-centered and more ruthless in the pursuit of its ends than the individual. . . . If we did for ourselves what we do for our country, what rascals we would be."[20]

When and how should whites break their silence? There are many whites who want to effect change but do not know when and how to do it. I assume that the UUA has called this consultation because you want to break the silence and do something about making the journey toward wholeness a way of life in the church and in society. I am here because I support you in your efforts.

I urge white theologians, ministers, and other morally concerned persons to break their silence immediately and continuously. It is immoral to see evil and not fight it. As Rabbi Prinz put it at the March on Washington, "Bigotry and hatred are not the most urgent problems. The most urgent, the most disgraceful, the most shameful and most tragic problem is silence." Theologians and ministers, churches, synagogues, and associations must not remain onlookers, "silent in the face of hate, in the face of brutality, and in the face of mass murder."[21] We must speak out loud and clear against the evil of racism, not for the sake of people of color but for ourselves, for our churches and theologies, for America and the world, and most of all, for humanity.

Talking about how to destroy white supremacy is a daily task and not just for consultations and conferences. If we talk about white supremacy only at special occasions set aside for that, the problem will never be solved. People of color do not have the luxury of just dealing with racism in church meetings. If that were true, it would not be so bad! No day passes in which blacks don't have to deal with white supremacy. It is found everywhere—in the churches, in seminaries, at publishing houses, in government, and all around the world. There is no escape. If whites get tired of talk-ing about race, just imagine how people of color feel.

The development of a hard-hitting anti-racist theology on the part of white scholars of religion is long overdue. What would an anti-racist theology look like? It would be, first, a theology that grows out of an anti-racist political struggle. Talk is cheap if there is no action to back it up. We must do something concrete about dismantling white supremacy. I know this task is not easy but a very difficult endeavor. Yet, do not be discouraged. Despair only supports the enemy. Working together with each other and with the Great Spirit of the universe, we can accomplish more than we ever dreamed. I want to commend you for the work you have done to "pound away at structural racism."[22] You seem to be serious—much more serious than I expected. Keep working at it. "Don't get weary," as the black spiritual says; "there is a great camp meeting in the Promised Land." That song is not primarily about the geography of heaven but rather a message of hope in dire circumstances. Blacks, with their backs against the wall of slavery, were saying that evil would not have the last word about their humanity. We have a future not made with white hands.

Begin the anti-racist struggle where you are. If you are in the churches, get together with other committed persons and analyze ecclesiastical structures and disclose how they reinforce racism. If you are in a seminary, start there and connect your struggle with others. If you are in a publishing house, start talking with those who are interested in making it more inclusive of people of color. While it is useful to bring in outside resource persons to assist you, there is no substitute for hard work. Set your pace as if you are going to do that work for the rest of your life. There is joy in this work, because it enhances your humanity. Justice work in any sit-uation is the most satisfying activity one can do. I just love it and would not trade anything for the opportunity to be involved in it. If you do not love racial justice work, then do not do it. We need and want people who love people of color, so that they are willing to take the same risks they would for their own kind.

One of the most important things whites can do in fighting white supremacy is to support black empowerment in the society, in the church, and in theology. Black empowerment means blacks thinking, speaking, and doing for themselves. The black church and black theology are black empowerment in religion. One reason why there are so few blacks in the UUA and other white churches is because they are ecclesiastical structures of white supremacy. For blacks to be members of white churches, it is necessary to follow the rules laid down by whites, unless whites are willing to help change the rules to reflect black history and culture.

To create an anti-racist theology, white theologians must engage the histories, cultures, and theologies of people of color. It is not enough to condemn racism; the voices of people of color must be found in your theology. You do not have to agree with their perspectives, but you do have to understand them and incorporate their meanings into your theological discourse. This is what whites almost never do. There are almost no references to black scholars or other people of color in any of the writings of major white male theologians. Even when white theologians talk about race, as Reinhold Niebuhr did occasionally throughout his career, there are no citations from black intellectuals who informed their thinking. How can anybody write about race in an informed way and not engage the writings of W. E. B. DuBois, Zora Neale Hurston, Ida B. Wells-Barnett, Richard Wright, James Baldwin, and Howard Thurman?

In America, we have a lot of racist theologies. Let us hope that white theologians, ministers, and other concerned human beings will end their silence about the evil consequences of racism so they can join people of color in their fight against white supremacy and connect the struggles in the United States with the fight for justice around the world. "What we all want," proclaimed W. E. B. DuBois, "is a decent world, where a [person] does not have to have a white skin to be recognized as a [human being]."[23]

The Response

"It is hard in a religious movement that prides itself on being non-confessional to confess, even to oneself, one's failings," **John Buehrens** admits, testifying to his own silence in the face of apparent police discrimination against people of color in the white enclaves of Dallas when he served as a minister there. "If my spirituality over the years has grown in any dimension," he adds, "I hope it is in this area of accountability."

To deepen the discussion of accountability, Buehrens offers the words of Wayne Arnason, a Unitarian Universalist minister and member of the UUA's Board of Trustees. In the following excerpt from an address to the board, Arnason drew on a fund of faith-related resources as he reflected on accountability as a "big theological issue":

> The founders of several world faiths believed that they were accountable only to God and not to any other sacred or secular authorities. Most theological traditions point to a source of authority that transcends this world as the ultimate reference for their accountability. Although some individual Unitarian Universalists do that, as a tradition, Unitarian Universalism does not require or covenant around a transcendent source of authority. Instead, as a covenantal religious community, we locate our accountability in *this* world, in our community of congregations, and in the values, principles, and traditions they represent.
>
> Calling ourselves to account can be a difficult thing for Unitarian Universalists. . . . Over and over again throughout our history, we have seen the struggles that have ensued when we called ourselves to account based on values we said that we held but denied in practice. Being accountable to each other is just as much a part of the theological covenant we make as Unitarian Universalists as respecting the worth and dignity of each other might be. In fact, I've begun to wonder whether we should affirm "accountability to each other for practicing these Principles with integrity" as a kind of eighth Principle.
>
> In saying we are accountable to each other, we make a statement about our whole lives as human beings. We acknowledge that the community of Unitarian Universalists in one sense represents the whole human race, past, present, and future, to which we are accountable—ancestors, people who aren't Unitarian Universalists, and people yet to be born.
>
> Aspiring to be anti-racist in practicing our Principles opens up these questions of who is in our community and to whom we are accountable in a new way.

Arnason then listed his communities of accountability as an anti-racist, beginning with the congregation that he serves as well as "other communities whose name I carry," such as the Board of Trustees, and capping the list with the "communities of color represented in my life by some of you who are also board members who name yourself persons of color, but also represented by people in communities of color that aren't Unitarian Universalist." Arnason continued,

> Buddhist theology has an important doctrine known as the interdependent chain of causation. Much like our affirmation of the interdependent web of life, this theological affirmation declares that no event, no encounter, no circumstance or occasion is disconnected from a great chain of causes that have led up to the present moment. Ultimately, each of our actions reflects and encompasses everything that has gone before and everything that comes after.

> If I truly take responsibility for racism, I bring to consciousness my place in that great chain of causation, and I own the actions I will have to take to shape the direction toward which that chain goes into the future. I recognize that in the interdependent web of life, what happens to communities of color happens to me, or happened to my ancestors, or will happen to my descendants— and the ways in which I can be accountable for and make a difference regarding what happens are both the content and the fruits of my Unitarian Universalist faith.

The Dialogue

The dialogue stretches to cover a wide range of issues. Some participants delve deeper into Cone's concept of "our common humanity"; some challenge him to respond to feminist and other critiques; and others seek clarification: Under what conditions can suffering be considered "redemptive"? Which should be the focus of anti-racism work: unpacking personal prejudices or struggling against structural racism? And just what is the relationship between *talk* and *action?* The following excerpts highlight these themes.

ROSEMARY BRAY MCNATT: I'm hoping to hear more about the very peculiar position that African American ministers in this particular faith community hold. Practically from the moment I heard about Unitarian Universalism, I have felt a tension: On the one hand, this is where I belong; this *is* my faith community. At the same time, I am often at odds with my responsibilities to the myr-

iad communities of accountability I serve, such as my family—I'm
a wife and a mother of sons in a world that is very threatened by
African American men—and my general community of accountability, that of African Americans. But I also think about my ministry in a small rural town in New Jersey, where *everyone* in that
community is white except me. I need to be a pastor to people who
sometimes can't see me as a human being, and I still have to care
for them because that is what I am called to do. There is a certain
amount of truth that they are unable to accept about that. Any
comments?

CONE: We have to always remember that we share a common
humanity despite our cultural, racial, and gender differences and
all the kinds of differences we have, and that common humanity is
more important than all the other things, even though the other
things are important. That is where I would begin my struggle
with them. To me our common humanity is not a debatable question; I would just live it, and speak it, and say it, and do it.

   You know, love is tough, but it also transcends the things that
separate us, and people can see and hear love even when they
don't like what they hear . . . . We have to love the struggle we
have and love the people who are in the struggle. God created
everybody, and we are committed to live out the calling we have—
I don't think there are any gimmicks that you can come up with to
deal with that tension. The main thing is to be authentic, and to
live and speak the truth, and to do it with love and care—not in a
wishy-washy way but with that deep, deep love and commitment
that can overcome the most intractable resistances within people
in our communities.

KEN OLLIFF: You stated that our common humanity is the point
about which we can maintain an absolute. Many religious liberals
would also make such an appeal, and I agree with you that a sense
of our common humanity is vital for the work of anti-racism. Yet
this appeal can also be used to downplay the significance of race:
"We share these elements, so we don't need to take the specifics
seriously." Can you flesh this out?

CONE: It's important to separate my perspective on common
humanity from that of liberal theology or from what is expressed

generally by a dominant group. A dominant group needs to use its own culture and history as the "common humanity," so that they won't even have to talk about anybody else except themselves and their history and their culture. When I speak about a common humanity, I am speaking about the cultures of everybody.

You can't find our common humanity until you search for it in "the other"! So it draws you to other people's particularities. That's what drew me to gender; that's what drew me to Latin America, to Africa, to Asia; that's what stretches me beyond my culture. I cannot be who I am until I am in solidarity with others. So I know that you really believe in our common humanity when your theology reflects engagement and wrestling with issues and people beyond the particularity of your own history and culture.

THANDEKA: As you know, Delores Williams[24] has been a severe critic of yours with regard to black theology, arguing that it is gender-based and that it focuses on the argument between black men and white men and thus is itself a form of oppressive power. How has your theology shifted during the past thirty years to take account of this?

CONE: I have been struggling with gender issues since 1976, when I wrote my first essay about it. At that time Delores Williams was a student, and we began our dialogue. I don't think it's possible for me to speak to anybody's issue in quite the way in which they want me to speak about it. I can only speak about it with the convictions out of which I live, and focus on trying to build a common humanity within which we can all search for truth and for right and for wrong. I want to learn as much from you and everybody here as I can. At the same time, that doesn't mean that I'm going to give up my deepest convictions about the faith. So what I've said here are basically my deepest, most passionate beliefs about the Christian faith and my commitment to struggle for a world that is for all and not just for some.

DIANNE ARAKAWA: Please name one theological idea with regard to anti-racism, with regard to feminists, and with regard to non-black people of color that you have considered and grown with and changed over the past thirty years.

CONE: If you don't change over thirty years, there's something wrong with you, because that means you're not learning from other people. The three areas in which I have changed the most are in the context of third world liberation theologies. I've been dialoguing with groups in Africa, Asia, and Latin America and they have taught me a lot, particularly in the area of economic analysis and class analysis. Women at Union and women around the world and in my community and everywhere I go have taught me a lot, particularly about the importance of gender analysis in one's work. I've tried to write about how I've changed, because for me it's not a matter of writing something once and for all; doing what I do is a journey, too. But there's one thing that I haven't changed my mind about, and that is I do believe in our common humanity. . . .

I have focused on racism because that is what I know the most about. I haven't excluded other issues; I just don't make other issues the point of the project, and I can't, because that's not where I actually start. . . .

Now, I didn't start to think about gender and class on my own. I had people to help me along, but when I was confronted, I tried to listen and I tried to hear. I may not have heard what they wanted me to hear, but you always have to speak out of where you are. If that's a limited place, the only thing you can say is I'm trying to be as open as I can and I'm trying to learn.

There are always limits, and we're always growing. . . . You look at someone's heart and struggle and where people put their minds, their hearts, their bodies, their whole beings into something, and you ask are they reaching out to other people and to other particularities? I try—I wouldn't be here at the UUA if I weren't trying to reach out to somebody, because this is not my particularity right here! It may be yours, but it's not mine, yet I'm here. I'm here because I think when you reach out, people need to see what your limits are. In becoming a teacher, the best thing you can do is to show people you don't know everything. And when they see that, they say, Well, if he or she doesn't know everything, then maybe I can get to be a teacher too! I'm not saying I know as much as I ought to know, but I am struggling to reach out, and I think that's what we all ought to try to do. And we ought to continue to do that as much as we can and never be satisfied with where we are but always continue to grow and move.

REBECCA PARKER: My question is about martyrdom. Do you agree with King that his physical death was the most redemptive thing he did? Could you comment some more on what you mean by *redemptive tasks?*

CONE: Let me comment on why I think King said that. Unlike the feminists who have spoken of the problems with sacrificial death, King deeply believed in it because for him, the heart of the faith was at the cross. He deeply believed that our suffering is redemptive, because through it we express our solidarity with those who are weak and powerless. For King, the cross of Jesus was redemptive because it expressed God's solidarity with the little ones. He didn't see how you could express that solidarity in any kind of redemptive sense unless you were prepared to die for what you believe. He believed, and I believe too, that when people see this deepest commitment, even unto martyrdom, they are redeemed by it—that is, they are inspired to also give *their* lives.

Now, I know and have read a lot about the danger of making suffering so central to the faith—the danger for women, the danger for blacks. But King believed that suffering can be redemptive, and his belief was so deep that he was prepared to give his own life—and by doing so, he transformed American society on racial issues.

I think both sides of the argument are right. I think there are some cases in which suffering is not redemptive, but I also think there are times when privileged people (and King saw himself as privileged) should give their lives for those who are less privileged. That means risking something very deep. If suffering leads the little ones to die or to give their lives for those who are victimizing them, for those who are trying to make them content with their suffering, that is not redemptive. What is redemptive is when people are inspired to say, What you do to my body cannot destroy who I am; there is an inner spirit of freedom and identity that is so powerful that what you do to the physical body cannot destroy who I am. I think that's what King was talking about. King was trying to say, I give my life for what I'm struggling for because I believe that I have an identity that others cannot destroy, no matter what they do. And that's where I am. I follow King in that.

FRED MUIR: As a white Anglo-Saxon Midwestern liberal Protestant at Union Theological Seminary from 1972 to 1975, I was one of those whom I felt like you silenced; there were others who were absolutely terrified to step inside James Cone's classroom.

CONE: Oh, really. . . . [laughter]

MUIR: Yes! It was a difficult time, and it was an amazing time at Union because the entire institution went through a transformation—I've never seen anything quite like it. But that transformation, for those like me, prompted a lot of struggle. It forced me to go inward, to look at my own personal prejudice, my own racism, which you tend to discount in your paper. You focus, and I agree with you, on structural racism, and yet within our movement there are many folks who say that that is not the way to go. They say we have to start with the individual, we have to start with personal prejudice; if we don't start with personal prejudice we'll never transform the institution. I'd like you to say more about the personal prejudice part and just where that fits in.

CONE: I'm a product of the 1960s Civil Rights movement. We did a whole lot of sitting around talking to whites about white racism—endlessly long nights. What we found out is that after all the talk across many many years, whites hadn't moved much. And they had talked you to death! And I just get tired of talking—I want to change the structures! I'm not saying that nobody should talk to you; just not me [laughter]. I want to talk about structural things; I want to talk about things that are going to affect me no matter what you think about me.

That doesn't mean that your personal struggle should not be dealt with, but that's why they have psychiatrists and therapists, and I just don't want to be your therapist. In the context of a conference like this one, I want to talk about racism in a structural way. In another kind of context, we can talk about it in a more therapeutic, intimate way. But I want to talk about white supremacy as a reality in the world, the same way Jews talk about anti-Semitism as a reality, and women talk about patriarchy; it's not "just what you feel in your heart." It is structural, it is real, and let's deal with that. That's how Union Seminary changed; it was not just sitting around and talking.

GEORGE "TINK" TINKER: I want to pick up on Fred's question, because it seems to me that until we understand that there is more going on in this social mix called racism, sexism, classism, and all forms of oppression than just some policies that have gone askew, some practices that have been violent to people, we won't really come to the point of genuine social transformation.

For me, one of the critical things is uncovering the structures of language, the structures of discourse, because culture and language are so closely related to one another. We have to understand that the methodology used in schools of higher education—seminaries, for example—is actually part of the culture and part of the problem, and that as a society we're not open to changing those patterns of discourse. Instead, we just perpetuate the past even if we do come up with some new policies, some current legislation that takes care of one particular issue at one particular time. What struck me in your question, Fred, is that for me, as an American Indian, the notion of personal conversion, of individual conversion, is so deeply rooted in white Euro-American culture that my first reaction was not to know exactly what to do with it!

My wife and I teach a course called "Race, Gender, and Class." In it, we set out to have a deeply theoretical conversation about race, gender, and class so that we can begin to devise strategies for changing the language, changing patterns of behavior, and transforming the social structures of the world around us. As long as we're only dealing with oppression on a person-by-person basis, it's kind of like—this is an analogy from the conservative Christian world—hoping that the Evangelist can finally convert the whole world, when we now know for a fact that that's a losing proposition, as other religions in the world have outraced the growth of Christianity.

At some point I want to push us to talk about the centrality of the European "self"—this model of individualism—and talk about paradigms of discourse more completely. That makes the question a whole lot more difficult.

BILL JONES: Getting theologians to talk, to break the silence, is only a necessary condition, it is not a strategy in itself. Getting them to talk does not indicate whether or not they are going to adopt the kind of strategy that is going to correct the problem. It's necessary but insufficient.

CONE: I agree with you 100 percent! Talking is not in and of itself going to solve the problem, but it sure is a starting point. If we don't get white theologians to talk, they aren't going to do anything.

JONES: Yes, but they start talking, and then they use their non-corrective talk as a way of legitimating that they are no longer oppressors—when the content of their talk is simply a perpetuation of the oppression in another form.

CONE: Well, that's why we're here, to make sure it goes beyond talking!

Study Questions

1. Although racism inflicts massive suffering, few American theologians have even bothered to address white supremacy as a moral evil and as a radical contradiction of our humanity and religious identities. Cone asks, "Why do white ministers and theologians ignore racism? Shouldn't they be the first to attack this evil?" How do you answer these questions? The author then recounts some of the liberation theology dialogues that address racism. He agrees with Martin Luther King's call for "temporary segregation" in order to achieve an integrated society. Do you agree or disagree with Cone and King? Why?

2. Cone argues that North American and European male theologians hardly ever mentioned the sin of racism in their public discourse during the 1960s and 1970s, and it appeared that they could not see that white supremacy was America's central theological problem. Cone articulates four reasons why whites rarely speak or write about racism. Do you agree with his perspectives? Why? How does your perspective differ? Which of the four reasons makes the most sense to you? Explain.

3. Cone states that awareness of racism is a problem of religious identity and not just a societal problem. Therefore, he says, it

is the first step toward engaging with racism theologically. Do you agree with Cone? Why or why not?

4. Cone argues that we may debate strategies for fighting white supremacy, but there can be no debate about whether the anti-racist struggle is a worthy and necessary calling of a religious institution and its theology. How does your congregation, the UUA, or your district express solidarity with this calling? Name some of the successes and failures of our religious movement's anti-racist struggle.

5. In his essay, Cone reflects on the nature of power. "Powerful people do not talk, except on their own terms and almost never at the behest of others. All the powerless can do is disrupt—make life uncomfortable for the ruling elites." How do you understand white privilege as an individual and as a member of your congregation or community? From your experience, how do you understand black rage as an individual and as a member of your congregation or community?

6. Cone contends that if you benefit from past and present racial injustices, you are partly and indirectly responsible for perpetuating America's institutional racism—which, according to Wayne Arnason, requires accountability. How have you confronted white privilege in *your* daily experiences? How have you challenged white supremacy in your congregation and local community?

7. Cone recommends "the development of a hard-hitting anti-racist theology by white religion scholars." What would an anti-racist theology look like? What actions are needed to support it? What knowledge and attitude must be brought to this work?

8. Cone advocates support of "black empowerment in the society, in the church, and in theology." How do you understand black empowerment? How can Unitarian Universalists engage the histories, cultures, and theologies of people of African, Arab, Asian, Latina/o, Caribbean, Pacific, Native American, and other non–Anglo-Saxon heritage?

9. In the dialogue following Cone's essay and presentation, participants wanted to hear more about his concept of a "common humanity." How does Cone understand the concept of com-

mon humanity? Do you agree with Cone that "You can't find our common humanity until you search for it in 'the other'"?

10. Silence among white theologians and breaking the silence in the face of white supremacy in our religious institutions are the themes and theological imperatives of this essay. How can our congregations and religious movement actively participate in breaking the silence? In your view, which is more important: unpacking personal prejudice or struggling with institutional racism? As a result of personal reflection on this essay, how did your thinking change? As a Unitarian Universalist, what actions must you take?

7.10.2003

The Problem of Theology
in the Work of Anti-racism:
A Meditation

ROSEMARY BRAY McNATT

Several years ago, in the middle of my seminary education, my literary agent called with an intriguing proposition. "Would I be willing to be considered as co-writer of Coretta Scott King's autobiography?" she wanted to know. I was one of several people being considered, but the book's prospective editor was said to be partial to me. I was more than willing to talk about it, and a meeting between Mrs. King and myself was arranged at the editor's office.

I didn't make the final cut of writers under consideration, but that is not why I tell this story. During an hour of wide-ranging conversation, I mentioned to Mrs. King that I was in seminary to become a Unitarian Universalist minister. What frankly surprised me was the look she gave me, one of respect and delight.

"Oh, I went to Unitarian churches for years, even before I met Martin," she told me, explaining that she had been, since college, a member of the Women's International League for Peace and Freedom, which was popular among Unitarian Universalists. "And Martin and I went to Unitarian churches when we were in Boston."

What surprised and saddened me most was what she said next, and though I am paraphrasing, the gist of it was this: "We gave a lot of thought to becoming Unitarian at one time, but Martin and I realized we could never build a mass movement of black people if we were Unitarian."

It was a statement that pierced my heart and troubled my mind, both then and now. I considered what this religious movement would be like if Dr. King had chosen differently, had decided to cast his lot with our faith instead of returning to his roots as an African American Christian. And what troubled me most was my realization that our liberal religious movement would have utterly neutralized the greatest American theologian of the twentieth century. Certainly, his race would have been the primary barrier. In a religious movement engaged until the 1970s in the active discouragement of people of color wishing to join its ministerial ranks, Dr. King might have found his personal struggles to serve Unitarian Universalism at least as daunting as the Montgomery Bus Boycott.

But even if race had disappeared as an issue, Dr. King might have found the barrier of theology insurmountable. Though from the very start of his theological training he revealed a decided bent toward liberal religion, by the time his faith had been tried by the Civil Rights movement Dr. King had said no to the sunny optimism of liberal faith, an optimism frankly untested in the heat of the battle for liberty and dignity for African Americans.

In his famous essay "Pilgrimage to Nonviolence," part of the Christian Century's series "How My Mind Has Changed," Dr. King made some trenchant comments about liberal theology that bear discussion.

> There is one phase of liberalism that I hope to cherish always: its devotion to the search for truth, its refusal to abandon the best light of reason. . . . It was . . . the liberal doctrine of man that I began to question. The more I observed the tragedies of history, and man's shameful inclination to choose the low road, the more I came to see the depths and strength of sin. . . . I came to feel that liberalism had been all too sentimental concerning human nature and that it leaned toward a false idealism. I also came to see that liberalism's superficial optimism concerning human nature caused it to overlook the fact that reason is darkened by sin. . . . Liberalism failed to see that reason by itself is little more than an instrument to justify man's defensive ways of thinking. Reason, devoid of the purifying power of faith, can never free itself from distortions and rationalizations.[1]

Long before I ever spoke to Mrs. King, I had sensed in some of her husband's writings the tension between liberal theology and the African American religious and cultural traditions that formed him. To read one of his first papers in graduate school on the role of reason and experience in finding God is to watch his earliest attempts to think through the connections between the experiential and relational God that is a bedrock of traditional African American theology and the use of reason in religion, demanded of humanity in a scientific age.

In the matter of experience, King writes, "religious experience is the awareness of the presence of the divine. Religious experience is not an intellectual formulation about God, it is a lasting acquaintance with God. . . ." He concludes that, "although experience is not the only way to find God, it is probably the primal way. It is a road . . . open to all levels of human intelligence."

With respect to reason, he continues, "It must be remembered that it is the duty of reason to examine, interpret, and classify the facts of experience. In other words, experience is the logical subject matter of reason. . . . Our knowledge of the absolute will always remain relative. We can never gain complete knowledge or proof of the real. This, however, does not destroy the stream of rational religion. On the contrary, it reveals to us that intellectual finality is unattainable in all fields; all human knowledge is relative, and all human ideas are caught in the whirlpool of relativity."[2]

Would Dr. King ever have found a place in a religious movement in which the dominant sense of excitement could be found in these words from Charles Francis Potter in 1930?

> So necessary is love and goodwill to the development of human consciousness that the highest conception of God that [humanity] has yet postulated is God as love, but it means only that man continues to make personal his highest ideal.

> But love is not power nor an attribute of power. The "power of love" cannot be taken literally.

> Love is a product of the flowering of human personality and can exist only between personalities. That love is an attribute of God according to theistic conception is consistent because God to them is a person though spiritual. . . . Every man will assume the responsibility for his own development but pledge himself that his efforts shall be in accordance with the best interests of mankind.[3]

Might Martin Luther King have one day joined a list of great Unitarian Universalists? Might his image have ended up on a tee shirt or banner at General Assembly? Would he one day have been enshrined in a religious education module? Perhaps no one with the power of Martin Luther King would have lived life in complete obscurity. But for him to have answered the call to a liberal religious faith, a faith that clearly resonated with him since his earliest days of graduate studies, would have meant a fatal separation from the sources of his power: a faith in a suffering God who stood with suffering people despite their mistakes and failures, and covenantal love between himself and oppressed African Americans, the people who grounded his passion for justice but did not restrict it solely to themselves.

The notion of the self-perfectibility of human beings was an inadequate theology in the face of the sustained hatred and embodied evil of the segregationist South. Yet Dr. King retained his faith in the great potential for goodness in humanity, his faith in the possibilities of human nature that Unitarians and Universalists would lift up as a corollary to our free faith. But it was reason and experience that revealed as much to Dr. King about humanity as about divinity, and what he thought and learned taught him the importance of both.

The great Universalist Clarence Russell Skinner wrote, "the ministries of religion are as many and as varied as the needs of men [and women]. What gives deep satisfaction to one group leaves another utterly cold; and what stimulates one person at one time may be useless . . . at another period of . . . existence. Standardization is thus out of the question."[4]

Skinner was referring to worship, of course, but the topic of theology and anti-racist work includes all of congregational life. Of all the many ways in which we struggle to be genuinely accessible communities of faith, it is the struggle against theological standardization that I think creates the most anxiety among us. Curiously, it was this aspect of our recent sensibility that came as the biggest surprise to me in my own journey of faith. I met in my early years at the Community Church of New York a host of folk across the theological spectrum, making room for one another with remarkable good humor. We were a congregation that fought about many things, but never, to my knowledge, about our religious paths, never about our theologies.

I had been a UU for eight or nine years when I moved to Detroit, Michigan. I was participating in a service at the Detroit church, and in my part of the presentation I had talked about God. An older woman approached me during coffee hour later that morning to inform me that as UUs, we had given up the notion of God. She demanded to know how I, as an African American woman, could possibly talk about God when that same reprehensible Christian concept had been used to justify slavery. I was dumbfounded by her vehemence, but not too shocked to remind her that it was that same conception of God—most particularly, a just and loving God whose movement was forever toward justice and freedom and wholeness—that had fueled much of the anti-slavery movement, and indeed, most of the major reform movements of the nineteenth century that we as Unitarian Universalists were so eager to claim. Finally, I informed her that I was just as much a UU as she was, and I had not given up on the notion of God.

I couldn't decide what was more frightening—the fact that she seemed oblivious to our historic roots as a liberal Christian community of faith, or her desire to make sure no mention of a higher power of any kind ever disturbed her worship experience. I asked myself then, as I have asked myself hundreds of times since, how much we mean what we say about inclusion, about becoming an anti-racist religious community, when we are not willing to acknowledge, incorporate, or engage the historic theological realities alive among many people of color.

Do we really understand that in pursuit of this goal of an anti-racist association, we are risking more than we realize? Do we realize that we are risking being informed by varieties of religious experience not entertained in our churches for decades, if ever? Are we prepared to know what it is that informs the survival strategies used by people often on the margins? Are we prepared to accept that even among people of color at comfortable economic levels—as opposed to those poor, uneducated people who don't know any better than to praise God—there may be not only a theological but a cultural understanding of the divine that travels with them into our sanctuaries?

Sometimes a person's experience is informed by structural oppression. Sometimes, it's just life itself that has weighed on them. But there are many people who have found help and hope and strength from a source greater than themselves in order to endure what has often seemed unendurable. Do we risk their sharing with us how they have survived? What if they tell us, "God brought me through"? Do we dare to make room for them to share and to celebrate, to witness to what they have seen and felt and intimately know?

What if our liberal religious brother Dr. King had come to one of our congregations on that dark night during the movement after being bombarded with threats on his life and the lives of his family? What if he had said, not to God, but to one of us, that he couldn't go on anymore, that he was afraid? What if he had said, as he did say to God, "I am here taking a stand for what I believe is right. But now I am afraid. The people are looking to me for leadership, and if I stand before them without strength and courage, they too will falter. I am at the end of my powers. I have nothing left. I've come to the point where I can't face it alone"?

Might members of our congregations have prayed for him, or with him? Or would he have been consoled with words like these from Potter:

> If man habitually leans upon God when the going is hard, and expects God's help when he meets a difficulty, he loses the strength of character which is gained by the extra effort in emergencies. . . . And when, at a time of crisis, man does pray and depend on God, and help does come, does that prove that the help came from God? Too often, man thanks God for what man has done.[5]

In the end, Dr. King chose to forego the liberal religious enterprise and lean on the God who promised never to leave or to forsake him, even in death. Yet many of us who believe in the work have not left this movement. Many of us, in the free and responsible search for truth and meaning, have found our way back to belief in God after a long sojourn elsewhere. Many of us who grew up in the black church, and many others who can say that the black church grew up in them, have followed our varied paths to the doors of liberal faith. Are we here to provide interior decoration for our congregations, here to do spiritual domestic work on behalf of those wounded by God, by racism, by white privilege, or by the circumstances of their own lives? Can we who are called to serve as religious leaders discern when we are doing ministry and when we are doing minstrelsy? Might our own wounds stand in the way of clarity? Will there ever be a time when we can authentically be who we are, believe what we believe, speak our own truth, sing our own song—and be with one another?

The work of becoming an anti-racist religious movement is not an adventure in which I am willing to participate under false pretenses. I want it all: for us to be anti-racist, religious, and a movement. I respect that the theological stance of others will differ from my own. But I am as hungry to be freed from the narrowness of our religious assumptions as I am to be released from the wary dance we engage in around race, class, and gender. I am as eager to see my congregants—and my ministerial colleagues—emerge from their massive blindness to the last thirty years of theology as I am to see what we might do in a religious community in which praxis is a given. I nurse a secret wish that one Sunday, my Pentecostal mother might wander into a Unitarian Universalist congregation and stay for services even if I'm not in the pulpit. Above all, I am praying for the transformation of the religious movement I love so much—and hoping for just one day when I won't have to explain why I might choose to pray.

The Responses

As Rosemary Bray McNatt explained before the discussion of her essay began, this paper really was a meditation, "something that I have been struggling with since I returned to church through Unitarian Universalism. . . . How could I reconcile the experience of a relational God, an experience that has a lot of resonance for me as an African American woman who grew up in an African American community, with my encounters with other people in Unitarian Universalist congregations who were humanist in a way that I found disconcerting because of their vehemence and their total reliance on human agency? What would life have been like historically for African Americans had human agency been the only power being brought to bear? Is there room in the Unitarian Universalist movement now for the variety of voices that belong to people for whom the Unitarian Universalist message—the message of hope and courage in the context of freedom—would be powerful? Or does this message get lost because of the sometimes pervasive hostility around God-language?"

José Ballester's response adds the variables of culture, economic status, language, and ethnic differences to Bray McNatt's examination of the "limitations of [Unitarian Universalist] theology in the work of anti-racism." Comparing the life and words of Latino liberator César Chávez to those of Martin Luther King Jr., Ballester points to ways that these two leaders could expand Unitarian Universalist notions of "freedom, tolerance, and reason in religion:"

> In the more liberal Protestant faiths, a hyper-individualism arose that became infused in many of the secular practices. For Unitarian Universalists this sense of hyper-individualism is best expressed by Earl Morse Wilbur, who saw our theology as a "progressive development of freedom, tolerance, and reason in religion."[6]

> It is precisely at this juncture where Chávez would disagree. For him, as for many Latinos, the sense of connection and relationship in community takes precedence. Freedom, tolerance, and reason are accomplishments achievable by an individual. What Chávez extolled were the qualities of life that could only be accomplished by being in relationship with a community. . . .

> Individual freedom [counts] for nothing if the community [is] not free. Thus Chávez and King both worked for the liberation of the whole community by stressing the needs of the poorest. "Perhaps we can work for the [time]," wrote Chávez, "when children will learn from their earliest days that being fully man and fully woman means to give one's life to the liberation of the brother or sister who suffers."[7]

> Tolerance seemingly calls for us to be accepting of individual differences and to create a community without prejudice. However, mere tolerance does not compel us to actively comprehend or appreciate our differences. We can become a gathering of individuals rather than a community working on behalf of others. Tolerance magnifies individual deeds and creates a false sense of accomplishment on the part of the group. Rather than tolerance, King and Chávez called for the various groups to use their collective power in actively opposing oppression. Ultimately, the justice-seeking community will be strengthened by association with others. . . .

> In her closing, Rev. Bray McNatt calls for our movement not to be limited. . . . She desires an expansion that will allow Unitarian Universalists to embrace all the diversities among us, including theological, so that we may be a true justice-seeking community.

While I share her vision, I desire more. It is my hope that our diversity crosses all lines and that we can be one in the struggle for justice. It is my hope that we, as a movement, realize that a just social order cannot be created only for the poor and the oppressed, and it cannot be created only without them. To work for justice that truly liberates the community requires the active participation of all people at all economic and social levels.

JoEllen Willis's response draws on A. Powell Davies' notion of people being "almost good." For Davies, goodness is a "possible choice . . . a temptation to leave the dreary paths of disappointment and frustration and live as [people] really want to live"[8]—but it is a temptation that most people resist. Willis continues,

> To engage in the hard work of dismantling racism has undeniable appeal—it is tempting. Yet we hesitate. What might be the cost? What will our friends, co-workers, neighbors think? What might we lose? So we resist the temptation and remain "almost good."
>
> The problem of theology in the work of anti-racism, I would suggest, lies not in its theory, but in its practice. It is not the acknowledgment of evil that restrains us. We have the will to acknowledge the imperfections of the world and the shortcomings of our society. We are almost good. What we lack is the courage to acknowledge that we ourselves are imperfect in our relationships with oppressed groups. What we lack is the perseverance to see such a task to completion. And what we lack is the grace to be humble.
>
> A word on courage: If we are to be anti-racist, we shall require the will to overcome our denial, our fear, and our apathy. We must be so tempted by goodness that we ignore the pundits who insist that racism is beyond destruction because it is embedded in systems more powerful than individuals. We shall need a faith deep enough and wide enough to challenge the structures of racism.
>
> Intellectual courage is not in short supply among us. We are brave in our reflections. We are not so bold in our actions. As a religious educator in the mid-eighties, I was proud to share the stories of our honorable past with our young people. From Theodore Parker to James Reeb, we have exemplars. And in many of our congregations we have inherited a fine legacy of

social action, particularly from the period of the civil rights movement. But that was long ago. So many of us lay claim to an inheritance that we ourselves have not earned. As heirs, these gifts are not ours to keep but to spend. . . . If a common thread of our many theologies is a belief in the inherent worth and dignity of every person, and if we come together to affirm equity, justice, and compassion in human relations, then we must invest that capital in turning the world toward justice. . . .

And, oh, if we could pray together! If those of us who have "given up the notion of God" could stand beside those whose lives have brought them to a suffering God, a compassionate God, a redeeming God, and hear their truth as clearly as we declare our own, then we would be transformed, each of us and all of us, by the power of varieties of faith. . . .

Rosemary Bray McNatt is right to question our ability to accept people of any color whose cultural and theological understanding of a church community includes faith in the God of Exodus and Easter. So many Unitarian Universalists are skeptics; so few are humble. Our temptation to be good must include the opportunity to consider that our answers may not be *the* answers and that our needs may need to yield to a greater need.

The Dialogue

How do the influences of culture restrain the impulses of inclusiveness? Do Unitarian Universalist styles of worship, for example, welcome all? In a primarily white denomination, what is the role of both clergy and laity (of all colors and cultures) in embracing more diverse worship styles? To what extent are worship style preferences related to race and culture? Finally, how do those struggling for racial justice keep their passion alive? These are the focal questions of the dialogue, which emphasizes the themes of hospitality, accountability, and motivation.

ELIZABETH ELLIS: In the community of Roxbury where I have ministered, people need a God who will not forsake them, even unto death. Their experiences of incarceration and of death from violence—both domestic and gang-related—to undergo all these experiences is to know Satan and to know God. There is a strong need for the positive theology of Universalism, but we Unitarian

Universalists are not really using that language. . . . We need to be talking with new groups—with people of color and people in poor communities—about the style and culture of our churches.

BRAY MCNATT: I love this idea. I believe our message gets lost because of stylistic differences. There is an undercurrent of belief among some folks that Unitarian Universalism is for a "certain kind of people." I don't believe that. I believe that our historical Universalist message has enormous potential to reach African Americans and people who have been—and are—oppressed. Evangelical Christian preaching emphasizes a belief in a God of love, forgiveness, and constancy; this is not incompatible with our tradition. There must be a way to bridge the gaps.

THANDEKA: You write about your Pentecostal mother in your paper. Are you making her a litmus test for the adequacy of Unitarian Universalist rituals? If not, what is the litmus test for the adequacy of worship, and what would inclusive worship look like?

BRAY MCNATT: No, I don't have a litmus test. But my mother is the best theologian I know. She *lives* Universalism. So I would say that any worship where she could be satisfied and could pray and sing and testify if she needed to, where the preaching is not just intellectual but speaks to the deepest longings of her heart—that would be truly inclusive worship. The things we most want in worship would be what my mom wants.

LEON SPENCER: Rosemary, your essay made me feel like testifying! You touched on my own woundedness and made me think about how that woundedness is connected to anti-racism work. As a Unitarian Universalist, I keep shifting back and forth from "Christian" to "person of color," as if I can't be both. What if we were to reclaim the multicultural self? There are many people who live in this "in-betweenness." My hope is for a theology that would be open and liberating enough that whoever the people are in the in-betweenness, they would be welcome.

TRACEY ROBINSON-HARRIS: Rosemary, you talk about "spiritual domestic work." I'm wondering, what do white folks ask people of color to do for us? I would suggest that we ask them to affirm us, to forgive us, to be our teachers, to bless us, and to like us. We must look at the spiritual labor of accountability. White folks ask people of color to bring the resources of community to us because we won't look inside ourselves for the spiritual domestic work, the resources, and the labor. When will we get a grip and move on?

BILL JONES: When I came into the Unitarian Universalist denomination, there was a sense that there would be a large influx of oppressed people, but that hasn't happened. Instead, what we seem to be doing is encouraging African Americans and people of color to join Unitarian Universalism in order to help whites become more whole—which may be healing the racism of white Unitarian Universalists, but it is not making the playing field more level. This makes us [people of color] the suffering servant, when this concept is supposed to refer to the person at the top, not the person at the bottom. Should I attempt to increase the number of African Americans in Unitarian Universalism if this is going to be their role? I haven't seen much in our anti-racism initiatives to make me think this is going to change.

BRAY MCNATT: There probably will be a point when a larger number of people of color will come into this movement for the right reasons—because it is a religious movement that speaks to them. Meanwhile, those of us who are already here will have to mediate for ourselves to what degree we rise to or reject the role of suffering servant. When we work in partnership with white Americans, we can't avoid provoking and being the conscience for the discussion. During my internship in Montclair, New Jersey, it became clear to me, to my senior minister, and to others in the congregation that my role was not to hold white folks' hands—and yet holding people's hands is what ministry is.

People of color in this movement must be supportive of each other in this draining work, and not do the work because it is sacrificial, but because it is the call we have accepted, the work we have chosen. What I hope for is a measure of accountability, and my challenge—my question—to white people is "Are you prepared to be accountable for this work, and if not, why not?"

MARJORIE BOWENS-WHEATLEY: What role do we Unitarian Universalist ministers of color have to play in addressing our woundedness, our internalized racism, and what challenges do you see for us in working as "wounded healers"?

BRAY MCNATT: We have to be conscious of our own woundedness first. Ministers are called to do things that challenge what hurts us the most. This is deeply spiritual work. The source of my growing capacity for this work is grace—and the recognition of our common humanity.

GARY SMITH: The line that leaps out of your paper for me is the one about "those who have found our way back to a belief in God after a long sojourn." I am on this journey, too. But part of my struggle is knowing what the Promised Land looks like. We tend to live in the "not yet" instead of the "as if." Do you have any thoughts about the Promised Land?

BRAY MCNATT: I have thought a lot about the truth of the Exodus story—that Moses doesn't get to the Promised Land. I know what I wish it would look like, but like Dr. King, I'm not sure I will ever see it. Still, there is a long tradition in the African American church of working to get to a place you will not see.

PETER MORALES: Both Rosemary and José spoke to the theme of how difficult it is for people who are liberal, who can see all the complexity, and who can speak from multiple points of view to have the passion and the motivation for change that folks with a simpler view sometimes seem to have. Sometimes the people best equipped to see the great reality lose the flame. You urge us to blow on the coal of the heart that keeps passion alight—and when you know how to do that, call collect anytime!

Study Questions

1. In her discussion with Rosemary Bray McNatt, Coretta Scott King reveals that she and Dr. King once considered becoming Unitarian Universalists. Why did they not? How might our faith community be different today had the Kings chosen to become a part of our religious movement? What would need to happen for our congregations to become havens for activism

around racial justice and the other issues of oppression that Dr.
King struggled to change?

2. Bray McNatt wonders how Unitarian Universalists would
   respond to Dr. King's search for allies and companioning in
   prayer during his most difficult time. She asks, "Might members of our congregations have prayed for him, or with him?"
   JoEllen Willis echoes that sentiment: "And, oh, if we could pray
   together! If those of us who have 'given up the notion of God'
   could stand beside those whose lives have brought them to a
   suffering God, a compassionate God, a redeeming God, and
   hear their truth as clearly as we declare our own, then we
   would be transformed, each of us and all of us, by the power of
   varieties of faith." How do you respond to Willis's desire for
   solidarity and transformation?

3. Claiming that there is a link between racial justice and theological diversity in Unitarian Universalism, Bray McNatt
   asserts that many Unitarian Universalists have not been willing to acknowledge or incorporate a reality that is important
   for many people of color: our historic roots as a liberal
   Christian community of faith. Furthermore, she questions the
   extent to which Unitarian Universalists are accepting and
   affirming of those for whom God-language and/or prayer are
   central theological precepts. Do you think that theology—
   specifically what Bray McNatt calls our "sometimes pervasive
   hostility around God-language" and "total reliance on human
   agency"—is an impediment to people of color becoming and
   remaining Unitarian Universalists? If so, to what extent do
   you think we can broaden our theological perspectives to
   affirm and embrace people of many colors and many cultures?

4. Bray McNatt asks, "Are we here to provide interior decoration
   for our congregations, here to do spiritual domestic work on
   behalf of those wounded by God, by racism, by white privilege, or by the circumstances of their own lives?" How do you
   answer this question?

5. "I am as hungry to be freed from the narrowness of our religious assumptions as I am to be released from the wary dance
   we engage in around race, class, and gender," writes Bray Mc-
   Natt. How do you understand the linkage between religion

and these various forms of oppression? Is there a hierarchy of oppression for people of faith? For Unitarian Universalists?

6. Citing the writings of César Chávez, José Ballester emphasizes the need for Unitarian Universalists to grasp the impact of "hyper-individualism" on the work of becoming anti-racists. He believes, as Chávez did, that "individual freedom counts for nothing if the community is not free." In your view, can a just social order, a non-racist society, be created by individual acts of good will? If so, how?

7. Elizabeth Ellis suggests that Unitarian Universalists tend to use negative theological language, and that through deepened engagement with communities of color, we can bridge a gap; she perceives this as stylistic and cultural in character. What would need to happen to make Unitarian Universalist congregations more welcoming and affirming to people of diverse racial, cultural, and theological backgrounds? Is the gap between many African Americans (for example) and Unitarian Universalists primarily theological, or cultural and stylistic, or both?

8. What needs to happen for Unitarian Universalists to rid themselves of doing what Bray McNatt calls "spiritual domestic work"?

Theology and Anti-racism: Latino and Latina Perspectives

PATRICIA JIMENEZ

The theological transformation of freedom, from liberty into creative agency, entails a shift of vision from self-centeredness and self-fulfillment into other-regard and other-service. The relational nature of all creative processes is more clearly perceived as an extension of our relational nature. We can better come to understand how every act of creation and every creative agent needs both the active assistance and passive witness of others.

—Ismael Garcia

My association with other Latinos and Latinas within our denomination has provided me with a community—a place, as well as a group of individuals—with whom to share experiences, ideas, and knowledge. I asked some of these individuals—including Rev. José Ballester, Rev. Lilia Cuervo, Rev. Peter Morales, and seminarian Marta Valentin—to share their ideas for this paper. I appreciate both their trust and generosity in sharing their thoughts and ideas.

If a theology of liberation suggests human transformation through active participation and "active agency" in one's life, it must also point to having what one needs to physically live and to achieve fulfillment as a human being. From a Latino and Latina perspective, a theology of liberation addresses not only the indi-

43

dividual and individual action, but the community as well. In addition to the "theological transformation of freedom," Ismael Garcia says,

> The theological transformation of liberty into creative agency also transforms our understanding of community. As the community is necessary for creative agency to take place, providing the creative agent with resources and a context of meaning within which his or her creation makes sense, it is equally recognized that the community itself depends, for its survival and well being, on the creative capacity of its members.[1]

Garcia points to interconnectedness, to the recognition of the commonality of responsibilities and interests that all of us have despite differences of race or ethnicity, class, sexual preference, or age. It is not a matter of merely agreeing with or being supportive of a cause, nor is it altruism. It has to do with recognizing, affirming, valuing, and defending common interests, feelings, purposes, and actions.

To be a creative agent means that one is not just allowed but also *actively encouraged* to tell one's story as an act of "active assistance" and "passive witness." In my work as a hospital chaplain, this is the single most powerful thing that I do. I ask people to tell me their story, and then I listen.

To become a creative agent, however, it is equally important to identify oneself. To name oneself is a way of claiming one's power. A name is not just an identification; it also provides a conceptual framework, a point of reference, a mental construct by which to think, understand, and relate to an individual. To name oneself is a dilemma that many of us face in many different ways. Do we get to choose how we identify ourselves or do others choose?

For the purposes of this article, I must find a way to refer to a large number of people, loosely affiliated and of great diversity. I will use *Latino* and *Latina,* knowing that these terms do not begin to describe the complex mix that we know ourselves to be, knowing, too, that someone will be or will feel excluded. That is not my intention.

Race. Class. Culture. Marta Valentin called these the "Un(W)holey Trinity." Even one of these has the ability to separate one from another, to build walls—mostly metaphorical, but sometimes real. For Latinos and Latinas the issues are complex. Where dis-

cussions of oppression center on race alone, and where race tends
to be cast in terms of a white and black dichotomy, the complexities of the Latino experience are lost. Our experiences are racial,
cultural, and linguistic. We cannot be defined racially, since all
races are a part of our people. Besides, if we wish to think in terms
of current scientific thought, we humans are all one despite the
fact that we see difference. In our experience, economic domina-tion
tion is directly linked to racial and ethnic domination. Our
racial/ethnic differences have been used to displace us from land,
to use us as cheap labor, to exploit our countries for their prime
resources, to insist that we give up culture and values.

With regard to race, class, and culture, the issue of names arises yet again. Among Latinos and Latinas, as perhaps among other
oppressed groups, names may carry political, cultural, social, and
racial meanings. For example, a name may be a political/geo-
graphical description that indicates national heritage, such as
Puerto Rican or Cuban; it may make a political statement, as with
the name *Chicano;* or it may be a racial description, such as *mulat-
to* or *mestizo.* In some countries, names may even indicate class.

Our names and descriptions of ourselves are colored by individual experiences of history and politics and geography. Some of
us, Chicanos and Puerto Ricans, are citizens of this country as a
result of U.S. conquest and colonization. Many of us have lived in
what is now the United States since the sixteenth century. Those of
us who have roots here among the indigenous peoples of this
hemisphere may count time even further back. Others have
entered the United States in more recent waves of immigration.

Often these names are controversial, and in the end, as my colleague Peter Morales wrote, "Any category is an idol, no matter
how powerful or useful that category may be. For behind any construct is a rich, multifaceted, complex, chaotic, messy reality. . . .
Using categories inevitably does a subtle kind of violence. I am a
Latino. But while that term captures a critical part of who I am, it
does not begin to capture the totality of who I am."

His comments bring to mind the U.S. census form, one of the
more recent examples of an attempt to name and categorize
according to race that left me frustrated and uneasy. Mixed, as I
know myself to be, I struggled to find a category that fit. There
were certainly more categories on the form than I remembered
from earlier censuses! Yet, I struggled to find a category that

described me. Finally, in a fit of pique, I checked several boxes and sent the form in—fully expecting someone to come after me. At the very least, I expected to get a letter stating that I hadn't filled the form out properly, and therefore didn't belong or perhaps did not exist. The form was yet another way that my reality—and probably that of many others—is not recognized.

Bilingual education generates another complex series of issues and questions. There is no agreement, even among Latinos and Latinas, about bilingual education as an educational tool. Keep in mind that there are Latinos and Latinas who speak only English; others who speak only Spanish, others who speak Portuguese or one of the various indigenous languages around the world, and still others who are not only bilingual but multilingual. Many Latinos and Latinas growing up in the United States in the days before bilingual education may remember when we were forbidden to speak Spanish at school or punished for doing so. Even with bilingual education, language is still an issue.

Bilingual education also raises questions that go beyond language, questions such as what it takes to succeed in this country and how success is measured. The answer to these questions is complicated, first by the fact that many people buy into the great myth that all one has to do to succeed is work hard, and second by the fact that success in this country is measured solely by individual success. It also raises the question whether or to what extent mastery of language alone is sufficient to escape the cycle of poverty. Even more critically, it raises the question of just how crucial language is to identity and what it takes to nurture family, community, and cultural ties. And finally, it raises the question of what it means to be a true citizen of this country. Implicit in many of the arguments around language—and how this applies as well to other minorities who speak other languages—is the assumption that true citizens speak English. What is left out of such arguments is what it takes for those living in poverty—or below the poverty level—to find the time and energy to learn English. It is also necessary to point out that not all immigrants are poor, and the need to be able to use English will affect immigrants differently.

The question of what makes a true citizen revolves around not only language but other forms of cultural expression, and there are class issues involved as well. Implicit in the assumption about the

United States as a "melting pot" is the belief that true citizens become like everyone else. Stanford anthropology professor Renato Rosaldo suggests that there is an inverse relationship between true citizenship and cultural visibility.[2] The truth of this statement may be experienced in many ways—from English-only laws to signs suggesting that a particular group should "go home."

What is astonishing about the belief in the "melting pot" is the assumption that there exists a single correct way of being. In general, this belief in assimilation assumes absorption into the mainstream at the expense of ethnic and cultural identity, but this does not reflect reality. Alternative theories, such as multiculturalism and pluralism, do not sufficiently address the problem either. *Multiculturalism,* as some individuals may use this term, often assumes a basic and unchanging culture in which minorities merely add color rather than create an altogether new entity. Describing the drawbacks of pluralism, William V. Flores and Rina Benmayor wrote,

> While pluralism allows for private and even some public celebration of difference, it tends to be the celebration of difference in publicly sanctioned settings of special holidays, parades, and social events, where we are permitted to be Jewish, or Italian, or Polish, or to claim any other ethnic heritage. Pluralism implies that in our private lives we can possess and exhibit different cultural identities, but that in the public sphere, except in these sanctioned displays of ethnicity, we must put aside those identities and interact instead in a culturally neutral space as "Americans." By taking for granted that public space can be and is culturally neutral, pluralism endorses the dominant culture as normative. More serious is pluralism's silence on inequality and power relations in the country. While expression of difference is permitted, challenges to power relations are suppressed.[3]

I noticed this private/public dichotomy in a particularly poignant way in connection with a Latino family in Michigan. I had been called, in my role as chaplain, to be with them; the matriarch of the family was gravely ill. Her husband arrived on the unit, along with twelve grown children and their children; great-grandchildren; and numerous other relatives by birth and marriage. Exuberant, emotional, and loving, they remained, for the most part, as quiet as such a large group of people could be, but occasionally one (or usually several) would begin to cry loudly. Often one or another would feel the need to apologize. As they sat in the lounge, stood in the halls, or entered the room, they consciously regulated their numbers. In conversations, they spoke both Spanish and English, and I was aware that sometimes they deliberately spoke Spanish, which seemed to exclude staff from their discussions.

Most of the time, I navigate between my private and public worlds without thought, but there are times when to live in that cultural borderland is lonely. It is easy to feel isolated—but occasionally, private and public merge and become one. I remember an experience in a hospital emergency room with another large Latino family. The patient died, and as the family was leaving, the grandmothers thanked me and blessed me. It was an action that recognized my actions as chaplain in the public sphere of the hospital emergency room. But by its very nature—a blessing rather than, say, a handshake or a hug—it also seemed to acknowledge both my spiritual and cultural connections to them. It brought to mind all the blessings I had received from my own elders, and I recognized my position in that borderland place between public and private. In that brief moment, for me, the public and the private became one.

One cannot talk about U.S. immigration policy without talking about skin color, language, culture, and class. Along the United States–Mexico border, physical violence to undocumented immigrants is commonplace. The story of the Cuban boat people—the marielitos, working-class and black—was front-page news for months. The toll in emotional, psychological, and spiritual well-being for all those affected is unimaginable. Mexican Americans living along the border may be asked to prove their right to employment and citizenship. Over the years, thousands of individuals have been deported without due process, some without regard to whether they might be U.S. citizens. In the United States, if one is a citizen, one is not required to carry proof. Nevertheless, to live on the literal border between Mexico and the United States means that officials may question one's right to be on one side of the line rather than the other. I recall going through checkpoints along the U.S.-Mexican border and worrying about whether immigration officials would believe me when I said "American" in answer to their question about citizenship, or whether they would just ship me off. Because of stories I'd heard, I was not convinced that my fears were groundless.

There are many ways to be on the boundary, the borderlands, the margins, the edges—between worlds. It is an experience shared by many minorities in this country and perhaps elsewhere. Sometimes it involves maintaining one's identity at great cost. Latina poet Gloria Anzaldua writes,

> To live in the Borderlands means
> the mill with the razor white teeth wants to shred off
> your olive-red skin, crush out the kernel, your heart
> pound you pinch you roll you out
> smelling like white bread but dead. . . .[4]

The metaphors are graphic, but to me not so far-fetched when it comes to that place where race, culture, and class intersect.

The process of telling one's story leads to greater understanding—not just for the listener but for the narrator as well. If the listener has developed the gifts of empathy, then it is in hearing the story that he or she may begin to understand. And sometimes it is with the telling of the story that the narrator hears, learns, and understands more deeply the significance and the meaning of the story. Transformation requires understanding that comes from the very center of our being—that place that sees and knows no difference between people across social boundaries.

A theology of liberation requires that we all—oppressors and oppressed alike—learn and understand what is oppressive. It is not always obvious. I see the process as a spiral. Sometimes we revisit an event, but we don't come back to quite the same place. Each time we return, we build on our understanding.

In addition, true liberation requires two more things. It requires denunciation of oppression, and then a further step, annunciation—telling what the future will be—regardless of whether the prediction comes true within our history or not. Telling what the future will be is an opportunity for us to dream. It is an opportunity to tap into the creative magic that happens when each person is encouraged and expected to be a creative agent. When the response creates a new community of love and justice, we become co-creators with the divine. Our survival and our salvation depend on liberation for all.

Betsy

The Responses

"At the core of Patricia Jimenez's essay is a wonderful vision of a community in which each one is valued and no one is misrecognized, unknown, or unnourished," **Thomas Schade** says in his response. This is the vision of a "beloved community" that holds the highest value in much of Unitarian Universalist theology. Schade's misgivings about the beloved community include the fact that its "underlying presumption . . . is historical materialism," with materialism's categories of race, nationality, gender, class, and culture. He continues,

> I do not argue that historical materialism is not a basic tool of understanding people, cultures, and history. People's thinking is shaped by their material experience, which is not only personal but also lived in groups that have material consequence in the world political economy. I *do* question its sufficiency as a theological understanding of humanity. . . .

> Movements that rely on historical materialism, as have most of the progressive movements in the United States, have painted themselves into various theoretical and ideological corners. They are seduced by the social theory of knowledge, which stifles free inquiry. They end up assigning political authority by historical materialist categories; leaders and led do not share mutual moral accountability. They end up in contentious arguments comparing the apples and oranges of different historical oppressions. They cannot account for wide differences between people of the same category—African American conservatives, the persistence of white liberalism. They become rigid and doctrinaire.

> I am an ex-Communist, one who experimented with the twentieth century's most catastrophic mistake. Now I am very alert to the ways in which the worldview of historical materialism creeps into the Unitarian Universalist movement. I believe that when we place the "beloved community" at the core of our religious vision, we have, without clearly thinking about it, adopted a thoroughly secular worldview. . . .

> I now believe that the "beloved community" is an idol, a false god. Not that there is anything intrinsically wrong with that vision. But partly because religious liberalism has so much trouble sharing an understanding of God, we seem intent on build-

materialist

ing the beloved community *with our own hands*. We are blind to Francis
to what is transcendent and beyond our control. Bacon

As the Hebrew prophets so clearly saw, the worship of idols creates
creates and furthers relationships of domination and subordination
within the community. Because an idol is a human invention,
those people who are instrumental in the production of the idol
will have greater power. The power of the divine, including the
most crucial power to judge and to forgive, gets attached to those
who mediate the divine. They have the power of approval and
disapproval; others must play up to them. Falseness enters all
relationships and authenticity vanishes.

The beloved community will occur not because we build it with
a political and social strategy, but as we recover a proper understanding of the human person in relation to the divine. The
beloved community will occur because each of us, having experienced a sense of God's judgment and forgiveness of our own
social being, will be able to see each other from God's point of
view. The beloved community is a *by-product* of religious awakening but not its cause or goal. The crucial fulcrum of that awakening is the sharing of our flawed, imperfect, sinful selves, our
hunger for forgiveness, and our compassion for each other's
sufferings.

"Patricia Jimenez and our Latina and Latino colleagues have
issued a challenge and a critically important perspective with
respect to our understanding of the nature of what is classically
called racism," **Marjorie Bowens-Wheatley** begins in her response.
"They ask us to see the context and complexity of their living
beyond any narrow formula or category. The 'black-white' paradigm of race is seen as inadequate to understanding the lives of
Latinos and Latinas in the United States." But isn't this paradigm
too narrow for *all of us?* she asks.

We are a country that exists in a sea of falsehood, a quagmire, in
its racial thinking. Our tendency is toward simplicity in the face
of complexity. Part of the problem is our cultural embrace of
philosophical dualism—or, to borrow a phrase given to us by
William R. Jones, *binary logic.* When a society such as ours holds
Eurocentric philosophical and cultural assumptions as normative, natural, and superior, those whose background and experience are rooted in and nurtured by a different reality find little
affirmation of their being.

Thus, our Latina sisters and our Latino brothers are calling us to acknowledge their full humanity, which includes but cannot be defined strictly by skin color, bloodlines, nationality, culture, language, or political identity.

In her essay, Patricia Jimenez asserts that to tell one's story is liberating and can lead to new understandings for both the narrator and the listener. Part of my story is more common than we like to think.

Most people see me as African American. But my mother is a product of British colonialism in the Caribbean; and so, when one adds "Caribbean" to the construct of who I am, it leads to deeper understanding. And that still masks the fact that my grandfather spent twenty-one years in the Dominican Republic cutting sugar cane because there was no work on the tiny island of Anegada, where he was born. It masks the fact that hundreds of other relatives migrated to various places: to the Netherlands Antilles, to Sweden, to France, to Harlem—wherever they could make a living. These patterns of migration led to intermarriage to the point that my family mirrors the United Nations in terms of skin color, culture, language, and politics. . . . This is my family— and I didn't even include the Cherokee and Irish blood that runs through my veins; they are not as great a part of the identity I claim. This multicultural self is unique—but in the United States, it is also ordinary. It is not, I suspect, significantly different from the complexity our Latina and Latino colleagues know so well. How, then, can we ask people to fit into a box—a narrow racial identity defined by others, a box that ignores so much of who we are?

Bowens-Wheatley then references Peter Morales' assessment that "any category is an idol" that masks a rich, complex, messy reality.

"Using categories," according to Morales, "inevitably does a subtle kind of violence." Theologians such as James Luther Adams and Paul Tillich suggest that *idolatry* (which is, for me, a religious term for false consciousness) gives credence and legitimacy to that which is unreliable at best and a big lie at worst. There is nothing trustworthy or reliable, for example, about the biological construction of "race." But having said that, we must acknowledge that racism is a social reality. In studies of identity, race is often a defining factor. But if we look around this country and the world, we know that religion, class, caste, culture, nationality, sexual orientation, and other manifestations of identity are equally important. To ignore this complexity is to accept the false premise of the "melting pot"—the assumption that there is a single correct way of being. It asks us to check a part of ourselves at the door, thus denying our whole being.

As Paul Rasor has suggested and others have affirmed, racism is the problem of "other-ing" people, of holding some up as superior and putting others down as inferior. It is embedded in our way of doing things in this country and gets played out in many ways, including personal disdain and hatred, institutional discrimination, and cultural domination. All of these represent power-over—domination, which is a fundamental evil, a theological problem that we are seeking to address.

Rev. Barbara Hebner reminds us that anti-racism work is religious work. "Thou shalt not other," she says, is the "one and only commandment," which subsumes the first ten. As we search for language that is more embracing, we must remember that "other-ing" includes the systemic power to keep some people down while others are lifted up.

And this represents another complexity, lest we assume that the power of whites is more powerful than God, the Eternal, the Spirit of Life itself. When we embrace this power beyond all earthly powers and principalities, we cannot see our neighbor as "the other." When we embrace this power, this Love, more fully, we will have moved a step closer to creating a beloved community, which Patricia Jimenez and others in this gathering have wisely lifted up, thus continuing the vision articulated by the prophet Isaiah, Jesus of Nazareth, Martin Luther King, James Luther Adams, and others who saw the coming of God's reign of justice. They remind us that we are co-creators with God in bringing about the *kin-dom* of God,[5] where humanity will transcend its loyalties of particularity and move from individual or group identity to recognition of our essential relatedness, our common humanity.

The Dialogue

The dialogue expands on thoughts about the relationship between identity and naming by looking at the crucial functions of language. Participants spoke to the conjunctions and disjunctions between language and understanding, between words and meaning. Peter Morales calls for more "real experience" with each other across social and cultural differences. Others address Thomas Schade's critique of historical materialism and the need for a transcendent commonality. And drawing on her work as a hospital chaplain, Patricia Jimenez questions whether the work of anti-racism should focus on personal or institutional transformation. Must it be "either/or?" she asks. Is there a "both/and"?

REBECCA PARKER: I want to express great appreciation to you, Patricia, for naming the exercise of creative agency as the heart of liberation, and for your embodiment for us of a kind of theological praxis that listens to a community and then brings the voices of that community forward in your own voice. I especially like the way you speak about denunciation and annunciation and how you're raising the question of "true citizenship." Would you say more about citizenship in connection with announcing? And here's the context for my question:

In California, we defeated the practice of bilingual education, and some people are now struggling to continue to do bilingual education even though public policy has shifted. As that debate was going on in our state, it became clearer to me that I would be a better citizen if I were multilingual. I would like to *announce* a future in which our educational system is committed to educating everyone to speak more than one language, rather than the reverse. What kind of future would you announce regarding languages and regarding citizenship?

JIMENEZ: Citizenship carries with it both privileges and responsibilities. For example, being an introvert and being generally quiet, I find it much easier to not speak up, but I've come to realize that citizenship *requires* that I speak and that I be able to name the truth. That's the *de*nunciation part—that I have to be able to name the oppression, I have to be able to name the evils.

The *an*nunciation part has to do with our dreams: What kind of world would we like to live in? Sometimes this vision is going to be very specific, like education for everybody and health care for everybody. Sometimes it's simply going to refer to a way of being with each other. Either way, it's what we work for.

I have learned many languages, when I was in school and when I was in India, because I wanted to be able to talk to people personally. I wanted to get to know them. But one of the things I've learned along the way is that even when you know the language, you don't always understand. You don't know whether a person's reaction to something—the death of a loved one, for instance—is related to that person's psychology, to her culture, or what exactly. It's very complex.

PAUL RASOR: *Doy las gracias a Patricia y José y Dianne y Tink por introducir la verdao sobe que se toma para entender el lenguage.* I thank Patricia and José and Dianne and Tink for articulating a truth about what it takes to understand a language. And I begin in Spanish not to be clever or cute but to acknowledge that we're often missing each other's *meaning* even when we think we're speaking a common language. The language we are using, even in this room—and I don't mean just "English"—has all sorts of socio-cultural underpinnings that color the way discourse happens. We need to be reminded that we're not always speaking the same language even when it *sounds* like we are.

I think the underlying assumptions of much anti-racism work, for example, are black-and-white assumptions. I try to use "race" as a placeholder that symbolizes or stands for something more; but, of course, it is a completely inadequate placeholder. We could use "oppression," which is better; but clearly, that's inadequate, too. I'm not sure what the answer is or whether there is an answer.

MEL HOOVER: As I was sitting here, I was hearing the words that I grew up with: "Say what you mean and mean what you say." It seems to me that language serves a number of functions. Sometimes it's about identity, but sometimes it is actually about *communication* and *meaning.* I have understood people whose language I did not know and could not speak; yet, we have communicated. In my international work, I have traveled all over the world, and even though I couldn't use those languages, I somehow found my way into being part of the families I visited.

Neurolinguistic theories tell us that we spend most of our time focusing on words and facts, but they're not the largest part of how we communicate. Words make up only 10 to 15 percent of our communication. We communicate with our bodies, with our gestures, with the way we move in space, with a whole set of interactions. Part of our comfort level depends on what we bring into a particular part of the world and whether what we bring is congruent with that particular culture and that particular setting. It may be that as we become more diverse, one of the things that we will have an opportunity to practice and learn is not just how to talk but how to communicate. If we could find ways to focus on hearing each other's *meaning*, the words wouldn't get in the way as much. This feels like something we need to wrestle with.

BILL JONES: You identify the concept of pluralism as a sort of inauthentic approach because it does not emphasize co-equality—the co-equal sharing of power and authority. I'm more familiar with a model that includes three ways of interacting across race and ethnicity: assimilation, integration, and pluralism. In this model, pluralism *stands for* co-equality. So is your understanding of pluralism different from the one I just described?

JIMENEZ: I think there is a good way of practicing pluralism that does mean co-equality. But I want to add *adaptation* to your model. When I go home to New Mexico and to my family, I am one person and I know how to operate in that private world, and then when I go into the public world I have another way of living, but to me that's *not* assimilation.[6] It's more like *adapting* to where I am, being able to go back and forth from this world to this world to this world. And I think lots of us practice adaptation in many ways, some of which we may not even be aware of.

PETER MORALES: One of the themes that is coming up is what a tiny experiential—not cognitive but truly experiential—base we share with each other. I think you'd have to go to the Amazon Basin to find as much cultural isolation, as little experience with different cultures, as you find among the young people in my congregation in the western suburbs of Denver. My hunch is that my church isn't atypical in that regard. I think traditional anti-racism training needs to be supplemented with something that actually gets people experiencing each other, conversing with each other. There's such a lack of that in this culture. Our praxis needs to be creating spaces where people can really interact.

JOSÉ BALLESTER: About your critique, Tom, of the beloved community and historical materialism, Latino culture has five components: family *(la Familia)*, faith *(la Fe)*, the arts *(las Artes)*, the community *(la Communidad)*, and our history or roots *(nuestra Historia, Cuenta, Diche)*.[7] All arise out of the interactions of that community and not out of materialism. When Latinos and Latinas get together, the first thing we do is try to establish our history, our roots, and our family. Then community arises out of that. Ada María Isasi-Díaz, *la Cubana*, writes that we as Latinos and Latinas do not *write* theology, we *live* theology. The theologians' job is to observe and to record the theology we live. The theology is truly coming out of us and not out of something outside of us.

KEN OLLIFF: I also want to pick up, Tom, on your point about our "theological understanding of community" coming out of what you call historical materialism. This is a really pressing question to address in talking about theological resources for anti-racism, and you lay out some of the issues very well. On the one hand, I take your point that we are *more than* our locatedness in history, *more than* all the labels that we attach to ourselves; there's something about human beings that transcends all this that we have to take into account. And you speak about this "something" in terms of the sovereignty of God.

But at the same time, I feel that we have to take very seriously our locatedness; we are historicized beings. The language that we use is shaped by the people from whom we learned that language, as Paul Rasor has said, and the values and elements that we can and cannot articulate are carried along with that heritage. We need to pay attention to these issues of locatedness in designing theological resources.

But I also want to pay attention to what James Cone was saying about a common humanity. Cone wanted to connect our particularities with our common humanity, but he didn't really spell this out. I think we have two choices: Either our anti-racism work (and our anti-oppression work) comes out of particularity—the thrust of which is respecting difference and the importance of difference—or (and perhaps it's a combination of the two) it comes out of some sense that we share a kind of core that transcends all our differences and our historical particularity, that there is some core essence of the human being that is inalienable and that is of vast value.

FRED MUIR: I keep hearing a particular theme in our conversation, and I know it's not dualistic, but for the sake of argument, I will make it dualistic. I hear people approaching the issues raised at this consultation from a story-based, personal model—one of personal transformation—and then I hear others who are looking at more materialistic, sociological, or structural transformation approaches. And we seem to keep going back and forth and back and forth, at least in my mind. In a lot of comments and in Tom's response, I hear people acting out their woundedness. So we've got to deal with our own woundedness. But, as Bill Jones has said, when we finally work through the woundedness or push the woundedness aside, the structural oppression will still be there. So how *do* we get on with it? How do we prevent our woundedness from getting in the way? Do we have to wait until we've done our personal work before we can go on? You can get so enmeshed in your story that you never get out of it and get on to some of the larger work that we've been talking about! How do you address that tension, Patricia?

JIMENEZ: At the hospital, I work with people who are living and dying. They're doing *both;* they're not doing one or the other.

This issue of focusing on personal woundedness vs. structural racism comes back to the concept of the spiral that I wrote about: We're doing the work, and at a particular moment something comes up that pushes a button, and so we have to stop and deal with it; and sometimes we go away and do it alone, or we do our spiritual practice for a while, and we talk to all our friends and to anybody who will listen. And we figure it out and we go on. And then something pushes our buttons again, but it's not quite the same; it's going to be a little different because we are a little different. We've worked through a little part of whatever this woundedness is.

In the papers and in people's comments, I hear the either/or you're talking about, and I want to ask, How can we do *both/and?* How can we live *and* die? How can we do our personal work *and* the institutional and societal work that needs to be done? It's not an either/or, and I don't think it ever can be, simply because we are human beings, because we are saints *and* sinners.

Study Questions

1. Referring to Latinos and Latinas, Patricia Jimenez states, "Our experiences are racial, cultural, and linguistic. . . . In our experience, economic domination is directly linked to racial and ethnic domination. Our racial/ethnic differences have been used to displace us from land, to use us as cheap labor, to exploit our countries for their prime resources, to insist that we give up culture and values." Is the experience of persons of African, Asian, or Native American heritage significantly different from that of Latinos and Latinas?

2. Peter Morales argues that "any category is an idol, no matter how powerful or useful that category may be." To use categories (such as race), he says, "does a subtle kind of violence . . . for behind any construct is a rich, multifaceted, complex, chaotic, messy reality." Do you agree or disagree with Morales' assessment? Why or why not?

3. Patricia Jimenez identifies language as an important dimension of identity, family, cultural heritage, and "true citizenship." She suggests that perceptions about success are integrally related to language and, by extension, to bilingual education. What does it mean to be a "true citizen" of the United States? How does language relate to racism? Do you agree or disagree with Jimenez that in the United States, there is an implied assumption that "true citizens speak English"?

4. Jimenez suggests that the natural consequence of assimilation (the "melting pot") is that people are asked to sacrifice their ethnic and cultural identity. Furthermore, she states that neither "multiculturalism" nor "pluralism" (as these concepts are sometimes promoted) resolves the problem. After reviewing Flores' and Benmayor's viewpoint (p. 47), do you agree or disagree with Jimenez? Does belief in the "melting pot" still have currency in our increasingly diverse country? Do you have an alternative view; and if so, how might this view be promoted?

By contrast, William R. Jones cites a model in which assimilation, integration, and pluralism are three approaches to social
interaction—with pluralism seen as a relationship of co-equality.
What is *your* understanding of pluralism as it relates to social
relations? Does it bend toward assimilation (or adaptation)
and sameness, or toward particularity and greater equality?

5. "The process of telling one's story" says Jimenez, "leads to
   greater understanding" and can lead to transformation. What
   stories about racism and racial justice have transformed your
   life? What methods will you use to continue to tell your
   story? How can the promotion of storytelling around racial
   justice issues be used in congregational life? What is the relative value of stories about racial oppression as witness or as
   testimony?

6. Patricia Jimenez introduces the idea of annunciation and
   denunciation in the work of anti-racism. If you could construct
   an anti-racist community, what kind of future would you
   announce? What would such a community look like? What
   would be its qualities and characteristics? How would it be
   sustained—protected by those who do not hold an anti-racist
   vision?

7. Tom Schade is critical of Martin Luther King Jr.'s concept of a
   beloved community because he believes that it is rooted in
   "historical materialism" and thereby "an idol, a false god."
   Such a view, he believes, is inconsistent with the idea of a sovereign or transcendent God. Ken Olliff, however, suggests that
   it is possible to hold two ideas simultaneously—to retain a
   "sense that we share a kind of core that transcends all our differences" (which James Cone refers to as "our common
   humanity") and at the same time to honor our particularities
   or "locatedness," which is rooted in history. José Ballester says
   that Schade's view does not reflect the experience of Latino
   culture. Where do your sentiments on this question lie?
   Should we consider a community of mutual regard based on
   particularities of identity to be idolatrous?

8. Peter Morales suggests that cultural isolation contributes
   to our lack of understanding of each other, and that experiential learning—"creating spaces where people can really

interact"—may be the fast track to becoming anti-racists. How do you respond to Morales' premise? Thinking about your personal experience, how have your interactions with people in cultures different from your own influenced your outlook? What opportunities for intercultural interaction do you see within your congregation or community?

9. Fred Muir addresses what he sees as a tension in anti-racism work—that our personal stories, particularly our woundedness, may be an impediment to dismantling structural oppression. He asks: "How do we prevent our woundedness from getting in the way? Do we have to wait until we've done our personal work before we can go on?" How do *you* respond? Patricia Jimenez argues that it's not an either/or—that we must do *both* personal healing and institutional or structural work at the same time. What is your view? What is the place of our personal histories in dismantling racist structures? Where there is deep woundedness, might this interfere with building healthy anti-racist alliances and coalitions?

7.16

The Other
Side of Route Two:
Some Autobiographical
Struggles with Theology,
Race, and Class

GARY E. SMITH

↩

I am a parish minister, and I have been one for the thirty years of
my adult life. I served the Unitarian Universalist Association for
three years in the mid-80s, but otherwise I have served parishes in
Middletown, Connecticut; Bangor, Maine; and, for the past twelve
years or so, in Concord, Massachusetts. Whatever theology I practice I practice within the context of parish life. These congregations
have been my teachers. I am sometimes a leader, sometimes a fol-
lower. Sometimes I am inspired. Sometimes I am tired and discouraged. I am a white Anglo-Saxon Protestant. I have lived a
mostly sheltered, clueless life. My world is beginning to open.

I grew up in central Maine. My father was, in this order, the
owner of a grain store, a traveling salesman, a car salesman, a
plumber, a teacher at night in a vocational high school, a clerk in a
hardware store, unemployed, and a worker for the state highway
department, negotiating the taking of property by eminent
domain. My mother was a registered nurse. My father's father
owned a grocery store and a grain store. My mother's father
worked in a mill, making wood products. My wife Elizabeth's
father was a stonecutter, as was his father before him. I went to a
public high school. I went to the state university. I grew up in

Maine, and only a tourist could like the slogan that greets travel-ers on the Maine Turnpike; "Maine: The Way Life Should Be." There's a great deal of poverty on the other side of Kennebunkport and the Bush family compound.

My roots are blue-collar. I served a decidedly blue-collar Unitarian Universalist congregation in Bangor, Maine, before applying for a job with the Unitarian Universalist Association in Boston, where my job title gave me access to the white wine and Brie crowd. It's been a ride since then. I often have to pinch myself. Sometimes I feel like a fraud. If I weren't the Senior Minister of the First Parish in Concord, Massachusetts, would these people talk to me?

I'm earning now what my father would have taken ten years to earn. I live in a house that cost twenty-five times what my par-ents paid for their home in 1957. When a house would come on the market in Bangor in the early 1980s for more than $100,000, the natives would drive by it, knowing for sure that someone moving from "out of state" would purchase it. If my children had gradu-ated from Bangor High School instead of Concord Carlisle Regional High School, the chances are slim to none that they would have gone on to the colleges they did, all their intelligence and talents notwithstanding.

You are thinking I should be down on my knees every night, with tears streaming down my face, giving thanks. Maybe I should be. (This is where the organ starts playing "I'm in the Money.") But, by Concord standards, I'm not even close. When we moved to Concord in 1988, I had some parishioners tell me how sorry they were that I had to live on the other side of Route Two, a main east-west artery that cuts Concord in two. Historically, Concord Center has been the place of old money. West Concord, "the *other* side of Route Two," has been the more working-class part of town. The distinctions created by this boundary are now blurring as the "mansionization" of Concord takes place. When we moved to Concord in 1988 and I was paid a salary I had never dreamed of making, I ended up visiting a parishioner in those first few weeks at the emergency room of the local hospital. Posted promi-nently on the wall was a mandated notification that my income level fell within the guidelines under which I was entitled to free care.

This paper contains pieces of a sermon about class that I preached to the Concord congregation in October of 1999. I said to them then, after I had outlined my working-class pedigree:

> If you are still listening, and you are thinking that you come from the same background as I do, and you find it amazing and troubling, I am grateful for your company. If you are still listening, and you have inherited or you have earned a kajillion dollars, and you have all the trappings to go with it, and you believe you are entitled to all this, I must tell you it is all a house of cards. Maybe, in your case, a big house of cards.

> When Jesus said, "It is easier for a camel to go through the eye of a needle than for someone who is rich to enter the kingdom of God," I think he was telling us here in Concord that it's all a big house of cards. I think he was telling us we're skating on thin ice. I think he was telling us we don't get it. Or in part of the letter of James, found toward the end of the Christian Bible, "What good is it if you have faith but do not have works? If a brother or sister is naked and lacks food, and yet you do not supply their bodily needs, what is the good of that? So faith by itself, if it has no works, is dead."

So I preached this sermon about class, about who's in and who's out. And I said to the Concord congregation,

> We're in! But the soul of this town and our souls are at stake. I think we're living in fear. And that's how we'll lose our souls. That's where we get stuck in the needle's eye. We've got it, and we don't want anyone to take it away from us. We are slowly becoming a *de facto* gated community. We're piling more and more things on our kids. We buy an expensive car and put an alarm on it. We build bigger houses and put security systems on them, put a guardhouse at the end of the road, fear the stranger. God forbid if someone looks or acts different. Please don't say a gay person is your best friend. Please don't say a person of color is your best friend. I am talking about a whole system in our society that needs our attention, that cries out for our attention.

> If I invite you to participate in City Year in Boston later this month, and you tell me that you'd prefer that we do charity closer to home, I will tell you that Boston *is* our home. These boundaries between towns are only lines on a map. If we are not part

of a solution to the neglect of housing and education and justice
in Boston, our style of life and our things are going to be a beacon of envy, and we will need a legion of security people to keep
the hungry and the naked and the neglected from our doorsteps.
And that's only the self-serving rationale for action.

In our unison benediction in Concord, we say, "Strengthen the
fainthearted. Support the weak. Help the suffering. Honor all
beings." Indeed. And the strengthening and the supporting and
the helping and the honoring go both ways. The great lie is that
there is a helper and the helped. The great lie is that we have it and
they don't. If the "it" is food and shelter and education, we do
have it. If the "it" is love and spiritual depth and faith and kind-
ness, who can tell? James says we can't tell—on the surface.

As with so many other of our Unitarian Universalist congregations, First Parish in Concord is partnered with the good people
of Skekeleykeresztur in Transylvania and the minister Jozsef and
his wife, Anna, and his children, Jozsef and Zsuzsanna. Eighteen-
year-old Zsuzsanna, in the year she lived with us in Concord,
would marvel at this town, its homes, its schools, its cars. It was
seductive. But she did not bend. She did not break. She knew that
the home to which she would return had riches she rarely saw
here. She never tired of asking me how many families lived in this
Concord house or that, and I would always say "one, Zsuzsanna,
just one."

I was raised in a New England Congregational Church. I was
baptized a Christian, "in the name of the Father, and of the Son,
and of the Holy Spirit." I went to confirmation classes. I went to a
Christian theological school. I was ordained into the United
Church of Christ and professed Christ as my Lord and Savior. I
served for eight years of my ministry as a Christian minister. I do
not regret one moment of this. I do not belittle it or deny it. But
somewhere in my ministry, as I preached from the Bible each and
every week, I actually heard the words I was saying, and I began
to doubt some of them. "No one comes to the Father except
through me," Jesus says in the Gospel of John. No one comes to
God except through Jesus? And I knew in an instant that One Big
Doubt had been planted within me. At the wise old age of thirty, I
knew there must be many ways to God, many ways to understand
what is holy. And then Unitarian Universalism came into my life,

and I knew I had found a home. I had moved from a creedal church to this covenantal one.

But I had also left behind the story of Jesus' life, there in between the birth story of Christmas and the resurrection story of Easter. Jesus' life story is a story of courage and of hard teachings and of compassion and of revolution, and that is the Jesus I am thinking I will lift up more in my preaching. The fact is that in the congregation I serve, we make the nod to Jesus mostly in the crowds on Christmas Eve and then again on Easter morning. But it was no meek and mild Jesus that led our Unitarian forebears to proclaim a "pure" Christianity—a religion *of* Jesus, not *about* Jesus. This is no "little Lord Jesus, no crying he makes." This is a man who waged war with the powers and principalities of his day, and who tried to turn the world upside down: The poor and the persecuted enter the kingdom, those who mourn will be comforted, the meek will get it all, those who hunger and thirst will be filled, the peacemakers will finally be recognized.

Dorothee Sölle, one revolutionary woman, says that Jesus "gave answers to questions [the people] didn't ask. Sometimes they didn't dare open their mouths anymore. Not because they hadn't understood that he was taking from them everything sacred and safe. He offered no guarantees. The down and out were his proof and actually he had as much assurance of victory as we in these parts do. None."

I am now in my thirteenth year of ministry in Concord. It is a church and a town of enormous privilege. I often find myself co-opted by the culture of entitlement there. And yet I try to stand outside of it, too. In sermons and in conversation, I refer to Concord as a "theme park," and I make fun of members' "trophy cars." And I laugh, and the congregation laughs, nervously. I take seriously the maxim one of the Niebuhrs used at the mid-twentieth century, that a preacher should learn "to comfort the afflicted and to afflict the comfortable." I try to maintain that balance. I believe I am called to do both.

I challenge First Parish, to the best of my ability, to live outside the boundaries of safety, to live with absurdity, to face death and uncertainty and tragedy and not give up on this world or each other. We have much to learn. I am not as clueless as I used to be. I remember the line from Audre Lorde, "When we speak we are afraid our words will not be heard nor welcomed, but when we are silent we are still afraid. So it is better to speak, remembering we were never meant to survive."[1]

I am wondering these days what it would mean to reclaim some of my Christian background and to preach from the Social Gospel of a revolutionary Jesus. I use the language of revolution in my ministry. Some years ago I challenged First Parish to go deeper spiritually and to reach out more effectively. In order to provide a space and teachers and classes for members of the congregation to go deeper spiritually, we began the Wright Tavern Center for Spiritual Renewal in the historic building we own next door. It began with three families putting money up front to hire a director and to show the parish that it could be viable. We colored outside the lines.

And at the same time we sought ways to be more effective in our witness for social justice, including making a commitment to becoming an anti-racist, anti-oppressive, multicultural institution. Following an anti-racism weekend with the Crossroads Program three years ago, I returned to Concord committed to finding ways to effect systemic change. I have said to this congregation more than once that if we wanted to bring about change, we could. We have the talent, the energy, the numbers, the expertise, the money, the power, and the connections to do anything we set out to do. Now, a small group similar to the one that launched the Center for Spiritual Renewal is meeting to consider new and radical ways to "do" social justice at First Parish. They are thinking of ways to color outside the lines.

Everything "sacred and safe" is at stake. As a leader of this congregation, I have much to learn. I have alternately felt challenged and chastened by the Association's "Journey Toward Wholeness" program. I have sometimes felt as if I am dealing with colleagues who are not walking with me but are instead sitting over in "Stage Five,"[2] shaking their heads at my cluelessness. This Journey Toward Wholeness effort could do with a little less self-righteousness and little more companioning. I *want* to do the right thing. My world is opening. I am increasingly finding the colleagues who know how to companion. This Concord congregation and its leadership are encouraging my leadership. I am encouraging their leadership. It is an amazing thing, this parish ministry. I would not be doing anything else. "We were never meant to survive," the poet says. We were never meant to be safe, the poet says. "Grant us wisdom, grant us courage, for the living of these days, for the living of these days," we sing, we pray.

The Responses

"The word *theologian* is not a term I would use to describe myself," remarks Gary Smith as he introduces the discussion of his essay. Instead, he says his "entry into this struggle" arose from his work with the executive committee of the Unitarian Universalist Ministers' Association, where he has *had* to "pay attention to racism and classism."

> Now my ongoing wish is to bring this struggle to the congregation I serve in a town of great privilege. . . . Still, when I'm writing a sermon about these issues or when I'm "raving" on a Sunday morning, I worry about driving the congregation away. Preaching becomes dangerous. After I preached a sermon on class a few weeks ago, people didn't really want to look me in the eye as they left. They shook my hand, but that was it.
>
> So all this is a big step for me. As I said at the beginning of my essay, I have lived the most sheltered, clueless life, but my world is beginning to open—and I'm really glad to be here.

With twenty-two years of experience as a community-based urban minister, **Elizabeth Ellis** acknowledges the challenges of pursuing a "truly radical and socially transforming ministry" within Unitarian Universalist congregations in often affluent communities where there is often a "felt need and powerful social force to maintain the status quo." She offers these reflections:

> My favorite professor, Dr. Marie Augusta Neal, Sister of Notre Dame and sociologist of religion, defined the role of the parish minister in affluent communities as "teaching the people that when the poor come for what is rightfully theirs, [the rich] should let go." . . . Historically, part of the challenge has been to discover ways to involve our Unitarian Universalist societies, mostly suburban, in offering empowering ministry in low-income communities. . . . Joseph Tuckerman[3] suggested that the rich had the most to gain from such relationships, but by the end of his ministry, he was discouraged by the lack of will on the part

of his affluent friends to be engaged over time in issues of economic and social inequality. At most, they were interested in discussing poverty and their relationship to it only occasionally and were not interested in making it a priority of their religious life.

In contrast, Ellis applauds the urban ministry successes of the First Parish in Concord, Massachusetts, under the leadership of senior minister Gary Smith and associate minister Jenny Rankin. The two have kept the "issues of inequality and oppression before the parish while ministering to its people," says Ellis, matching congregants' skills, desires, and personalities to much-needed tasks and collaborations with low-income communities.

> I lift up Gary's ministry and its success because I am concerned that our efforts in anti-racism can become removed from reality and ineffective if we are not willing to engage with others whose experience is different from ours—specifically, with those who experience the concrete physical, social, and economic impact of racism and oppression. We may all suffer from the effects of racism, but we don't all suffer equally. With all due respect, I am suspicious of efforts that focus too much on the suffering that racism causes white people. Gated communities may suffer from some level of fear or discontent, but that is not the same as suffering the effects of racism wrapped in poverty, causing not only social but spiritual devastation.

> We need to engage thoughtfully and respectfully with others who suffer the brutal effects of racism and poverty, and we need to engage with them for the purpose of providing concrete help and resources even as we tackle the larger systemic and spiritual evils of racism and poverty. Let us begin to define community differently, so that we form communities across racial, economic, and urban-suburban divisions. The world divides too easily between activists concerned with systemic change and advocates of direct community involvement. We need a movement weaving them together, and only a faith movement can effectively do this. In short, we need to be engaged directly with others, to address systemic problems and white racism within Unitarian Universalist societies, and to be sustained in this work by faith.

> As a Unitarian Universalist Christian, or Jesus-follower, I believe that generally Unitarian Universalists miss a wonderful opportunity to embrace Jesus and the Christian tradition in freedom,

with imagination and creativity. While we might have significant disagreements with some traditional Christian doctrine, we still allow others to name and define Christianity for us and then we reject *that*, instead of acting with respectful, intelligent freedom and defining a Jesus movement for ourselves. Gary, like many others, left the Christian path because of its exclusive claims, but there are other ways to live within a Christian understanding. Universalist, free from fourth-century doctrines and creeds, we have a unique opportunity to engage the Jesus story from both a practical and a spiritual place. . . .

Jesus addressed the large question of God's vastly great and ongoing life and the issues of justice and love among the people. Unitarian Universalists, like all our sisters and brothers, stand in need of both God *and* a just and loving human community. Whatever spiritual disciplines and traditions we incorporate into our movement to end the evil of racism, we cannot do so without the power and sustaining nature of larger faith.

Fredric John Muir's response opens with this thought from E. B. White:

It's hard to know when to respond to the seductiveness of the world and when to respond to its challenge. If the world were merely seductive, that would be easy. If it were merely challenging, that would be no problem. But I arise in the morning torn between the desire to improve the world and a desire to enjoy the world. This makes it hard to plan the day.[4]

The luxury that most Unitarian Universalists face every morning, Muir says, "is that we have a choice: Improve or enjoy, save or savor." Not everyone has this luxury. Muir explains,

To this choice, the members of Unitarian Universalist congregations bring a backpack of factors that contribute to and affect the decisions they make. Among these factors are wealth and social or cultural capital. Dalton Conley suggests that wealth is shaped not only by income, education, and occupation but also by property, assets, or net worth.[5] Conley shows that the impact of wealth is long-term; . . . the impact of social or cultural capital can be equally significant. The availability of role models, connections, and peer influences shapes personality, attitude, and the future. With both wealth and capital, we Unitarian Universalists have the power to create our story, a personal and institutional narrative, in a way that those without these two factors cannot. . . .

While everyone in our faith community may not have both of these factors in their backpack, most have at least one, which is enough to write their own story and affect their day. It so happens that most of these Unitarian Universalists—not all, but most—are white. . . .

My experience informs me that while religious liberals may wish to do the right thing, it is difficult, maybe impossible for them given their wealth and social or cultural capital, to see beyond their individual and family journey, the shaping of their story. An outcome of this individualism is that we are reluctant to share our wealth and capital in any meaningful and decisive way, any way that might result in changes to our story. As a condition of moving out of their narrative, some want assurance that their story, their pain is real and understood. Gary is right: Folks want someone to walk with them; they seek a companion. But a condition of companioning can be to walk down a new path. . . .

The "myth of religious individualism" says Muir, has led to "an isolating personal spirituality and a divisive congregational polity." We must, he says, "name this lie and re-imagine our faith." This, he suggests, is a way to break silence with racism as called for by Dr. James Cone.

Authenticity means naming the implicit and explicit ways in which our individual pasts have undermined, resisted, or just ignored the demands of our faith. What personal demons have possessed and stalled—and continue to possess and stall—our hope and desire to be among the prophethood of believers?

Personal authenticity—honesty—is a prerequisite to accountability, which occurs when individuals shape their community and their congregation. Accountability is the institution naming, resisting, and removing the social demons that have possessed and stalled our hope and desire to be the beloved community, the actualization of our covenanted vision.

Authenticity plus accountability equals credibility, a personal and institutional force that must be reckoned with. Religious credibility is prophetic and liberating, rooted as it is in honesty, understanding, and passion. "Your ancient ruins shall be rebuilt; you shall raise up the foundations of many generations; you

shall be called the repairer of the breach, the restorer of streets to
live in" (Isaiah 58:12). We do have a theology and spirit that are
rooted in, among other places, the "Social Gospel of the revolutionary Jesus"—a gospel that demands faith by works, a faith
that is built on the foundation stones of authenticity and
accountability.

The Journey Toward Wholeness and this consultation are efforts
leading toward credibility. As leaders of our association, we
embrace them—our members are watching. No one said it
would be easy; no one promised security: the creation of authenticity and accountability are spirit-shaking. We have a choice—
improve or enjoy, save, savor, or serve.

The Dialogue

The dialogue carries forward several overlapping themes, among
them: congregants' longing for engagement, the need for ministerial leadership, Unitarian Universalist attitudes toward money,
and resources to renew our liberal Christian roots. Questions arise
for which there are no ready answers.

ROSEMARY BRAY MCNATT: From the start of my ministry, I have
felt that the members of our congregations have a longing to
address the issue of racism, even though they can't always articulate that longing. Racism comes up in their personal lives and in
their working relationships, and anti-racism work has meaning
and resonance for them. I always feel affirmed in this work when
I talk with members of our congregations. But I don't always feel
that way when I talk to Unitarian Universalist ministers. What I
really appreciate is that the three of you—all ministers—from the
different positions you hold, are willing to grapple with racism for
real. You don't agree about everything, but you take it seriously
enough to address it directly. This holds out the possibility that I
might genuinely have colleagues—and that is incredibly affirming
for me!

MEL HOOVER: You three ministers have great courage. I'm asking
you to help me. As I travel around the country, doing workshops

being rich and smug

on the Journey Toward Wholeness, many of our congregations say that they are open to diversity, but they are not prepared for structural change. "We don't know how to do that," they say, "we need to be companioned, to learn how to do it." People in the pews indicate that they want the leadership of ministers, but too many ministers are not prepared for or committed to the work.

JoEllen Willis: Thank you, Gary, for naming your fear about driving congregants away. That's one of those practical issues: What we say on Sunday will not only affect whether we draw people toward what we believe in and hold in common but may also determine whether we will be able to keep standing up there to preach! Your returning to your Christian roots, for example, can be a double-whammy: Taking a prophetic stance on this can make people uncomfortable—touching that tender part of our faith where, as one of my seminary teachers said, Unitarian Universalism is the "ABC (Anything but Christian) religion." Yet the story of Jesus is such a powerful one in helping us frame all kinds of oppression. If there is a way we can hear it, this story seems very valuable.

Paul Rasor: All three of you are touching on a place where I get discouraged. I don't have anywhere near the experience that Gary has in a parish, but I did have some similar experiences in preaching prophetic messages about economics in an affluent community. I'd get the polite "Oh, that was great, oh yeah, we really need to do that. . ." but at the end of the service, I would wonder whether anything would actually change after they went home.

A few people who are already involved in something like the Unitarian Universalist Urban Ministry take these messages in, but 95 percent just don't hear them, or aren't willing to let go of anything, or they don't see themselves described in neocolonialism. In light of the cultural inertia that draws us back to conformity, what do you do with the vast majority of congregants who don't get it? Especially since, as I have said before, there are longstanding tensions in the liberal tradition between being prophetic and at the same time being accommodating to the surrounding culture.

Like you three, I have had my own struggle reclaiming my Christian roots. I can't help but think that it's not an accident that some of the best urban ministry work we've done in our association is being done by congregations that are specifically Christian. . . . One hundred years ago a lot of Unitarians and Universalists rejected Christianity because it was not rational. Today a lot of Unitarian Universalists reject Christianity because it's too hard to do if we really take it seriously.

SMITH: I was feeling extremely cynical about Christmas, but it became more powerful for me as I read the stories—beyond the birth and the death stories—about what Jesus actually *did*. I felt an authority standing beside me.

REBECCA PARKER: I spent ten really happy years as a parish minister. In my experience, the members of my congregation were not coming to church to have their comfort blessed; rather, they were coming to church because of something they felt and hadn't been able to fulfill. There was a collaboration between the minister and the congregation around a *desire for life*.

I've been thinking about why I maintain my connection with the United Methodist Church when I am committed to Unitarian Universalism and hold a leadership position within the denomination. But there are things that I need to bring to the context of Unitarian Universalism that this context drains away from me. In Unitarian Universalism alone, I cannot sustain my faith in a source of life and grace larger than all of us on which we can depend. I find lots of *collegiality* around such a faith, but I do not find a *community* that shares it. So I think leaders must sometimes have multiple commitments and multiple contexts in order to be sustained.

Now, here's the thing I find most difficult and even incomprehensible: I cannot understand Unitarian Universalist style and attitude about money. There is no intuitive understanding of class differences in Unitarian Universalism; I know this is a problem. But without the Christian context that says the earth is the Lord's and the fullness thereof, without a theological foundation for stewardship and generosity, I don't see how we can do anti-racism work effectively. This is heartbreaking and discouraging. In my experience, when actions are taken for people other than the white majority, it is difficult to get money. When you move in a different way about race, a lot of negativity comes up, and this negativity gets expressed in terms of money.

My anti-racism work includes teaching Unitarian Universalists to tithe. Tithing is a spiritual practice that transforms our understanding of the world. Could we talk more here about what happens with money and resources for anti-racism? Could you be a pastor to me?

SMITH: We have had a commitment to tithe since I arrived in my congregation: 5 percent of annual income. [There is laughter and discussion among the group about what "tithe"—a "tenth part," according to the dictionary—actually means.] Well, okay, so I say, "If you can double it, do!"

A lot of what I do around money is pretty shame-based, I admit. I say, "All I want for a pledge is what you're going to spend on your February vacation going to Vail."

But what I love about parish life is that it is such a living thing. You build equity and you spend equity all the time. So I do really good memorial services—that's building equity. Then there is always a fine line: Have I built up enough equity to do the anti-racism work?

JOHN BUEHRENS: To maintain joy in leadership and ministry, as Gary does, is a struggle. To fuel our effectiveness in justice work, we need more joyful ministers who will move toward those in our pews who have amassed a certain level of accomplishment and financial success yet who are yearning to lead more compassionate, meaningful lives yearning to do what Sister Augusta Neal asks them to do, let go when the poor come for what is rightfully theirs.

Two weeks ago I co-led a retreat with one of Gary's parishioners, someone who is studying for our ministry but who is also the chair of his own venture capital firm. Our retreat was for fifteen Unitarian Universalist CEO types; the theme was "Power, Authority, and Spirituality." . . . There was not a single person there who wasn't yearning to live fully into the ideals that we come together every Sunday to espouse. But people who take joy in accomplishing things in the world and in making a success of their lives are not immune to messages from our movement that they are unwanted by virtue of their very success. There was a fair amount of pain expressed in that gathering about how often these people feel scorned for their very accomplishments. We systematically drive these people out of our churches, instead of creating ministry and leadership networks that will help them develop a deeper stewardship and a deeper sense of spiritual connection to the real problems of our time. So one of the things that I believe we need to think about, both strategically and theologically, is how we can more authentically companion people who are yearning to give back out of what they have achieved.

I agree with you, Rebecca; I find that the biggest cheapskates in the movement are those who are still running away from religion. The people who are willing to be generous are those who are often on a pilgrimage of return to their deepest spiritual roots and to a yearning not only for a liberal but for a *prophetic* religious community that is connected to the whole network of humankind. I find this yearning far more pervasive these days in Unitarian Universalism than many of us have been willing to trust. And it needs to be trusted, particularly at the activist end of our movement. To the extent that we build ideological barriers filled with rebuke against any of our members, I think we make not only a strategic mistake with respect to the effectiveness of this movement, but also a deeply spiritual and theological mistake.

Study Questions

1. Gary Smith, his respondents, and the dialogue above reflect an intuitive understanding that to eliminate racism requires sharing wealth and power, and that the will for such action on the part of the privileged is a theological problem. How does your theology address this issue?

2. Elizabeth Ellis argues that radical social transformation cannot happen in the absence of building new relationships across race and class or in the absence of direct community involvement. Do these relationships exist between Unitarian Universalist congregations and the community where you live? Can we, in fact, live a life of accountability without these relationships?

3. The social ministry of Jesus is lifted up as a model by several writers and speakers in this chapter. What does the ministry of Jesus suggest to those engaged in anti-racism work today? Are

there other models that can help us to engage in an anti-racist, anti-oppressive ministry?

4. Rebecca Parker asserts that anti-racism work cannot be done separate and apart from tithing as a spiritual practice—and that generally speaking, Unitarian Universalism lacks a theological foundation for stewardship and generosity. Do you agree or disagree with Parker's assessment? How can stewardship help us to move from individual charitable giving to strategic funding of anti-racism work and build cross-class collaborations? How does this relate to Fredric Muir's notion of the "myth of religious individualism"?

5. Much of this chapter explores various understandings of what it means to live in community with others across social boundaries. Several challenges are raised. Gary Smith urges us to venture out of our "gated communities." John Buehrens calls us not to exclude—but rather to welcome—the wealthy and the successful in our congregations. How can we companion both the oppressed and the privileged in our efforts to create new relationships beyond our congregations?

7.17

Racism and Anti-racism in a Culture of Violence: Dreaming a New Dream

GEORGE TINKER

Leslie Marmon Silko, a Laguna Pueblo author, begins her great American Indian novel *Ceremony* with a poem dedicated to Spider Woman, the creatrix of Laguna mythology.[1] In the Laguna explanation of the world, Spider Woman creates by thinking, "and whatever she thinks about appears."[2] In this poem, since creation is never complete and done with, Spider Woman is thinking into existence the very story that Silko is writing—the story of the healing of a person, of a people, of a whole world.

It is no different for non-Lagunas. All of us live in an imagined, thought-up world—a social and mental construct. Our task is either to imagine the future of this world into existence together or to let it be imagined for us and to play out the roles that others will impose on us. I want to suggest that we can and must begin to create our world anew, to think it anew, to dream it anew, and to dream out of existence violence, and especially that racialized violence implicitly signified in the globalization of capital and the domination symbolized by the World Bank, the International Monetary Fund, multinational corporations, and the World Trade Organization; to re-imagine out of our world the abuse and subjection of women and the racialization of blacks, reds, yellows, whites, and browns. If we are not intentional about engaging such a process, I fear we are doomed to mere repetitions of the past. As George Santayana insisted, "Those who cannot remember the past are doomed to repeat it."

The world that we have inherited is a world of increasing violence, a world that has been dreamed into existence over a millennium or more. The violence to which we have become heirs today includes youth gang violence and the violence of white middle-class kids at schools like Columbine High School, but it has a much longer history. It is a persistent violence that saturates both the private and public spheres of our contemporary existence. It has persistently manifested itself as a violence perpetrated by states and their militaries. And it will take a major movement and a major shift in our thinking to change this story and dream a new one into existence.

Robert Williams traces this history of violence from before the rise of modernity to medieval Europe, Pope Innocent III, and medieval canon law. He demonstrates that the "rule of law" and the legal codices that evolve from it—the very foundations of modern constitutional democracies—almost immediately become implements for perpetrating state violence. Historically, the Rule of Law has also been an imagined construct, created as a device for controlling the "other." As such, the rule of law, which sounds like the foundation of fairness in the world, became the foundation for every Euro-Western colonial adventure, from the Americas to Asia and Africa. An example of the rule of law at work is the U.S. legal corpus referred to as "federal Indian law." Deloria and Wilkins offer an analysis that is most persuasive that the entire corpus of federal Indian law is completely unconstitutional, a work of fiction created out of whole cloth to serve the acquisitive desires of the United States and its settler population.[3] The point of all three scholars is that under the vague notion of the "rule of law" the United States carefully created and used these legal traditions in its conquest of American Indians and its continuing control of Indians following the conquest. Note carefully the opening paragraph of Williams' volume:

> At the dawn of Renaissance Europe's discoveries in the New World and conquest of the American Indian, Europeans already enjoyed the singular advantage of possessing a systematically elaborated legal discourse on colonialism. This discourse, first

successfully deployed during the medieval Crusades to the Holy Land [and, I should add, eventually in the English colonization of Ireland], unquestioningly asserted that *normatively divergent* non-Christian peoples could rightfully be conquered, and their lands could lawfully be confiscated by Christian Europeans, enforcing their peculiar vision of a universally binding natural law. This is to say that for centuries our churches have been involved in the colonization and conquest of the world on behalf of Europe.[4]

Replace the word "Christian" in this paragraph with its modern religio-economic counterpart, "capitalism," and the sentence rings more true today than ever. Noncapitalists can rightfully be conquered (economically, militarily, or by police action), and capitalist Euro-Westerners, enforcing their peculiar vision of a universally binding natural law, can lawfully confiscate (i.e., buy, exploit, manipulate) their lands. Think of the coercion exercised by the World Bank and the International Monetary Fund to force Third World countries to privatize their economies and to open their markets—under the clear directive of Ronald Reagan or Bill Clinton. And then notice the religious dimensions of what gets called "development" in contemporary economic and political theory.[5]

More than half a century ago, Felix Cohen, author of the standard mid-century text on Indian law in the United States,[6] wrote that American Indians are the miner's canary of U.S. society. Just as the death of the canary would alert miners that it was time to abandon the mine for lack of oxygen, so the health and well-being of American Indians should reflect back to North Americans how healthy our own society is. That is to say, the fate of American Indians is reflective of the spiritual condition of the rest of U.S. society, and the malaise of Indian peoples is deeply symbolic of the ever-growing U.S. dominance in this "new world order" we now more gently call globalization—even if we actually mean "Americanization."

I want to address the problem of racism and the task of anti-racism in the United States today from a patently American Indian perspective and to clearly connect racism with the enduring American and European history of violence. Yet, because of our aboriginal status as the indigenous owners of the North American landmass who have been dispossessed of that land by invading settler populations, we are still today the miner's canary of North

American society. I particularly want to talk about racism both as a structural problem—in which anti-Indian racism is merely one part of a larger whole rather than merely a personal or individual problem—and as a part of an even larger systemic whole in which racism is only one contributing factor.

Five hundred years of violence: Racism, as an acute but chronic problem affecting Indian peoples, can be easily assessed on one level simply by noting social welfare statistics—if one can locate them, since they are usually well concealed from the American public. Newspapers report statistics typically for "White, Black, Hispanic, and other," where Indians are squeezed in with a variety of folk (e.g., Asians) in the "other" category. When we finally surface in the statistics, Indian people are at the bottom of the list in virtually every category of social welfare: highest unemployment rate of any ethnic group in the United States (chronically, 60 percent nationally); shortest longevity (nearly twenty years shorter than the U.S. average); higher illness rates (six times the U.S. diabetes rate; seven times the tuberculosis rate); teen suicide rates three to ten times the U.S. average;[7] and a school dropout rate stuck at 50 percent. These statistics are the tragic result of more than five hundred years of the violence of conquest, colonialism, civilization, and conversion (religious and cultural)—each representing a different strategy of white racist oppression of Indian peoples. The statistics are a constant reminder that racism and its genocidal results continue in a variety of ways to hold Indian communities down.[8] They are the residue of a continuing history of racialized violence.

Violence—and racialized violence—is not something new to American history, however. It began with Christopher Columbus—Cristobal Colón—in 1492 and was continued by the Pilgrims and Puritans in Massachusetts, by Episcopalians in Virginia and by Spanish Catholics in the U.S. Southwest. Violence marked the formation of the United States and continued at a legal and intellectual level with the purchase of the Louisiana Territory by Thomas Jefferson and his sending of Lewis and Clark to *explore* the new piece of property.[9] The massacres of Indians, which began in North America with Miles Standish at Plymouth, Massachusetts, in 1622[10] and John Winthrop's Puritan army at Mystic, Connecticut, in 1637,[11] became habitual repetitive behavior throughout the U.S. conquest of the West. Massacre behavior was repeated in Vietnam and in the Gulf War as the use of violence as the ultimate American solution was soundly affirmed. The strategic use or threat of violence has continued today both in connection with economic strategies and in organizations like the School of the Americas and will continue in whatever economic and diplomatic institutions are devised to replace the School of the Americas. The practice of violence that so permeates American history and life is and has always been heavily racialized; it has been class-biased from the beginning; and it has consistently been and is today increasingly genderized. From the private sphere to the public, violence and resort to violent solutions have become as American as apple pie.

Michael Hardt and Antonio Negri go a step further in assigning violence a central role in the emergence and development of modernity in general. The United States, by this accounting, is simply part of a larger European and European American pattern of behavior, rooted in the intellectual, political, religious, and economic development of the West.

> The legacy of modernity is a legacy of fratricidal wars, devastating "development," cruel "civilization," and previously unimagined violence. Erich Auerbach once wrote that tragedy is the only genre that can properly claim realism in Western literature, and perhaps this is true precisely because of the tragedy Western modernity has imposed on the world. Concentration camps, nuclear weapons, genocidal wars, slavery, and apartheid: it is not difficult to enumerate the various scenes of the tragedy.[12]

America has a European history of violence that has been unaccounted for and even at times rigorously denied. When the first Europeans came to the Americas—the Spanish to the Caribbean, the English to North America—they came with clearly preconceived notions of conquering indigenous peoples, and theological and intellectual grounds for justifying and legitimating their exercise of violence. In New England, the Puritans were the "new Israel," self-righteously displacing the aboriginal Canaanites.[13] The ensuing religio-political doctrine of "manifest destiny" that motivated the westward expansion of the United States across the continent seems to fuel our contemporary domination of the world and even the globalization of capital.

Violence has become a key theme in U.S. history because violent behavior, whether public or private, personal or corporate,
has a distinct tendency to become an addictive pattern of behavior
and racism very early became a key strategy for rationalizing violence. Violent responses to Indian peoples created the need for—
and provided the logic to support—further violence on the part of
European Americans in their conquest. Analogously, in a typical
case of spousal abuse, the abuse does not end with a single incident; battering will and must, by some perverse logic, continue, in
order that the woman might come to assent to it. It is not enough,
as Albert Memmi already noticed in his 1956 classic anticolonialist
work, for the colonizer to think that he is right in his abuse of the
colonized; he also needs the colonized to believe that his conquest
is just and right.[14]

White male privileging can be tracked from the systemic to the
interpersonal level, from white control of systemic structures of
power to the blatant racism and sexism of private joke telling. The
defense of white privilege requires clarity about the racialization
of the "other." Even jokes communicate important information
both to those in the center of the power field and to those con-
demned to the periphery. Ultimately, the defense of white privilege requires that black, brown, yellow, and red people
acknowledge, and in some measure consent to, the hierarchical
structuring of privilege in which white is superior to color.
Whether the message is encoded in the usual coloration of political leaders or in the statistical percentages of young men of color
locked up in prisons, the privileged status of whiteness is regularly reinforced and re-entrenched. In the same way, the privileging
of men is consolidated and imposed on women—even in our contemporary moment of feminist resistance.

Williams argues that the conquest must continue until "normative divergence" is completely wiped out. To understand international politics, we need to move from the private sphere and the
abuse of women to the globalization of capital in the public sphere.
The United States must insist, as President Clinton did shortly
before leaving office, that "freedom can only be measured in terms
of free markets." The United States is invested spiritually in its
economic conquest of the world, so it becomes necessary to
reinforce American privilege and the superiority of American
(economic) ideology. Hence, we must tell Third World countries—

through our economic mission agencies, the World Bank and the International Monetary Fund—that they must have free market systems in place in order to do business with us.

Clinton's remark mimics the rationale of the Spanish *conquistadores* five hundred years ago. In a document called *"Requirimiento,"* the Spanish made clear that the aboriginal peoples of the Americas had no choice but to do business with their conquerors. Not to agree left the aboriginal peoples, the owners of the land, at risk of a Spanish declaration of a "just war" of conquest. The document was dutifully read in Latin, on a hilltop some distance from the village, and if the Indians did not respond quickly, the Spaniards were free to attack and kill them. The picture described by Bartolomé de las Casas, an important Spanish critic of the conquest, is not pretty: The Europeans engaged in wholesale slaughter of Indian communities because they refused to acknowledge the reign of Ferdinand and Isabella over their lives, refused to acknowledge the Gospel of Jesus Christ, and refused to allow the Spaniards to trade with them. The Indians could not understand any of the words, of course, but they understood the blood, and Las Casas, an eyewitness to the slaughter "conquest" in Cuba, reports that blood ran through the villages like rivers of water.[15] The result has gone beyond economic and political domination, but has also entrenched spiritual and cultural domination—all of which is replicated through today's popular culture.

Violence, an American value: The pattern of addictive behavior associated with racialized violence has meant that the public practice of violence over several centuries has now deeply penetrated the sphere of the private. Violence as a solution has become a key American value, even part of what we call family values. We teach it to our children from an early age—in Hollywood productions, on TV, and in cartoons, for example. My own children, when they were of elementary-school age, were fans of the *Teenage Mutant Ninja Turtles.* These typical cartoon characters were not police officers or some other official part of a legal justice system; they acted outside the law—serving some perceived higher "rule of law"—to apprehend the bad guys and put them behind bars. This is children's entertainment, of course, and as a result, the plot is seldom marred by death. Rather, as in *The A-Team,* with its stereotypical Mr. T, the bad guys are merely beat up and tossed around—only a moderate quotient of violence, some would say. The message, however, is clear, and what our children are learning is this: As long as you think you are right, you can engage in an act of violence on behalf of justice and righteousness as you define it.

This is what American individualism has come to and what our children are learning from their parents who work in the corporate world of competition and free markets. America's middle- and upper-middle-class children watch their fathers act with viciousness in corporate takeovers, or in competitive free market enterprises where the task of business is to put other companies out of business. They learn early that it is never enough to have a market in which to sell goods—the successful business must corner an increasing market share to sell more this year than last year. This is capitalism at work! That such capitalism is inordinately white—as one surveys the Fortune 500 and its executive ranks—is only a small part of the critique of the system.

We wonder why so many children behave the way Klebold and Harris behaved at Columbine High School. These killers were, of course, the same age as the children they killed. Yet we can excuse ourselves of any social or moral responsibility by claiming school murders to be an aberration, even though we know that their violence is the same colonial mimicry that we decry in Third World dictatorships or civil wars. Some would say that gangs in American cities, typically young men of color, are young people who have failed to understand the American value system. Yet the opposite case can be made, as Jim Wallis of the Sojourners Community, a white minister living for some thirty years in a black community in Washington, D.C., says: children in gangs *have* understood the American value system and are attempting to implement it as best they can.

If we are to re-imagine ourselves, to think a new way of being into existence, we must begin to speak and live a new narrative. Re-imagining thus requires the action of continued resistance to the status quo. In Denver last year, we again resisted the celebration of Columbus Day, turning out some two thousand protesters to disrupt the Columbus Day parade. This protest quite unintentionally violated the participants' "freedom of speech," on the basis that "hate speech" is not protected. The quandary, of course, is that Columbus Day, as a federal holiday, is state-supported hate speech.

We did not engage in our protest because of what Columbus did, which indeed was bad enough, but because of what Columbus symbolizes for white Americans. As governor of the Indies, Columbus was directly responsible for the death of some four million aboriginal owners of the land he invaded during the first eight years of the invasion (1492–1500).[16] Yet the symbolic role of Columbus as the quintessential white American hero is far more important a reason to protest—and reason to object to our protest on the other side.[17]

Listen carefully to what the press had to say about Indian protests in Denver in the year 2000 and are already repeating in 2001. They consistently said and say (in print and over the airwaves), "Indians allege that Columbus was a slave trader and a murderer." At precisely this point, the press becomes a part of the systemic (and racist) problem—finding a subtle but irresponsible way to question the legitimacy of Indian protest. Of course, we protesters (Indian and non-Indian together) do not *allege* these things about Columbus: The man murdered people and shipped enslaved Indians back to the slave markets in Seville. These are facts. Read the texts. No one allows the press today to say, "Jews allege that Hitler killed six million Jews." So why would the press take such a clear stand against Indian protesters with this subtle use of language? There is, I believe, a critically important underlying reason, one that we anti-racists had better note well if we seriously intend to change the world in which we live. The safety of every abused woman is at stake and not just the welfare of Indian people or other people of color. The underlying problem is that violence and white male privilege work in tandem, constantly reinforcing each other in ever more creative and nuanced ways. As anti-racist activists, how can we stay one step ahead?

First, we must recognize that the celebration of Columbus Day is an example of what addictions therapy would call denial. Celebrating this holiday is an act of denial on the part of white Americans with respect to the history of violence that has been at the core of the American colonial project. It is further a denial on the part of perpetrators of the consistent history of violence reflected in the atrocities that accompanied each phase of the European conquest of the Americas and now enable the capitalist conquest of the world. This is to begin to say that Columbus is really a white men's hero.

Secondly, we must understand that Columbus Day functions to sustain structures of oppression and racism. It becomes a legitimization of the conquest, an act of self-righteous self-justification by white men in North America. It is thus an act in defense of both white privilege and male privilege. Columbus Day is a sexist, racist, and classist act of self-validation. Bringing together all three categories of race, gender, and class, it becomes a part of the same systemic whole that justifies the International Monetary Fund and the World Bank, the School of the Americas, and the U.S. presence of control and exploitation in Central America, Vieques Island in Puerto Rico, or any Third World context. It justifies the imposition of the globalization of capital and capitalist ideas of development on peoples, whether they want that kind of economic system or not. It justifies the exploitation of natural resources and labor in Third World countries. And Columbus Day is all the more pernicious because it is an official federal holiday.

We need to understand that all these things are related. Columbus Day symbolizes all these things for Indian people today. It stands for the continuation of violence both in the public sphere and in the private sphere, from international politics to homes and small local communities.

What is our solution? What can we do? It is incredibly complex; sometimes, it feels as if we are each involved in two or three justice and peace issues and we just do not have the energy to connect our issues with those attended to by others. I can get so bogged down in the confined world of my own concerns for justice that I fail to see that what I am doing is connected with what others are doing. It is so complex that it can seem overwhelming to try to put together all the pieces of the jigsaw puzzle. But if I am right, and this is a problem of massive communal addictive behavior and we are part of it, then we just cannot fail to make the connections.

Nor is there any possibility of a simple political solution, given the nature of the systemic whole. Just electing the right candidate, for instance, is not enough because the very forces we are struggling against control the whole electoral process and maintain the mere illusion of what can only be called a "procedural democracy." So we needed clarity long before the 2000 election that this systemic force was going to be perpetuated in a most decisive manner by either Al Gore or Bush, Jr. We—and the world—would not have been much better off if Al Gore had been elected. There would have been some social programs and some policies that would have been less patently violent under Gore, but never forget that Bill Clinton sent Gore to give Russia the green light to invade Chechnya. There are no heroes at that level of the U.S. government. The problem is so systemic that no one can rise to the top without committing himself or herself to the violence—and the racism—of the system.

Addictive behavior: If we are going to find a solution to this addictive behavior, we must remember what we have already learned from studies of addictive family systems. It takes people roughly as long to recover from an addiction as they spent being addicted. If someone was an alcoholic for twenty years, it will take twenty years of sobriety and self-conscious therapy to put their life back together again. Adult survivors of child abuse, who typically come to some understanding of the abuse in their thirties, will be of retirement age before they are able to achieve a healthy state of life, and then only if they do some really good therapy along the way. This same dynamic of healing applies at the corporate (systemic) level, as well.

The addiction I am talking about has been going on for 509 years in this hemisphere. If we put it off until next year, it will take 510 years for this country to get healthy again, so we might as well start now. It will take the energies of our children and grandchildren and great-grandchildren at least seven generations to bring things back into harmony and balance. Take a deep breath. We are in this for the long haul.

The churches need to create a new kind of liberation theology that moves beyond what our Latin American, African, and Asian brothers and sisters developed in the last third of the last century. We need to dream a liberation theology that makes a preferential option for the poor and the oppressed,[18] but also talks about how each one of us can become free. Indian peoples will never be free on this continent until white Americans are also free, until men are freed from the systemic structures of sexism, which automatically give privilege to men in this society, even to those of us who struggle against our own privileging and claim to be listening to our feminist colleagues.

Those who are white are still privileged in this world, whether the privilege is wanted or not—just as the systemic whole privileges men, even those of us who try to object self-consciously, to resist our own privileging. It's part of what we've inherited and what we are struggling against. We need to be freed from those systems that cause us to be involved in the oppression of others even when we think we are struggling against them.

Those who are involved in the anti-racism movement already know these things to some extent. We know we cannot be free apart from the freedom of everyone else in this globalized world. Chiapas cannot be genuinely free until Mexico is free. Mexico cannot be free until the United States is free, in the real sense of liberated freedom. We are today caught in an international web of violence and greed, of mass consumption and manufactured desire, where each of us has got to have the newest and hottest thing on the market. Our minds have been manipulated so that we no longer find it possible to write without a really good laptop computer, loaded with the most recent software. We cannot struggle against the forces of development, progress, and technology without a really good cell phone to allow us to make the best use of our time.

The only way out of the web is to dream a new dream, to reimagine ourselves in a new story, and to tell a different story to our children and grandchildren to counteract the story they are already learning from Hollywood. That is our only hope for counteracting the negative and destructive image that a movie like *Dances with Wolves* creates for Pawnee people—primitivizing and savagizing them, even while Kevin Costner, the *good* white man who comes as another white Christ figure, tries to save the good Indians (the Lakotas) from the savage (bad, really bad) Pawnees.[19] And this is liberal Hollywood at its best!

Indians, along with all racialized others in the United States, exist on the periphery of society, marginalized by the system both economically and politically. Today, those who commit themselves to the anti-racism movement have moved one step further away from the center and toward the margins—where all my people live. Given the complexity of our high-tech, heavily populated world, we may never again rise above some form of hierarchy and domination. The key question is: Have we structured our society to leave open a space for resistance; for alternatives; for allowing the voice of the other not just to be heard, but to have merit? Does the voice of the "other" have sufficient structured power to influence a radical change in the course of policies, practices, etc.? This will require some intentional dreaming—on the margins and even among those closer to the center. We start by beginning to distance ourselves from the language of the center and learning to speak the language of the periphery.

White, European American people of good will who work in the churches must remember that the churches participate fully in this new religious movement called the globalization of capital just as they participated in the initial invasion and conquest of this continent.[20] Not only are church people employed in the system, but church people also staff the highest executive offices of global-ized capital. Indeed, what is being globalized are white European American standards of well-being and social organization—along with, particularly, White American hegemony. Thus, when church people boldly act in resistance they are actually acting against their own immediate and narrow self-interest on behalf of the poor, the oppressed, and the colonized and marginalized "other" of the world. This is the courage that will generate a new dream, that will imagine into existence a future of harmony and balance for our world and all those who inhabit it.

I am just completing the revision of this essay in the aftermath of the September 11th carnage at the World Trade Center and the Pentagon. As the days go by, it is increasingly obvious that our anti-racism task has immediately become more difficult. Key Bush advisors are suddenly announcing that police racial profiling is not all that bad.[21] American xenophobia has reached new heights as the general population has come to fear color—associating it with the threat of terrorism. And the president of the United States now constantly poses the crisis of the day as a confrontation between civilization and the uncivilized, between good and evil. Overtly religious categories—once used occasionally by Ronald Reagan and much more sparingly by Bush, Sr.—now dominate the national consciousness. And the language of civilization, which was used for more than three centuries to rationalize and justify the white, Euro-Western theft of aboriginal lands in North America, is now being used to justify and rationalize the new globalized expansion of American capital, for the moment, in the form of a military attack on Afghanistan. The need to generate a new vision of balance and harmony in the world has immediately become both more difficult and more pressing.

The Responses

To open the discussion, George Tinker links the systemic nature of oppression to issues of violence, language, and cognition, and places them in the context of U.S. history vis-à-vis American Indians:

> I am what's called "mixed blood," which means that I'm part Indian and part white; I'm also called a "man," even though only one of my parents was a man. [There was a pause, and then a burst of laughter from the group.] The problem of mixed blood versus full blood is not intrinsically an American Indian problem; it is a white problem. In the Indian world, you are Indian or not Indian, a man or a woman or one of those in-between categories called *burdash* or *winkde* or *nablé*. In other words, we have more than two genders in our communities traditionally.
>
> It was the U.S. government late in the nineteenth century that decided to start tracking Indian blood. There have only been three peoples I know of in the world who have had to carry cards to demonstrate who they are to the body politic: Jews in Nazi Germany, blacks in South Africa under apartheid, and American Indians today. I have (somewhere in my files, and I refuse to carry it) what is called a CDIB card, a certificate of degree of Indian blood. You see, the one-drop rule for African Americans works in just the opposite way for us. In Canada until recently, for example, any Indian woman who married a white man was immediately removed from the rolls of her tribe by the Canadian government. There's a reverse discrimination going on with the certificate of degree of Indian blood, because the government would like to get rid of Indians so that the pangs of conscience over stealing land can fade into historic oblivion.
>
> In my institution I try to get students to deal with these issues without collapsing into guilt, because guilt ain't gonna solve the problem. I tell them, "If this stuff really bothers you, take a step away from the center out toward the periphery and look back at the center again as something that's hurting you as a white American as much as it's hurting Indian people, blacks, Hispanics, Latinos, and Asian Americans. Get angry instead, and do something about it." Maybe if we reflect on that thought, it will be helpful here too.
>
> When I argue that *language* is critically important in getting at the systemic whole of oppression which surfaces so virulently in

racism (but also in sexism, classism, colonialism, and globalization), I'm really talking about more than just hate speech; I'm talking about categories of cognition that function every day without anybody usually giving them a second thought.

When the disruptions began in Zimbabwe late in the spring of 2000, as black former revolutionaries began taking over white farms, I was stunned to hear the U.S. ambassador to Zimbabwe announce that what was at stake was the "rule of law" and that these black "bandits" who had taken over white farms had "violated the rule of law." But he didn't show any concern for the violation of the rule of law that had put that land in the hands of white people 150 years ago! The language of the "rule of law"—which is everyday stuff here in the United States—is at the heart of the oppression that you and I are talking about.

For example, there is one category of law in the U.S. codices called "federal Indian law." It's taught in all the law schools, but there is not a single piece of Indian law in the whole codex that is constitutional. Every last bit of it is extraconstitutional, things that Congress or the courts *made up* as they went along. . . .

Today, the poorest of the poor in the United States are American Indians, with more than a 50 percent unemployment rate, chronically, from year to year. I want to emphasize that this is a *systemic* problem; I'm using American Indian people to talk about this larger problem. The categories are so interrelated—race, gender, class, colonialism, economy, capitalism, globalization—they're all so deeply intertwined that it's going to take a major effort to unpack all the layers of oppression, but that has to happen before we can create a more useful and happier future for our children and our grandchildren seven generations from now. The question is not whether this systemic problem is so complex that we ought to just drop it. The question is: Are we in it for the long haul? Are we ready to live through uncloaking this beast, working toward eventually trimming its size, killing it off maybe, and replacing it with something that is more humane, something that can allow us to celebrate what James Cone has called the common humanity that we share on this earth?

Using as a refrain Jesus' words on the cross—"Forgive them, for they know not what they do"—and plumbing the "deepest Christian message of love, forgiveness, and human kinship," **Anita Farber-Robertson** challenges the assumption that "not knowing" how whites participate in sustaining racism is achieved through the "universal capacity for designed blindness." She names this capacity as sin:

> Designed blindness is the capacity to remain unaware of that which is knowable . . . [by screening] out information that we do not want to know or that conflicts with our map of reality. Thus, it is not only possible but in fact predictable that we will continue to be unaware of that which is knowable when it is at odds with our map or our perceived self-interest.[22]

> Designed blindness allows us to understand apparently contradictory truths: (1) What we do to participate in and perpetuate racism is knowable, and (2) some of us really don't know it, or don't know all of it. Thus, those of us who reap the benefits of racism can report that we do not benefit, because we have so skillfully and effectively learned to design our blindness. Yet when exposed, such blindness can be unlearned.

> In theological terms, designed blindness is sin—sin we cannot avoid. It permeates our culture; we take it in with all our lessons about language and relationship. It is inevitable that we will participate at times in the sin of not knowing what is knowable. Not surprisingly, it is an open door through which evil enters the world.

> When liberal religion cast sin out of its theological lexicon, it sacrificed its most powerful and effective concept. We have constructed a religion that only wants to hear good news. But the bad news that the good news was addressing is still with us. Sin dwells in the world and dwells deep within us. For the good news of love, healing, and reconciliation to reach us, we must first acknowledge our wounds, facing the pain of our guilt as well as the pain of our affliction. "Forgive us, for we knew not what we did."

> So what *do* we know? We know that people who have been allowed to participate [in "whiteness"] . . . have access to resources that people of color either do not have or have to a greatly limited degree. These resources are material and therefore finite. In the perceived conflict over finite resources and the anxiety about potential scarcity, the dominant white group has staked out its claim, intending to ensure its survival. Dr. Tinker describes how this looks in relation to Native Americans. When allowed to run its course, this dynamic is genocidal.

But there is a dimension that we do not know, which poets try to grasp in verse, theologians in doctrine, and preachers in prayer: the life of the spirit. We have confused our model of the physical world with the reality of the *spiritual* dimension. Though we acknowledge the infinite and our accountability to the eternal, we have functioned as though there were a scarcity of the holy. We have behaved as though it is not possible for there to be enough God, or enough of the Good, to go around. We have behaved as though limited love, conditional love, is the only kind there is. But the one who lived two thousand years ago— the one who so enraged those in power that they hung him on the cross—knew of love unbounded. "Forgive them, for they know not what they do." . . .

People of color are well served by a faith that focuses on their resources, that offers worship that affirms and sustains them as persons precious, important, beloved. With such a faith, they can marshal those resources to face the world. White people, I believe, are threatened by that. Embarrassed by the overabundance of resources we hold, we hide them, deny them, try to keep them under cover. Because our perceived resources are material, they could be taken away. So, we hoard them.

Material wealth is functionally symbolic. Money is the way we have tried to validate our intrinsic value, ensure our place in the universe, and build a hedge of protection around what we believe to be our essential selves. It doesn't work. Security does not reside in things. As long as we believe that it does or can, we are marks for the Great Seducer, easily lured into selfish, destructive, and oppressive behavior. A theology of scarcity begins with confusing the surface for the essence, the persona for the person, our stuff for our soul.

My Universalism is fierce. It has no patience with a theology of scarcity. We are beloved—like it or not. If we could only believe and accept that, we would not need to oppress, or control, or hoard the resources, because as God's beloved, we belong. Neither life nor death can separate us from that love. When we know that, there is very little else we need.

For **Danielle Di Bona,** the "addiction of violence" has engulfed even "people of color, the marginalized, and the poor." She elaborates:

Dr. Tinker says, "The problem is so systemic that no one can rise to the top without committing himself or herself . . . to the violence—and the racism—of the system." I would suggest that in addition to those rising to the top, all people, including the marginalized and oppressed, are committed to the violence and racism of the system *precisely because* it is our history and it is what we know. It has become a self-perpetuating cycle.

The more subtle and insidious violence includes deniability and invisibility. When the media say, "Indians *allege* that Columbus was a slave trader and a murderer," they are denying a historical reality that can quickly be confirmed in the reference department of your local library. But experiencing such denial is a regular occurrence for people of color. When a person of color describes an incident or gives an example of the racism he or she encounters each day, the experience is often diminished by their white audience. Comments like "You must have misunderstood," or "I'm sure she didn't mean it that way," or "That couldn't have happened" perpetuate an insidious violence upon people of color that comes out of the power and privilege of the white community. The power and privilege of the white community include the reality that their story is *the* story. Therefore, the story a white listener hears from a person of color is so much out of the realm of possibility that he or she cannot fathom the truthfulness of it. This perpetrates a violence upon the very soul of "the other."

Related to this violence of deniability is the violence of invisibility. It seems clear that if the story can be summarily denied, it is a short step to denying the very existence of the storyteller. Let me tell you a story: Over twenty years ago, the Wampanoag people went before the courts of Massachusetts to demand recognition of the tribe by "the government." The leaders of the tribe stood before the court and heard from the judges that they would not grant that recognition because the Wampanoag people were "extinct." The violence of this act of denial is overshadowed only by the violence of the act of making a people invisible.

The issue then becomes one of survival. If the story is denied and the people are made invisible, survival demands adaptation. But adaptation is a kind of surgery. If in order to be seen and heard, a people must become what the dominant culture defines as normative, then the violent act one commits is akin to surgical intervention.

I wonder then if it is possible for this society to "open a space for resistance," because I am not convinced that this society can hear and give merit to the voices of those who have been made invisible. I choose my language carefully: It is a case of *being made* invisible, not of *being* invisible.

Change requires going to and staying in the margins. People of color, oppressed people, do indeed live on the margins. Those of us who refuse to commit violence upon ourselves in the guise of adaptation are at the margin. When we demand that our story be heard and validated, we are moving to the margin. When we insist upon being seen, we cling to the margin. And for our brothers and sisters who are committed to anti-racism, you must make the journey toward the margin, always fighting the centrifugal force of the dominant culture that will pull you back to the center. This work that we call anti-racism is dangerous work, and our participation in it makes us dangerous people. We are committing acts of revolution, even in this gathering as we talk about race. Certainly, when the community goes forth to do the work of anti-racism, the community is a revolutionary and radical community.

As religious and spiritual people, we are called to respond to the status quo of this culture's institutionalized violence. The traditions that we Unitarian Universalists hold dear—all of them radical religious traditions—call us to stand against those aspects of the culture that destroy body, mind, and spirit . . . and challenge that culture into change.

The Dialogue

George Tinker brings a systemic theological analysis of culture, conquest, and violence to the dialogue, reflecting on the lived experiences of American Indians. The dialogue also focuses on the social consequences of racism, and questions whether "designed blindness" is a "sin"—whether "sin" is a willful moral failing, or an unavoidable cultural norm.

JOHN BUEHRENS: Tink and Danielle, I particularly appreciated your introducing the concept of moving from the center to the margins. It is my observation that for Unitarian Universalists today, it matters tremendously *which* margins.

When I came into Unitarian Universalism, I found this movement running to the wrong margins, congregations abandoning the inner city to move to what they thought was their new center—the center of where "our people really lived"—in the suburbs, abandoning relationship with the rest of the mainstream religious world by becoming theologically defensive, feeling weak and misunderstood. We participated in a theological self-marginalization, abandoning even a humble catalytic role in promoting interfaith cooperation for justice, which is a strand I want to hang on to. But you challenge me to think about a new set of margins to which we need to be accountable, to think about becoming accountable to marginalized people who have been put on the margins through our participation in domination.

On the other hand, ours is also a tradition with tremendous ambivalence and ambiguity about the center. I would like you to comment a little bit more on the concept of the center as you're using it. At one level it seems to be "safe space" that needs to be opened up, while at another level, it seems to be the place of domination. What's the primary meaning of "center" as you are using it?

TINKER: I think the center is a safe place for those who have power and can centralize their exercise of power. But the center is never completely identifiable at any point in time because as soon as you identify it, it shifts. It is constantly shifting, especially when there is a change of power in the world's "hyper-power"—that is, in the sole superpower. I think that people have different relationships to the center and different senses of dislocation from the center. White people (understanding that "white people" is a socially constructed norm that has no genetically or biologically verifiable elements in it whatsoever, but still it is a social construction with considerable power) stand closer to the center than red people or black people or brown people or yellow people—people of color, shades of color.

I teach in a seminary, which puts me closer to the center than other Indians, probably closer to the center even than other Indians who work for the Bureau of Indian Affairs—we call them the "Washington Redskins." [Laughter.] *We* can use that name in a sentence, but they shouldn't have a team in Washington by that name. There's a clear exercise of power behind such names.

I'm constantly fighting to survive as a marginal person. My faculty keep trying to co-opt me, to tame me so that I learn to speak *their* language—the language of the center—and abandon the language of resistance, which is the language on the margins. They are deeply frustrated that I cannot see the rationality of their language of the center. One colleague keeps trying to establish some notion of a "common culture" in America—which *really* sounds like an exercise of the center to me—and every time it comes up I criticize it, and every time he just shakes his head and says, "Well, Tink, I don't think you and I can talk anymore." It's that simple: The response doesn't have to be rational; it just has to have enough muscle to tell Tink where his place is, and that "you and I can't talk anymore." So there's a center right there in my school that replicates the center found somewhere along the axis between Washington, D.C., and Wall Street.

JOSÉ BALLESTER: I have two comments and a question, and they all center around, for lack of a better word, invasion. For the past four years, my program Just Works[23] has worked very closely with the Lakota people. One thing we have noticed of concern is the rise of gangs on the reservations. We've seen more and more young people trying to pick up on the power that they see in images and imports from the West Coast. We speak about the "American way"; well, these gangs understand the American way very well, and that's what they're picking up on.

On the other hand, I've also seen many of our Unitarian Universalist colleagues arriving with Just Works and trying to invade the reservation. They try to bring their view of what the native people are; they even try to instruct the native people in what is the correct way for them to behave!

Finally, it seems to me that the "traditionalists" look upon anyone who is not traditional, but is Christian among their people, as not being part of the center but being very much on the fringe. How do you, as a Lutheran minister, as a native person, react to this?

TINKER: First of all, on Easter Sunday in 1993, after I sent off the manuscript for *Missionary Conquest*,[24] I told the people at Four Winds in Denver that I would never again call myself a Christian, and I haven't. I'm still a Lutheran minister, but I'm not a Christian. I don't know whether that makes me a Lutheran Unitarian [laughter].

The center that you're talking about at Pine Ridge, José, isn't the center in any real sense. The traditionalists may represent a small local center, but the center of power in Pine Ridge is Pine Ridge *Village*, which is a government town. That's where the Pine Ridge "government" is and where the office of the Bureau of Indian Affairs for Pine Ridge is; that's where the power is, not in the traditional ceremonies.

Now, the traditionalists have been *forced* to be more negative about the churches because the churches have tried consistently to destroy both traditional ceremonies and traditional government at Pine Ridge since the nineteenth century; priests even provided police services to the U.S. government after the U.S. government outlawed the native religious ceremony. That is, priests would go in and disrupt the ceremony and simply take the medicine man's altar, so that Red Cloud Mission and St. Francis Mission over at Rosebud are filled with sacred items taken away from the Lakota people.

For the most part, the traditionalists on those reservations are really very open to the Christian Lakotas; in fact, many of the traditionalists are themselves Christians, in some manner of speaking. The medicine people may only go to mass once a year, but they go, and they encourage others to do both—both the Christian masses and the traditional ceremonies. And a lot of people do. It's the Christians who have trouble making room on the reservation for the traditionalists, because the Christians have been taught all too well by the missionaries that their former selves were sinful. In other words, the missionaries have preached, coached, and taught self-hatred as a value.

REBECCA PARKER: I wanted to say to you, Anita, that I don't think you have to make the move that a denial of knowledge is sin. Sin is a religious category that implies moral failing, a willful act, while "designed blindness" is "unavoidable," as you say. There is so much that is problematic in how we think about sin.

My question for you, Tink, is this: In what ways and to what extent do the thievery of resources and the failure to have right relationships in using resources influence your theological thinking? In other words, how do you think about resources theologically?

TINKER: That's a really complex question, because it involves not just the theft of Indian land but also the theft of Indian resources from what is *still* Indian land. Seventy percent of U.S. uranium reserves in the West are on American Indian reservations, and all of the open mining in the United States is on Indian land; so we are dealing with waste products that threaten both our environment and our employment. We're dealing with a model of development that is temporally based, which comes right out of European and European American cultural experiences. It might not ever have been the Indian choice to exploit these resources. So one of the questions that we have to ask is: Do Indians have the choice not to develop the resources on their land, *not* to mine?

In Wisconsin, the Indian people have come together with environmentalists and sports people—an unholy trinity if there ever was one, because sports people and Indians have fought over Indian fishing and hunting rights for the past thirty years. But now they have come together to fight against Exxon, because Exxon has been eyeing the huge zinc deposits in northern Wisconsin. But zinc mining will destroy the wetlands, with all their resources, in northern Wisconsin and will make the fish and the animals that survive inedible because of the mercury compounds that would necessarily leak into the water as part of the process.

A similar thing is happening in Ontario with the hydroelectric dams. The dams may give Ontario a way to achieve some genuine sovereignty, but they will also force the Ojibwa people from their habitat and their communities by destroying their livelihood. So the issue of resources is not just about economics but it is also about destroying the *livelihood* of a people. And this kind of economic injustice is part of the systemic whole.

SUSAN SUCHOCKI BROWN: Based on my own experiences of working in the alcohol and drug treatment field for many years, I was struck by your use of the concept of intervention, Tink, and I got to thinking about that in terms of spiritual discipline. In the addiction field, we intervene because we need to break the complicity, break the silence, and we need to offer a new vision, a new thought. It's soul work. It involves developing trust and the belief that something else might be possible—a belief *in* something or someone else. And unless that happens, not only will the person drink himself or herself to death but he or she and everyone else around them will suffer a spiritual bankruptcy. I really appreciate thinking about the work of anti-oppression as an intervention; it gives me a systematic way of looking at this work. It helps me to understand what motivates me in my work and validates the experiences that I bring forward. Thank you.

TINKER: We have far too much experience with addictions in my community. One of the signs of late colonialism is alcoholism.

THANDEKA: Thank you for bringing up colonialism. I would like to know how you would critique Anita's description of "designed blindness."

TINKER: There is a sense in which all of us are victims of what our parents, our grandparents, and generations before us have done. We become heirs of those patterns of behavior. We know that the damage perpetrated by abusive parents on children is nearly impossible to shake loose from, even with some serious therapy. At the same time, we know from addiction therapy that people *do* blind themselves; they go into what we call denial.

At one level, I tell white people and Indian people different things; I have to. I tell Indian people that we know where these addictions come from; they come from five hundred years of oppression under white power, colonialism, and conquest. But I also tell them that it won't help just to blame white people; you have to take care of yourself—*we* have to take care of ourselves. But I tell my white students in the classroom that white people have to take care of themselves too. . . . So, it's both/and.

Study Questions

1. What Native American peoples lived on the land you currently inhabit? If they were removed, how? What is your theology of land use and our relationship to the land?

2. George Tinker says, "Violence as a solution has become a key American value." Do you agree with this assessment? If so, brainstorm examples. Are there concrete ways in which

your congregation could begin work to counter violence as a solution?

3. Anita Farber Robertson says, "When liberal religion cast sin out of its theological lexicon, it sacrificed its most powerful and effective concept." Do you agree or disagree with this statement? What theological perspective, if any, do you have on the question of sin?

4. Dialogue partners in this chapter discuss the social geography of living in the center (supporting the status quo, including the structures of oppression) vs. living on margins (resisting oppression and the status quo). John Buehrens asserts that Unitarian Universalists have had great ambivalence about their place in the center. What are some of the ways in which your congregation—whether consciously or unconsciously— functions to support the margins or the center (or not)?

5. What could be done in your religious education program to help children and youth understand the moral, theological, and social implications of what George Tinker describes as the American "addiction to violence"? How could we help them resist perpetuating this culture of violence?

6. George Tinker cites Columbus Day as an example of denial of the "violence that has been at the core of the American colonial project," which sustains racism and oppression. How do you respond to Tinker's analysis? How might you change Columbus Day and Thanksgiving activities in your congregation so that they do not disguise the genocide of Native Americans or sustain racism and oppression?

7. Consider a current social policy issue (such as drugs, crime, poor literacy, public health) and discuss the following: Who is defining the problem? Who is being blamed for the problem? What racial or other fears are being appealed to? Who is left out of the discussion? What is being proposed as a solution? Based on the proposed solution, which ethnic groups would gain the most? Who would lose the most?

8. Throughout his essay, George Tinker clearly *de*nounces violence as a central tendency of oppression, and he *an*nounces a

new future, thus taking up the task posed earlier by Patricia Jimenez. What would you denounce and announce for institutions in our society (including the Church) to eliminate racial oppression?

Reclaiming Our Prophetic Voice: Liberal Theology and the Challenge of Racism

PAUL RASOR

In this paper, I examine three related themes that raise important challenges for liberal theology as it confronts the evil of white racism. Each reveals a particular tension or set of tensions that we must face squarely if our anti-racism work is to be effective. Left unattended, these tensions tend toward an equilibrium that sabotages our own best intentions and reinforces a comfortable status quo.

First, I argue that inherent within religious liberalism is a fundamental tension that undermines our efforts to become an effective prophetic voice in a society that badly needs one. Second, squarely confronting the continuing evil of white racism and our own complicity in it can shift the balance of this tension and help us reclaim our prophetic voice. Yet, anti-racism work reveals some additional tensions and tendencies within liberalism that make this effort difficult to sustain. Third, the evil of racism lies deeper than institutional structures and systemic power relations; it has a spiritual dimension that liberals all too often fail to recognize. As a result, despite our clearest analysis and noblest intentions, we sometimes fail to truly engage and call out the evil that holds us in its grasp. Yet, ironically, it is the spiritual dimension that can not only ground our anti-racism work but contribute most to recovering the prophetic power of our own voice, which too often lies dormant or speaks only weakly.

Before I continue, I need to acknowledge the obvious. I am speaking as a white theologian, a straight white male who grew up as a clear but unwitting beneficiary of a structured system of privilege that I only later came to recognize. As such, my observations are necessarily limited by my own perspective and life experience. My immediate aim is simply to make a small contribution to the dialogue represented by this gathering. In a larger sense, my remarks are aimed primarily at the European American middle-class liberals who constitute the vast majority of Unitarian Universalists; those who want to do good works but aren't sure quite how to move forward, whose hearts are struggling with both love and fear.

Let me begin with the stark assessment of Cornel West:

> The crisis in contemporary American religious life is profound and pervasive. . . . To put it bluntly, American religious life is losing its prophetic fervor. There is an undeniable decline in the clarity of vision, complexity of understanding and quality of moral action among religious Americans. The rich legacies of Sojourner Truth, Walter Rauschenbusch, Dorothy Day, Abraham Heschel, and Martin Luther King, Jr., now lie nearly dormant— often forgotten—and the possession of a marginal few.[1]

I believe West's words pose a particular challenge to religious liberals. In an earlier article,[2] I called this the "justice crisis" or "prophetic crisis" and linked it to a fundamental tension inherent within liberal religion, involving its relationship to society and the larger culture. On the one hand, liberal religion has always accepted the social, scientific, and other cultural realities of its own time, and has consciously tried to adapt itself to them. In this way, liberals have sought to remain credible and relevant to contemporary society. Indeed, this adaptive or accommodating stance is sometimes said to be the central characteristic of what it means to be a religious liberal.[3] On the other hand, liberal religion has always understood itself in prophetic terms, as offering a critique of culture. Liberals have long sought to call society to account for injustice, to challenge the cultural status quo, and to work for reform. James Luther Adams called this the "progressive element" in religious liberalism.[4]

These two liberal tendencies, the accommodating and the prophetic, exist in tension with each other. My own observation is that the accommodating side has been the stronger of the two, and that this has tended to limit the effectiveness of our justice work.[5] I was certainly not the first to see this. A half-century ago, H. Richard Niebuhr noted that the easy accommodation of religion and culture tends to produce a certain level of intellectual and social comfort. As a result, religious liberals tend to be "nonrevolutionaries who find no need for positing 'cracks in time.'"[6] Cornel West agrees, arguing that the prophetic voice in American religion can be recovered only by "counter[ing] and contest[ing] the widespread accommodation of American religion to the political and cultural status quo. . . . This accommodation is, at bottom, idolatrous."[7]

An important factor in this liberal tension is social class. Since I examined this issue in detail in my earlier paper, I will not do so here. I do want to note, however, that the white middle-class values of liberal religion tend to tip the balance toward the accommodating and away from the prophetic. This too is not a new idea. H. Richard Niebuhr noted the link between denominationalism and social class over seventy years ago. As he saw it, middle-class churches tend to emphasize individual self-consciousness, personal salvation, financial security, and an ethic of individual responsibility.[8] Parker Palmer makes a similar observation from a contemporary perspective:

> The religion of the American middle class sometimes seems to mock the Gospels; it aims at enhancing the self-esteem of persons who have material comfort while ignoring conditions of poverty and pestilence which deprive a whole class of people of life itself, let alone feelings of self-worth.[9]

Throughout American history, middle-class religion's association with the social and economic establishment has limited its ability to engage social justice issues at a deep level, since overturning the existing system would be contrary to its own interests. I believe this danger remains present for European American liberal religionists, including Unitarian Universalists, as they seek to become anti-racist.

This brings me to my second theme, the link between this prophetic tension and the issue of racism. Facing the challenge of white racism needs no justification; it is simply something we must do. But I believe our anti-racism work can help create a significant counter-force to the accommodationist inertia that weakens our prophetic voice. Indeed, legal scholar Anthony Cook argues that the progressive religious voice cannot be truly recovered without attending to this unfinished business.

As Cook sees it, the liberal-progressive coalition that emerged around the Civil Rights movement disintegrated because it couldn't fully deal with the legacy of racism in America.[10] Ironically, this disintegration began at the very moment of one of the movement's greatest victories, the passage of the 1965 Voting Rights Act. The problem was that while this law was indeed a victory, it was only a formal victory. As Martin Luther King Jr. and others understood, a "colorblind" federal law prohibiting discrimination wouldn't really change much unless poverty and class were also addressed. Yet white liberals were largely unwilling to do this. They were afraid of King's new call for a more radically inclusive coalition; they were even more afraid of the explicitly race-conscious agenda of the Black Power movement. As Cook puts it, "the liberal coalition reached its philosophical limits with the signing of the 1965 Voting Rights Act."[11] James Cone's trenchant analysis of these events is similar. White resistance was so great that King "had to move closer to Malcolm [X]'s perspective and begin to see white liberals as phony advocates of freedom for the black poor."[12]

I argue that these liberal failures reflect several tensions and ambiguities that continue to plague us today. First, as the social agenda has moved from issues of formal equality and basic human decency to genuine equality and systemic oppression, many white religious liberals seem reluctant to talk about race at all. We may hesitate to talk about existing disparities among racial and ethnic groups, for example, because to do so feels somehow like buying into racial stereotypes, and because they remind us of the continuing structural racism we once thought, or at least hoped, had been addressed. From the perspective of the "colorblind" ideals of an earlier era, this kind of race talk can even seem "unliberal." For many white liberals, it is no longer comfortable even to talk the talk, much less walk the walk.

A related tension within religious liberalism emerges, ironically, out of one of our great strengths. Our traditional emphasis on rationality leads liberals to do good conceptual analysis. This is important work; indeed, it is essential if we are to address the systemic and structural dimensions of racism. But, as with the Voting Rights Act, this sort of analysis can get stuck in a kind of formal rationality that can all too easily keep us at a respectable and safe distance from the very problems we are attempting to address. Like Linus, who in a famous *Peanuts* cartoon remarked, "I love mankind—it's people I can't stand,"[13] we liberals are often better at formality and abstraction than at getting our hands dirty and our feet moving. Liberals deeply want things to be right in the world, but we also want them to be tidy. Justice work is messy, and our discomfort with messiness, which I believe is another symptom of our desire for control, weakens the prophetic power of our words and actions.

Our efforts to become genuinely anti-racist are hampered by another liberal ambivalence that history helps to make clear. This ambivalence surfaces as we begin to learn the importance of community in anti-racism work. Liberals want to create a strong and inclusive community, but we often want to do it without giving up anything, without letting down the barriers we erect around ourselves in the name of individual autonomy. We wade into the waters of community up to our knees, but we're afraid to let go of the dock and plunge in with our whole bodies. As Cook says,

> The central problem of liberalism . . . is that the liberal conception of community is based too much on fear and too little on love. It is fear of the "other" that generates in liberal thought the fundamental paradox of liberal theory. The liberal subject both desires and fears, needs and is threatened by community.[14]

Cook's observation is telling, yet I think the problem lies deeper. Our deep-seated fear of community, when combined with our tendency toward formalism and abstraction, leads to a deep fear of otherness that we have barely begun to recognize and address. Fear of the other manifests itself in such liberal ideals as autonomy, self-reliance, and the like and prevents us from seeing that we are truly social selves.[15]

Liberal political and social theory, too often echoed in liberal religion, tends to protect the individual from the community, from true engagement with the other. This kind of negative freedom tends to produce a constricted sense of self. But a love-based understanding of community would extend the individual and expand the self outward *toward* the other. This sort of reconception of community seems essential if we are serious about our anti-racism work.

Let me turn now to the third part of my argument. My claim is that the tensions I have identified will continue to weaken our prophetic voice and interfere with our anti-racism work unless we recognize that racism is an evil that poisons not only our institutions, but also our hearts. We must, in other words, attend to its spiritual dimensions. And in order to do this, we must begin to see racism not only as a matter of institutional structures and social power disparities, but as a profound evil.

This is a difficult message for liberals to hear, so let me be as clear as possible. I am not simply making a moral judgment that racism is wrong, nor am I making an anthropological claim that human beings have the capacity to do horrible things and create oppressive institutions. These statements are, of course, true; in fact, they represent the way religious liberals usually think about systemic evils. Instead, I am making a theological claim. Racism is an evil, a profound, structural evil embedded deeply within our culture and within ourselves. It is a "power" in the biblical sense.

It is hard for liberals to talk in these terms because we have no real theology of evil, and therefore no language or conceptual reference points adequate to the task. Indeed, this language has been difficult for me. But as I have thought about white racism in the context of our ongoing denominational struggle, I have come to believe that any other approach is inadequate. Treating racism as an evil, a power that has us in its grasp, may help us realize more clearly what we are up against. This does not mean that we need to think of it as a disembodied, supernatural demon or the like. White racism is of course a cultural construct, the invention of human beings in specific historical settings and social contexts. But to approach it as a human construct and nothing more misses its profound power over us. We are tempted to think it can be dismantled with the right motivation, proper analysis, and good programs. It will take all of these and more, but these, by themselves, are not enough.

Instead, racism, once unleashed onto the world and embedded within human structures and institutions, takes on a life of its own. Like all cultural and institutional structures, it eventually becomes self-perpetuating and, to some, self-justifying. Despite our best and most persistent efforts to dismantle it, it keeps coming back in newer and more subtle forms. As Bill Wylie-Kellermann says, "no force in U.S. history has proven more relentless or devastatingly resilient than white racism. It is empirically a demon that again and again rises up transmogrified in ever more predatory and beguiling forms, truly tempting our despair."[16]

When we begin to see it from this perspective, we can more easily recognize that the evil of racism poisons our spirits as much as our institutions. It gets inside us despite our best efforts to block it out, eating away at our hearts, eroding our capacity for expanded community. New Testament scholar Walter Wink even suggests that the hold this sort of evil has on us amounts to a kind of possession:

> Our involvement with evil goes far beyond our conscious, volitional participation in evil. To a much greater extent than we are aware, we are possessed by the values and powers of our unjust order. It is not enough then simply to repent of the ways we have consciously chosen to collude with evil; we must be freed from our unconscious enthrallment as well.[17]

When we acknowledge this unconscious captivity, we begin to open space for healing and then for expanded community based on love.

In other words, the evil of racism is not only structural and institutional; it is also spiritual. This means that all of our analysis, no matter how sophisticated, and all of our programs, no matter how well designed, will never be sufficient by themselves to make us anti-racist. We must also be "willing to do the difficult soul work necessary for spiritual transformation."[18] This aspect of our task reveals another ambivalence for religious liberals. As much as we say we want more spirituality in our lives, we are often reluctant to go too deep to find it. Part of this is no doubt due to our traditional emphasis on rationality, which many of us erroneously place in opposition to spirituality. Another factor, I suspect, is an awareness that sustained spiritual practice can take us deep inside, exposing aspects of our selves we may rather not see. We lose the security of safe distance that purely intellectual analysis permits. As Wink says, any attempt to transform a social system without addressing both its spirituality and its outer forms is doomed to failure. . . . Only by confronting the spirituality of an institution *and* its concretions can the total entity be transformed, and that requires a kind of spiritual discernment and praxis that the materialistic ethos in which we live knows nothing about.[19]

This paper is not the place to work out a full-blown theology of evil for liberals, or even to suggest specific spiritual practices or techniques for addressing the particular evil of white racism. As a necessary first step, however, we must at least recognize these dimensions of the struggle we are engaged in. We have been shaped by the very powers and structures we now want to dismantle. The social transformation we seek requires spiritual transformation as well. Without this, our anti-racism work, like other prophetic practice for social change, becomes difficult to sustain or retreats into the safety of disengaged analysis or internal debate.

It is too soon yet to tell whether this will be the fate of our current anti-racism work. I hope not. In the meantime, we will have to dedicate our heads, hands, and hearts to the task. And in so doing, may we reclaim the prophetic voice that is constantly tempted to become lost in our accommodation to the very culture we seek to change.

The Responses

"The kinds of things we write about reflect who we are, where we are, and our own struggles at the time" is how Paul Rasor opens the discussion of his essay, highlighting its main points:

> Some of my earlier articles have addressed the tensions in our movement. There are so many inertias at work, allowing us to settle into a comfortable status quo. It is important to keep these tensions in front of people so that we can approach this work with a long-haul view and with determination and focus.

> But in talking about racism as evil, I'm somewhat less confident, and I'd be very interested in your responses. I'm trying to find a way to talk about racism, and especially about white racism, that begins to bring home its seriousness in religious language, using religious ideas that liberals are sometimes uncomfortable with.

I'm really struggling to find a language for this, so in this essay I am floating the idea of reclaiming a true theology of evil and of applying it to racism.

Ken Olliff calls for Unitarian Universalists to acknowledge their historical location within the liberal religious tradition, recognizing its limitations as Rasor does ("its failings in accommodation, rationality, and community") and "doing the hard work of reconstructing it" in order to deepen its theological reflections on race and class, as well as to make it more effective in dealing with these issues. Olliff points to resources within the tradition for this reconstructive effort:

> By looking at different strands within the liberal tradition (such as early Universalism, the variety of sects within the Radical Reformation, and Unitarianism in Transylvania), we might find the resources for addressing our current weaknesses on the issue of class. We might also draw on the diversity of perspectives that exists within liberalism to counter currently prevailing conceptions. For instance, John Dewey's philosophy of education holds a conception of the self as strongly embedded in community—as compared with much of Enlightenment liberalism, which lifts up individual autonomy. . . .[20]

Whether acknowledged or not, theological understandings and priorities lie behind our work on behalf of anti-racism. In order to most effectively go about this work, I believe we need to be as clear as possible as to the "why" of anti-racism. What about our liberal faith calls us to do this work? What is at stake for us? This is a particularly difficult task for Unitarian Universalists, as we are largely uncomfortable with making explicitly theological claims in a public forum. We also know that we will not come to theological consensus, and perhaps it is better to concentrate on the work that we can do together rather than argue over why we do it. But without a theological component our roots remain shallow: We can only articulate anti-racism in terms of "shoulds," but we are unable to express why working on behalf of anti-racism goes to the depths of who we are as a people of faith. And we need deep roots in order to sustain us through a long and difficult journey.

Rasor suggests the need for a theology of evil for liberals as a theological rationale for anti-racism, which I believe is a crucial step in providing theological foundations for effective anti-racism for

Unitarian Universalists. . . . If racism is evil, it is an aberration and must be confronted at all costs. I would add, however, that we cannot speak about the evil of racism without raising an anthropological question as to the nature of human beings and the brokenness of our lives and the world in which we live—which raises the question of sin.

While it is also not a particularly comfortable topic for religious liberals, I would like to suggest that along with a conception of racism as evil we also need to take seriously racism as arising out of a condition of estrangement and alienation, which in Christian theology has been addressed under the topic of sin. In my own wrestling with racism, I have found Paul Tillich's conception of sin as estrangement from self, other, and the ground of being to be crucial in providing a theological explanation for the brokenness that I experience in the world.[21] Nothing in my progressive Unitarian Universalist upbringing allowed me to account for the estrangement from my own best self, from my fellow human beings, and from God that I have experienced in the pernicious-ness of racism. In other words, the way I was raised offered me a vision of the world that did not account for what I actually see in the world.

Thus I agree with Paul Rasor that, along with solid theological analysis, anti-racism requires of us a spiritual transformation, a *metanoia*, a change of heart and mind.

In Rasor's description of "otherness" and his "insight into the role that fear plays in preventing us from creating true communi-ty," **Peter Morales** discovers "possibilities for creating a new lan-guage that builds on anti-racism and yet is flexible enough to speak to issues that transcend race." He observes,

I also believe that we have here the seeds of a language that can speak to the spiritual work we must do to confront the evil of racism—and other evils as well.

First, however, I should say a few words about the need for a new language. The language of anti-racism grew out of the expe-rience of African Americans and European Americans, out of the experience of slavery and the efforts to dismantle the racism that has oppressed African Americans. This language of anti-racism has focused our attention on real evil—evil that is pervasive, per-nicious, and frighteningly resilient. Anti-racism focuses our attention on power and privilege.

And yet I am convinced that we desperately need a new language. . . . I believe that if we continue to use the language of anti-racism, if we continue to build our efforts on the concepts that grew out of the experience of African Americans and "whites," we are doomed ... to become ineffective and irrelevant anachronisms. . . .

I am not for a moment suggesting that racism is dead, or that it is not a pervasive evil that poisons our society. I am suggesting, however, that the language of race is utterly inadequate to speak to the experience of recent immigrants from Mexico and Nicaragua. It does not speak adequately to the experience of Vietnamese or Hmong immigrants. It does not come close to capturing the issues confronting Native Americans. The language of anti-racism cannot speak compellingly to the experiences of tens of millions of Americans who are of mixed race and mixed ethnicity. . . .

Can we create a language that speaks to racism, to issues of social class, to issues of culture and ethnicity? And how about the issues of gender; bisexual, gay, lesbian, and transgender concerns; and ableism—all of the oppressions that our Faith in Action Department attempts to address? I think we can, and I believe Rasor's thoughtful comments on "otherness" are a good place to start. Rasor speaks of our individualism and fear of community. The idea of defining the "other" also speaks to the persistent, innate human evil of tribalism (perhaps the language of original sin is not too strong here). This, too, is founded on our sense of vulnerability—a visceral, animal fear of the unknown. We collectively draw lines around those who are part of us and safe, and those who are "other" and to be feared. And once we have defined a group of people as "other"—whether black, brown, Bosnian, Jew, or gay—violence and oppression will follow.

Rasor ably describes how defining another as "the other" has an emotional and spiritual component as well as a collective and structural dimension. This insight into the spiritual dimension opens the door for a dialogue about how we address the fears that breed oppression and that prevent us from creating the blessed community.

How do we best do this work? I wish I knew. My hunch is that part of the spiritual work can be done in our congregations by creating a safe place to confront our fears. Clearly we need better models. And we need to create experiences of "shared work" that help break our racial, class, and cultural isolation. I am increasingly less optimistic about the enduring value of anti-racism workshops. I wonder if, in the jargon of education, our workshops are "developmentally appropriate." At the very least, we need to supplement them with experiences that allow our people to cross the barriers of race, class, and culture. Rasor's analysis points us toward doing more work that is not only spiritual but *relational*. Our language and concepts are important as we evolve a new praxis, for our language can help us to see things more clearly, to see opportunities and to ask the right questions. . . .

My fear for our movement and for this consultation is that in our devotion to addressing the evil of racism as it bears on African Americans, we will attempt to shove the experiences of Latinos, Asians, and Native Americans into containers that cannot hold them. The experience of Latinos, for example, has much more to do with issues of culture and class than with race. We are a different "other."

Together, though, we can create a language that makes us not *less* anti-racist but *more than* anti-racist. We can develop a language that can speak to our different oppressions and to our deep fears about the community we long for . . . a new language of human liberation and compassionate community.

The Dialogue

The definition of evil, the importance of language, notions of God and "otherness," the relationship between the individual and the community, the possibility that heartlessness is a product of the culture in which we live—these are the topics that absorb participants during the dialogue.

THANDEKA: I'd like you to clarify, Paul, what you mean by the term *evil*. I offer three possibilities: You suggest that evil is a kind of structural evil; so by "structural evil" do you mean evil in the way that Schleiermacher meant evil, which is that it is a social creation of a specific community, handed down from generation to generation? As you know, he rejected the doctrine of original sin. When you say that evil takes on a life of its own, are you talking about Weber's ideas? Is this Geertz? Or, third possibility, are you talking about Satan?

RASOR: When I was writing this essay, I realized that I didn't really define "evil," but I decided to let it ride, partly because of the word limit and partly because I wasn't there yet. I *don't* mean number three [group laughter]; it could be "all of the above" with respect to numbers one and two.

My idea is that theologies and worldviews are constructions; they become a thing as you work on them, but they are really social constructions. And that *thing* that I want to call evil— racism, really white racism in the modern European sense—is a product of culture over time; it's created, particularly with power and violence. It's certainly a social creation that is handed down and that I believe takes on a life of its own. It becomes *in the nature of* a biblical power or something that perpetuates itself because it's so deeply embedded that you don't notice it, or if you do notice it, it's considered normal. . . . I'm hoping that if we construct a way of looking at racism that takes it as demonic, that looks at it as a kind of thing with a life of its own, then whether we buy into a supernatural view or not, we will be jolted into taking it seriously.

JOHN BUEHRENS: This discussion opens up for me the question of whether liberal theology can begin to understand that theological language is inherently culturally mediated. It is our tendency to strive for universals; thus we strive to abandon the language that's specific to theological traditions in favor of languages borrowed from the social sciences.

We are in the midst of a global debate about the language of race [with the United Nations Conference on Racism] . . . . How will people begin to analogize the differing experiences of people in the Balkans with the insistence of the *dalit* groups in India that what they experience is another form of racism and with the experience of, say, the Maya of Central America, who see their treatment as aboriginal people as partaking of the characteristics of race and racism within the Spanish culture?

The language of "oppression" that we have attempted to make the great umbrella language in the Unitarian Universalist Association has some inherent problems, just as the language of race does. I've been insistent with the Faith in Action staff, for example, that we need to pay attention to the fact that we are operating within an American culture and in a Unitarian Universalist culture that are both particularly subject to what Christopher Lasch has called the "culture of narcissism." One has only to go to Unitarian Universalist worship these days to notice the self-referential and self-display aspects of that "culture of narcissism.". . .

Maybe we would do well not to try to find one single universalizing language of race or theology but to develop more nuanced ways of understanding evil at differing levels. For instance, to your question, Thandeka, I would answer, "All three, *including* the last one." From my personal relationship with the demonic force of the powers and principalities that are inherent in the culture, I find that I am dealing with the Devil, whose greatest trick is to try to convince us that he or she doesn't exist in our own lives. So color me part medieval, if you will. I'm holding out for a multi-layered approach to some of these issues.

BILL JONES: Paul, I agree with your concept of evil as a social construct, but it means you're going to have to go back and take out the places where you give evil an independent, ontological status. With the social construct status, the object has two components: There is an objective "thing," and then there is a human addition to it, a label that we've put on it. Evil, then, is not an essential active agent operating on any object. Rather, evil is the way a certain agent looks at a neutral state of affairs.

RASOR: I am torn between the thought that these things take on a life of their own, and the thought that this very idea is *itself* a social construction. I think that it *is* a social construction—but even so, to treat racism *as though* it's an independent ontological reality has some bite.

FRED MUIR: Language is so important. If you have the language and are structuring the argument, then you've got the power. Peter says that the language of anti-racism grew out of the experience of African Americans and European Americans—this is an issue of power. I feel that the language of anti-racism has grown out of European Americans' *interpretation* of the experience of African Americans. . . .

I'm still confused and perplexed about the language of "race." We all use the word *race*, which creates a problem right from the beginning, because my understanding is that there's *one* race—the human race. To break it up is evil; that's the power of the language that European Americans have foisted onto the rest of the world. What are we going to do about that? James Cone spoke of our common humanity, which is the fact that we are all one race; yet throughout these essays, we talk about "race." Do we really mean that, or do we just use the word for convenience because that's the language our society uses?

KIM BEACH: This is what I wrote during the journaling time: "No one language will speak to all forms of . . . *what?* If not racism, then what are we talking about? This pushes us toward a more fundamental language of human brokenness—the brokenness we experience in our relationships with ourselves; with our communities of work, of learning, and of worship; and with God, the ground of our being."

I think one of the reasons we liberals get worried when we talk about evil is that we feel we're dipping into dualism, and we've been taught again and again that dualism is bad and monism is good. But if there's evil, there is a certain amount of dualism going on in the world.

James Luther Adams had a great deal to say about evil; he even brought in the term *demonic* to refer to the "principalities and powers" of the New Testament. Adams made an interesting distinction between the demonic and the satanic. He referred to the satanic as pure evil; it's the mythical and mythological notion of an independent ontological power that is totally separate, like Satan coming in from a supernatural realm. The demonic, on the other hand, is the distortion of the good. So if you think that the creation is fundamentally good, then whenever and wherever this original goodness is distorted, that is the demonic. In this spiritual notion of evil, evil is seen as self-perpetuating and self-justifying, which is what makes it so strong. Hitler was a great example of evil; his was a demonic power.

The other notion that runs through Adams's work is idolatry. To reduce it to its simplest form, idolatry is misplaced devotion. Insofar as our faith has to do with those things and those ends to which we are devoted, we seem to give idolatrous devotion to our own success, or to our "beautiful institution," or to our beautiful building, and so on. Those are demonic loyalties, because they are distorted. They may be caused by demonic powers in our world; you can talk about that without worrying too much about the supernatural. Tillich also used the language of the demonic; that's where Adams got it.

RASOR: Adams is complex and hard to nail down. He seems to say that humans can do great evil or great good, but he presupposes that the *creation* is all good at first. I'm not sure it is all anything *first*.

ANITA FARBER-ROBERTSON: Paul, you talk about the fear of "the other" and how it manifests itself in such liberal ideals as autonomy, self-reliance, and the like. To what extent is that fear of the other reflected in our fear of a God who is other, and in the way in which our current liberal tradition does not allow for the otherness of God? So that—speaking of the narcissism that John was talking about—the "Spirit of Life" becomes *like us!* It strikes me that the dilemma you raise is also reflected in our whole dilemma around God-talk, around accountability and the tension between community accountability and individual accountability. I think that our relinquishing the otherness of God feeds into this tension.

RASOR: That's very interesting. Liberals have historically rejected concepts of God as wholly Other. This makes being accountable to an "other" and how we construct an "other" difficult. Being accountable to an "other" and seeing ourselves in an "other" are all related to how we see God. There is a liberal tendency to bring it all *inside ourselves*, so that our only reference is ourselves—that's essentially the whole modern liberal tradition. We tend to "immanentize" God until God loses all meaning.

TOM SCHADE: I was moved by the cadenza of Ken's ending—that your training as a Unitarian Universalist did not prepare you for the reality of the world you met. I was afraid that was only my experience and the experience of my daughter!

I'm trying to connect two arguments that I hear going on: Paul has made the argument that we need to confront the reality of evil and sin. Then there's another argument, which I first became aware of at the Robert Bellah speech at General Assembly and which places the contradiction between the individual and the community.[22] This argument claims that the errors of the past have derived from our being excessively individualistic and that the way to the future is for us to become less individualistic and more community-minded—and that *this* is the battle between evil and good. I am *extremely* distressed to understand that individualism is bad and community is good, having lived through the last half of the twentieth century and seen what we've done and having had my experience with communism.

Now, does either one of these arguments—about good and evil, and about individualism and community—offer a way to respond to the inadequacy of Unitarian Universalist theologians in preparing our children for the real world?

RASOR: I don't think that it's quite what Bellah had in mind, and certainly not what I have in mind, to say that there's a contradiction between the individual and the community. I think that's a false dichotomy. One of the things that liberals have a tendency to not see well—and this was part of Bellah's point—is that individuals and communities emerge together, that the individual is *always* already embedded in a community and a social reality. The idea that liberals have, that they are individuals and then together they form community, has it backwards. Individuals are already social beings from the start. We need to learn to think about the individual and the community simultaneously.

MORALES: And there is an important distinction between a community that is based on interest, in the Marxist sense, and a community based on affection and compassion.

GEORGE TINKER: This is a *fascinating* discussion; I'm really appreciating it and enjoying it. I'm also increasingly aware that I am from a culture different from anything you have experienced. And I say "experienced" because in American Indian culture, we *experience* the world, we *experience* our intellectuality. We tend to have some things in common: I think American Indians are very quick to admit the personalization of a universalized signifier of evil like Satan. But we are not supernaturalists; we are thoroughgoing naturalists. I just think we admit to a much larger natural world than you do! [He chuckles, and the group laughs heartily.]

We struggle with evil, too, and we see the counter to evil in balance and harmony. But we don't mean by balance and harmony any notion of New Age individualism, because it's a balance and harmony of the whole. If the whole isn't balanced and harmonious, then it's impossible for me to be balanced. And any notion of balance is temporary; the balance is always changing, always being established and re-established.

We experience a spiritual aspect in the world that is very hard for me to talk about here in this context. Our understanding of this spiritual aspect is that it's neutral—it's not good or bad, even though ultimately the power force that we call *Wakume* in my tribe can be helpful and useful and good. It can also work with whatever energy is inside us to create patterns of behavior and ultimately systems of behavior patterns.

For me, the systemic whole as an evil in the world is probably best signified by the existence of the modern state as a form of governance; today it seems as if the state were the *only* divinely mandated form of governance, the divine right of states having displaced the divine right of monarchs. I say that the United States as a modern state *must* oppress people; I believe that the well-being of the United States absolutely depends on oppressing American Indians. The economic well-being, the stability, of the United States *depends upon* oppression. Capitalism is built on necessarily oppressing other people. The power and force of capitalism derive first of all from access to cheap natural resources—to somebody else's stuff, right?—and then from the exploitation of human labor, which is somebody else's energy.

The United States economy is built on the government's illegal, immoral, and unjust claim to the U.S. land mass. If the Indians ever get healthy and strong enough to make a claim to the land again—not even *all* the land, but just the 30 percent that's not covered by any legitimate treaty (never mind that the rest of it is clouded by the failure of the United States to live up to its treaty negotiations with Indian peoples)—then the economy would have to fail very quickly, and the power relationships would shift as the true owners of the land would begin to make decisions about how to use the land productively, with different imaginings of what *productive* might mean.

RASOR: There's a deeply ecological theme underlying your comments. Capitalism not only presupposes oppression as being the creation of poverty at the margins but also commodifies *everything*, including human beings, relationships—everything is seen as marketable. I think this relates to Anita's question about "othering" someone, because the "other" becomes commodified and therefore marketable. If we ever concluded that "we" and the "other" were the same, that would have a profound impact on our relationship to capitalism, in which we are all so deeply entrenched.

REBECCA PARKER: I want to come back to the very first thing you said, Paul, that you're trying to find a way to speak about racism that brings home its seriousness, and you're experimenting with using the language of evil for that. I want to suggest that we not only give attention to the social construction of *ideas* but also to the social construction of our feelings and the social construction of our senses. Your concern that we come home to the seriousness of racism might be addressed not in inquiring so much about our concepts—though I think that's really important work—but also in inquiring about what has led those who are not serious about racism to not be serious. I would suggest that perhaps the reason lies in the social construction of heartlessness or numbness of feeling.

RASOR: You are articulating something I wasn't able to articulate even to myself about what I meant when I said that we also need to deal with racism as a spiritual thing. The "social construction of heartlessness"—yes! Thank you!

Study Questions

1. Paul Rasor says that racism is a human construct and a "profound structural evil . . . that has us in its grasp." What meaning does the term *evil* have for you? If not "evil," what language would you use to describe racism?

2. Although in the past, religious liberals were on the cutting edge of advocacy for racial justice, Paul Rasor argues that since

the 1960s, there has been a shift toward liberal social action based on an accommodation and acceptance of the cultural status quo. Do you agree or disagree with Rasor's analysis? Have religious liberals lost the "prophetic fervor" that calls us to account for racial injustice? Can you give examples?

3. Another challenge that prevents us from more fully engaging in the work of anti-racism, according to Rasor, is that religious liberals have a deep-seated fear of community that is rooted in fear of "the other"' He says, "Liberals want to create a strong and inclusive community . . . without letting down the barriers we erect around ourselves in the name of individual autonomy." Have you experienced or observed this tension? If so, how has it manifested itself? What is the place of spiritual practice in bridging the gap between the desire for individual autonomy and the desire for community?

4. Peter Morales argues that the language of "race" and "anti-racism" does not sufficiently address the experiences and concerns of Latina/os, in part because these concepts are rooted in relationships between African Americans and whites. John Buehrens, however, points out that language is "culturally mediated" and expresses itself differently in different national and cultural contexts. To what extent do exclusion, discrimination, and oppression manifest themselves in significantly different ways around the world? Does our "tendency to strive for universals" inhibit our understanding of the ways in which racism expresses itself as an international phenomenon?

5. George Tinker points out that the American Indian approach to struggling with evil is holistic—based not on individualism but on balance and harmony: "If the whole isn't balanced and harmonious, then it's impossible for *me* to be balanced." What would it take for Americans to engage in cross-cultural learning to increase our understanding of evil in general and of racism in particular?

6. Paul Rasor and George Tinker assert that capitalism presupposes oppression, and that racial oppression is one manifestation in the United States. Is there a contradiction between capitalism and democracy? Beyond the relationship between capitalism and class, is our economy based on *racial* oppres-

sion? If you respond affirmatively to either question, how do we approach this ethical dilemma?

7. Rebecca Parker suggests that *feelings* are as important as *thinking* about racism and its consequences, and that our feelings about racism have been anesthetized, numbed. Is your primary tendency to express your feelings about racism or to intellectualize them? What causes the numbness and the tendency to suppress our feelings? If more people expressed their *feelings* about racism, might this move us further along the path to eliminating racism?

The Paradox of
Racial Oppression

THANDEKA

~

Racism and self-hatred: Recently I received a letter from a man (whom I'll call Jim) who had suffered pervasive feelings of ethnic and racial shame. His minister had helped him make sense of those feelings. The letter begins with Jim's account of his confession to his minister: "No matter what situation I am in, I am easily made to feel as if I don't know how to do the right thing, despite positive feedback from others that I indeed do [know]." Jim then chronicles the genealogy of his discomfort—in three generations of ethnic identity issues and prejudices.

His paternal grandfather, who was "part Gypsy and part English," was "very dark, with high cheekbones and jet black hair, and was often denied service in the local bar because he looked like he was Chippewa."

His father "lives in constant despair of being caught out somehow" because he was "the darkest child [in the family], had a hooked nose . . . and didn't look anything like the blond-haired, blue-eyed kids around him." Compared with his extremely fair, blond brother, Jim's father was "always found lacking."

Jim himself, despite his own blond hair and blue eyes, doesn't believe that he looks right, either. "No matter how hard I try," he writes, "no matter what beauty products I use, I never quite look Anglo. There is something around my eyes, in the shape of my face, in my skin tone."

Having read my book *Learning to Be White: Money, Race and God in America*, Jim's minister helped him make sense of these experiences. The minister noted that Jim's stories were strikingly similar to the stories recounted in my book about people who are ashamed of their ethnic background because it isn't "white enough."

After listening to his minister's comments, Jim had what he calls an "Oh-my-God experience." Writes Jim, "Suddenly the uncomfortable parts of me 'fit.'" He could now talk about those "uncomfortable," non-Anglo parts of himself. They had a name: *Gypsy.*

Jim then describes his next insight, which concerns what he describes as his grandfather's "rabid racism against other people of color." Jim now understood that part of his grandfather's racism was "self-hatred." The grandfather had learned to fit into a world that despised him by despising the despised part of himself. Jim talked with an aunt about his insights and experiences, and the two "have begun healing and hope we can, together, help heal our families." Furthermore, Jim found that he "no longer felt compelled to 'pass' [as white] anymore."

It is clear from his letter that Jim experienced a personal transformation. This happened, I believe, because he became aware of the link connecting his and his family's ethnic self-hatred with his grandfather's racism toward "other people of color." As he learned how to think about issues of race and identity in new ways, he came to understand and begin to overcome the self-perpetuating cycle of racism and self-hatred in his own family.

In order for the rest of us to catch up with Jim, we must learn to think about race in new ways. A good place to begin is with definitions.

The lexicon of racism: The term *ethnicity* comes from the Greek root word *ethnos,* meaning nation. The term thus refers to national origin, carrying with it particular cultural traditions, geographic locations, and collective histories.

The term *race,* from the Italian word *razza,* refers to a tribe or family of persons who have descended from a common stock. It refers to a biological state (genetic inheritance) rather than to a politically constructed, national state. In this biological sense, all human beings are members of the same race: the human race.

Confusion begins when the term *race* takes on a different meaning. You know that such talk has begun when words such as *whites, blacks,* and *people of color* are used to describe cultural identities as if they were biological facts. People talk about different "races," and members of each of these "racial" groups proceed to identify their own common ancestors as different from the ancestors of other "racial" groups who live in the same nation. These putative "racial" differences are then used by members of one of these "races" to legitimate their right to economically exploit and govern the racial "underclass." Rule is now talked about as a racial right, and the privileges, power, and prestige of the ruling elite are discussed as a racial fact.[1]

The term *racism* refers to the theories constructed to explain race-talk. The theories justify the conflation of class status with race. Racist theories begin with the premise that all members of the ruling race are genetically suited—through intelligence, moral aptitude, or some other biologized social factor—to enjoy the power, prestige, and the privilege of governance. In short, the term *racism* refers to a set of theories used to explain why the "superior race" has the right to rule—and conversely, why the "inferior race" is fit only to be ruled. We need to understand the theory.

The economic and social function of racism: Racism is a theory about social control. When practiced, it works as a punishing regime. Michel Foucault describes the genealogy of the practice in technical terms: "One has to take into account the points where the technologies of domination of individuals over one another have recourse to processes by which the individual acts upon himself. And conversely, one has to take into account the points where the techniques of the self are integrated into structures of coercion or domination. [These machinations of governance] assure coercion and processes through which the self is constructed and modified by oneself."[2] In nontechnical terms, racism is about how people learn to subvert their own self-interest.

George E. Tinker uses an analogy to make this practical point. "Just as an abused child slowly but inevitably internalizes a parent's abuse as a consistent demonstration of the child's own shortcomings and may even regard the life of the abusive parent as exemplary, so communities of oppressed peoples internalize their own oppression and come to believe many of the stereotypes, explicit and implicit, spoken by the oppressor."[3] The oppressed, in colonization schemes, become agents of their own oppression.

The late Frantz Fanon, psychiatrist and freedom fighter for Algerian independence, describes the economic aspect of these oppressive lessons. His terms are technical. The racial inferiority complex in the colonized "other," Fanon writes, results from economic exploitation that is then internalized. To describe this process, Fanon coined the term *epidermalization,* which might express itself as economic inferiority.[4] Such disempowering racial strategies, Fanon concludes, are part and parcel of colonialism.

Rabbi Michael Lerner, editor of *Tikkun* magazine, brings the theory home to white America with an amazingly practical term, *surplus powerlessness.* In his 1986 study of union workers and other wage earners in California, Lerner uses the term "surplus powerlessness" to identify a "set of feelings and beliefs that make people think of themselves as even more powerless than the actual power situation requires, and then leads them to act in ways that actually confirm in them powerlessness."[5] Lerner contrasts this notion with the idea of "real powerlessness," which defines the American reality we live in: a class society.

Lerner reminds his readers that the rich do not have all the power. Members of the small, elite class who have the real wealth and power in America do not have absolute power: "Things could be quite different if people were engaged in the struggle to change things." But the American people aren't so engaged. Why? Surplus powerlessness. It prevents the vast majority of America's citizens from making and sustaining a concerted struggle to improve the overall economic quality of their lives. It's a power blocker for the poor and a power stopper for the rich. Surplus powerlessness is a structural requirement needed to keep the economic elite in power. It helps the few to rule the many. Those they exploit help them stay on top. Race-talk is a form of surplus powerlessness.

White surplus powerlessness: Martin Luther King Jr. did not use the term, but he described the condition of surplus powerlessness in white America. By 1968, King had come to believe that American capitalism must be confronted before racial equality would be achieved. King knew that racism's "twin" was classism, the economic exploitation of the vast majority of the working and nonworking poor in this country by a ruling elite. To break this system, King organized the Poor People's Campaign, an interracial mass movement of the poor against the power elite. But King's plans were dashed by a seemingly intractable problem. He discovered that "white America [was] not . . . psychologically organized to close the gap" between the rich and the poor in America if this meant that the uplift of the "Negro" was entailed in such a venture.[6]

King knew that the self-defeating political behavior of poorer whites robbed them of the power to improve their own economic condition. They exchanged the potential for real power achieved through coalitions based on class interests for a surplus powerlessness based on racial identity. White power thus became a way of keeping those below them more oppressed than themselves. To hold onto white power, they gave up class power.

The power, prestige, and privilege of whiteness thus became a punishing regime. Poorer European Americans "epidermalized" their own economic degradation as "whiteness." By so doing, they lost the ability to engage in coalition work with other "races." Everyone was the loser in this scenario. White supremacy, King concluded, can feed the ego but not the stomach.

The so-called "privilege" of being called "white" is a remarkably successful way to make European American wage earners feel like their own bosses. It's a ruse. Such feelings of white grandiosity keep personal feelings of economic inferiority from surfacing. Most Americans, after all, are part of the working poor. Sixty percent of working Americans make less than $40,000 a year.[7] That's not enough money to make it in today's America. Most Americans thus live in houses they can't afford, drive cars they don't own, wear clothes they've bought on credit, and toward the end of each pay period, use their charge cards to buy food. This pervasive system of economic depreciation is often accounted for in racial terms. "Blacks" become the racial scapegoat for the economic resentment of white middle-class and lower-class poor people. Such racial resentment prevents white Americans from working with black Americans to improve the overall economic status of all working Americans. This was King's point.

White racial resentment "encodes" the political thinking of white Americans so that they vote for their perceived racial interest rather than for the real, immediate economic and social changes required for their well-being and that of their own families. This is also the point of social theorists Thomas Byrne Edsall and Mary D. Edsall.[8] The objectively groundless fear of raced "others" on the part of white Americans makes white voters prime targets for manipulation by political and economic interests who use race-baiting tactics to achieve their own ends.

Racial resentment by white Americans blinds them to their true self-interest. It dismantles their ability to significantly improve their economic predicament as members of the largest economic class in America, the working poor. This is how 95 percent of the wealth of this country can remain in the hands of 1 percent of the population. Class grievances are turned into racial feelings of resentment.

Thus the paradox. White racial resentment against black Americans self-demotes most white Americans. It is a self-deprecating sentiment that mirrors the real source of the problem: underpaid, overspent consumers. In other words, white racial resentment cripples the ability of white Americans to think clearly about the class strategies needed to improve their own economic conditions through interracial work with others.

White racial resentment is thus a form of surplus powerlessness. It functions as a structural requirement needed to keep the economically elite on top. Feelings of white racial resentment are a racial barrier that prevents one group of wage earners from uniting with other wage earners for their collective economic advancement. This racial barrier is a wall that imprisons white Americans as class victims.

Here we find the psychological condition King referred to as the congenital illness of white racism. This illness, I am suggesting, is a form of surplus powerlessness that prevents white Americans from thinking clearly and systematically about their own economic status as members of the working poor. Effective coalitions for social change must address this self-abusive mental impasse.

Home-grown racial abuse: We must go back to basics. Racial abuse is homegrown. As I note in my book *Learning to Be White,* the process of "racing," and thus raising, a child to think of herself or himself as "white" often involves child abuse. The child's own natural sense of agency and personal integrity must be dismantled because children are born with an innate ability to relate and bond to others. Otherwise they would not survive because they are unable to fend for themselves. Children thus have to learn how to internally destroy their own ability to relate and bond with those who are not acceptable to their parents or authority figures. Only then can they learn to deny what their feelings affirm: the importance of openhearted engagement with others.

Children learn to deny their true selves, their own feelings, by separating themselves from their own initially positive feelings toward others who do not conform to the patterns, racial ideals, and expectations of the parental figures in their lives. In this way, the child learns to feel ashamed of her or his own original, openhearted feelings toward others. The child's own feelings are now thought of as bad and wrong. The child learns that if these feelings are expressed, he or she will not be loved. The parental figure, in turn, learned this lesson early in life, as it is handed down from generation to generation. Feelings of shame thus become core emotional content around which white racial identities are formed.

Not surprisingly, to protect themselves from further emotional abuse children conform their feelings to those of their parental caregivers by denying, repressing, splitting off, or in some way suppressing positive feelings toward "wrong"-colored persons. This walling-off of the child's own feelings requires the child to separate herself or himself from her or his own true self. The resulting breakdown amounts to the child's own internal loss of coherence and integrity. This primal experience cannot be retained in consciousness because children have to depend on their caretakers for survival. If their caretakers abuse them, children tend to blame themselves rather than their caretakers. Children thus forget that the persons who ostensibly loved them were abusive.

To keep core feelings of brokenness from surfacing, three defense mechanisms often come to the fore: explosive rage (white racist acts), false pride (white supremacist sentiment), and self-deprecating sentiments (an ongoing sense of being "not white enough"). Each of these defense mechanisms is a form of surplus powerlessness. Each feeling makes coalition work across color lines impossible.

The social system of "racing" American wage earners white is also homegrown, with its own peculiar history of institutional abuse. Economic powerlessness and feelings of racial inferiority went hand-in-hand in colonial America. In late-seventeenth-century colonial Virginia, for example, indentured servants of English and European descent were raced "white" by the planter class in order to sepa-rate them from the other members of the serving class who were of African descent. Until then, indentured Africans and Europeans were thought of as members of the same race: the poor. They were thus alien to the ruling race: the middle-class. To divide the ser-vant race against itself, the planter class biologized ethnicity to cre-ate a psychological allegiance among all members of the newly created "white race." The new legal entity—the "white Christian servant"—was now kith and kin to his or her exploiter. Or so s(he) was told.

In nineteenth-century industrializing America, the "racing" of European "ethnics" continued. Industrialists coerced their immi-grant European population of industrial workers (75 percent of the labor force) to give up their "ethnic" Slavic, Catholic, Jewish, Irish, or Italian ways and become "American"—not only in order to work but also to survive. These workers had to become "Ameri-can," which meant they had to become racially "white" and cul-turally Anglo-Saxon Protestant. Paradoxically, these newly white workers gave the nation its first form of national entertainment: blackface minstrelsy. The ethnics taught themselves how to be white by ridiculing all the parts of themselves (the "darker" parts) that were not Anglo-Saxon Protestant enough to "fit" their new racialized, ethnic ideal.

White racism in America is a self-defeating act. It hides from view something that most racial oppressors and the racially oppressed have in common: self-defeating acts of abuse against self and others. White racial resentment against black Americans is one form of this pervasive system of surplus powerlessness.

Resolving the paradox of racial oppression: As president of the Center for Community Values (www.the-ccv.org), I recommend small group ministries as one way to heal the divides within us and between us. United we stand, divided we fall. Together, we can heal ourselves and make the world a better place for us all.

The Responses

Thandeka begins the discussion of her essay by noting that she "was inspired by our conversation following Gary Smith's presentation because it took up the issue of class." She then cites statistics relating to class in the United States and suggests ways in which these conditions relate to issues of race and racial oppression:

> The median income for middle-class people in this country is $33,000–$37,000, and 67 percent of Americans earn less than $50,000. This means that most Unitarian Universalists are middle class, part of what I define as the "middle-class poor," the working poor. I believe that a lot of the issues of power and privilege that we have discussed pertain to "class passing." . . . So why is there all this pretense about being part of the rich and powerful and respected? . . . The work that I have done shows that middle-class European American poor people are so close to the line that God help them if anyone were to discover that they should be classified as poor whites.

> My work is to help European Americans pay attention to their actual class status and to recognize that they really have a great deal in common with the vast majority of the other-colored peoples in this country who are also part of the working poor. I believe that if there is empathy through true self-discovery and self-understanding, then European Americans will be able to discover what they have in common with other Americans—and *then* there is the possibility of coalition building.

> What I call the "paradox of racial oppression" is that it prevents European Americans from doing something even as simple as identifying themselves as "European Americans," and thus they slip ever so slightly out of the relational realm wherein there is a parallel with Native Americans, African Americans, Asian Americans, and Latino/a Americans. Instead, European Americans are supposed to be called "white." "White" is a way of hiding their true status in this country because the American dream does not work for most people, and this is very hard to take. My point is that any full analysis has to take into account not only the structural problems but also the psychological makeup of the person.

George "Kim" Beach briefly takes up the concept of "surplus powerlessness," suggesting that it parallels James Luther Adams's "analysis of the corrupting effects of powerlessness." Kim Beach then explores the theological implications of Thandeka's work, asking first a "question sure to raise lively debate among us":

What lies at the root of our faith commitments to compassion and human transformation? Can they be attributed to the sectarian standard of the "Principles" of the Unitarian Universalist Association by-laws? Or are these values rooted in much broader theological and moral traditions—traditions reflected in the second part of the UUA's Principles (the Sources), especially in the references to "prophetic" and "Jewish and Christian" traditions?

The doctrine of original sin, for example, includes the recognition that though we claim to act from purely righteous motives, we are deceiving and self-deceived. It is a salutary reminder that doing justice is never just "doin' what comes naturally" but requires humility and moral discernment—that is, deliberate steps toward self-transcendence. . . . Liberals tend to say, "We can solve these problems by 'trying harder'—because we are, of course, people with rational understanding and goodwill." This allows "right-thinking liberals" to claim that they are not complicit in a social system that enforces racism.

Anti-Calvinist though William Ellery Channing was, an idea of the "original" or root sin, domination, was central to his thought. Insofar as all persons and groups tend to strive for domination and in the process claim "superiority" and others' "inferiority," racism can be seen as a condition both inflicted upon and suffered by an entire society and all individuals who acquiesce to it.

Our task is to enable persons-in-community—that is, in covenant—to remember and thus recover the image of God in which we are made (not *were* but *are* made) as whole, healed, saved beings and to be healed of the physical, psychic, and social brokenness of racism.

In sum, racism is a condition suffered as oppression and economic exploitation, and at the same time, it is a deeply rooted psychic complex of mixed self-loathing and fear of otherness. It is a possessive, demonic power. Our vocation as a covenanted people of faith is to remember who we are, recalling our original humanity and knitting together again our broken humanity at both the psychic and social levels of existence.

James Luther Adams called us to "take time seriously," and in the process, he renewed our awareness of the eschatological, future-directed task of a liberating faith. Thandeka similarly calls us to recognize the "paradox of racial oppression," and in the process, she renews our awareness of the healing, as well as the judging, vocation of a liberating faith. And so, we begin to recover our theological voice!

Leon Spencer brings his "glasses of suspicion" to the theory of "surplus powerlessness." He asks whether it is just another psychological theory that can be used to maintain institutional racism:

> Racial and cultural identity development is complex and cannot be viewed from a monolithic perspective. People of color and other oppressed groups have a deep sense of suspicion concerning the use of theories and research in areas of identity, as well as in areas of "helping" and "healing," because their actual experiences with research, theory, and practice have not been positive. Psychologists and sociologists have misused their research in order to create and support models ranging from "genetic deficiency" and "cultural deprivation" to "racist multiculturalism" as ways of explaining the life experiences of people of color. Could "surplus powerlessness" be another such model?

> Psychological theory itself has been oppressive by striving to explain the experiences of people of color within a framework that has not included their worldview and their contextual realities; nor has it recognized their resilience. The survival mechanisms of peoples of color, for instance, have sometimes been viewed as pathological defense mechanisms. As we used to say in grad school, when I trained in psychology, everything was white, including the mice. Everything was looked at from the perspective of a white person, so that much of our psychological and sociological research has ended up blaming peoples of color for their status and condition in life while equating what is healthy with whatever experience is closest to being white. This in itself has become a part of oppression. Is the notion of surplus powerlessness, then, any different from other theoretical positions that make for good discussion and *encounter*[9] but not for *transformation?*

> I believe that the notion of "surplus powerlessness" among whites may be another means for them to remain oblivious to their white skin power and privilege. Peggy McIntosh describes white skin privilege as the "invisible package of unearned assets which I can count on cashing in each day, but about which I was 'meant' to remain oblivious. White privilege is like an invisible weightless knapsack of special provisions, maps, passports, codebooks, visas, clothes, tools, and blank checks."[10]

In my experience, most white people seem *not* to think about race. Those whites who identify as white yet have an ongoing sense of not being "white enough" seem to be the exception rather than the rule. White people who feel not "white enough" tend to have experienced some kind of *encounter* around the issue of race that challenged their status quo and precipitated an examination of what that encounter meant to them. They then also have to explore the meaning of this encounter for others like them and the context in which the experience occurred. Eventually they come to an understanding of internalized oppression, much as Jim does at the beginning of Thandeka's essay.

I believe that what is described as Jim's "transformation" is indeed a life-changing event for Jim, but it is more accurate to call it an "encounter" rather than a "transformation." . . . Jim has internalized the oppression he experienced during his socialization as a child, as Thandeka describes. It was his attempt to be "white enough" that produced the conflict that ultimately led to his personal change. *But this personal encounter does not change the institutional racism and systems of oppression from which he was seeking relief.* The feeling of not being "white enough" is not enough to dismantle racism or to end race prejudice. It leaves the system of white skin privilege intact.

Is surplus powerlessness, then, a redefinition of internalized oppression? It seems to be used rather as a definition of internalized *superiority,* to explain why poor whites are unable to unite in their poverty with peoples of color who are poor. "Surplus powerlessness" seems to be a *mechanism* of whites' resistance to change, rather than a means of *addressing* this resistance. How can we address this issue, and how can we address the issue of whites not seeing themselves as members of a group? How can we address the destructiveness of individualized white identity and cultural values that victims of racism are trying to embrace or have embraced? My concern is that we are all victims of racism, but if we portray whites as the original and continuing victims without recognizing the reality of white institutional power and control, the status quo will remain the same and there will be no transformation. What hope does this offer peoples of color, and what spiritual direction and guidance does it provide for whites' own liberation? Focusing on the psychological and the individual does not provide concrete systemic strategies for addressing issues such as these. It fails to bring all the varying and equally important understandings of racism and white privilege together for the betterment of the church and community.

The word *church* means a "community that has been called out." It is the place where that which is holy and sacred is known, and where compassion is a way of being. It exists, in part, to nurture its members as they gain new identities through shared perceptions, values, and worship.

With Thandeka and the Journey Toward Wholeness, I believe that compassion is important in healing our brokenness. Compassion as a way of being moves us away from the many securities offered by culture, such as material goods, status, identity, nation, success, righteousness. As Marcus Borg suggests, compassion allows us to see the distinctions that are generated by the world through various forms of oppression as socially created products that provide no abiding home. Compassion calls us to leave such a "home," but it does not just pull us away from home or away from culture. For it is not an individualistic vision or action but an action that *creates community*.

The Dialogue

Differences in emphasis and in participants' approach to analyzing and undoing racism sparks heated discussion among the participants. A portion of this part of the conversation is excerpted here. Participants return again to the themes of "racism as sin" and of "self in community."

BILL JONES: My first point has to do with the issue of surplus powerlessness. . . . Michael Lerner's analysis emphasizes that people speak of themselves as being even more powerless than the actual power situation requires. If you look at this situation in terms of institutional power relative to whites and blacks, the situation in no way confirms whites as more powerless. . . . The actual institutional power relative to whites and blacks has been there in the past and is still there in the present. So I think Thandeka has misread Lerner.

With respect to Kim Beach's response, I feel that the parallelism between the corrupting influence of powerlessness that James Luther Adams talks about and the Lerner theory is incorrect. The notion of the "corrupting influence of powerlessness" comes out of the Black Power statement that there are two ways to create a corrupting influence: (1) regard yourself as *more* than what you are, and (2) regard yourself as *less* than what you are. The corrupting influence of powerlessness was an effort to show that the actual situation of powerlessness for blacks relative to whites made certain kinds of actions totally ineffective.

But the major point I want to focus on is that I think your model, Thandeka, is trying to convert whites over to compassion for blacks. I think basing that possibility on their seeing the interdependence of existence or oppression and having that trigger or bring about compassion is really ruled out when we look at the dominant characteristics of oppression. It's similar to the kind of problem James Cone was trying to deal with, in rejecting the idea of white "conversion" in light of the history of white denial of racism and so forth. This represents the same problem that Martin Luther King had with the premise that if people in power will recognize the problem of oppressing others, they will stop. This is not an accurate premise, because the hierarchical system of oppression starts off by redefining and relabeling the oppressed as *not* a part of the human family or *less than equal* in terms of the circle of the human family.

THANDEKA: In my work, there is an analogy between the powerlessness of blacks and what's going on with European Americans. If you take multiple perspectives in analyzing powerlessness, then it's not always part of a black-white mode.

About converting whites over to compassion for blacks: Most of your response, Bill, is a distortion because you're reading my work through your lenses—which, of course, you have a right to do; all I can do is show that you're distorting it. I will give you an example of some of the stories that I teach to explain the principles of my methodology. I began to work with men who had abused their spouses and their kids. Because I'm starting from the basis of self-psychology, the framework is empathy: You cannot judge the person with whom you are working; you simply have to look into them and find [the points of connection between yourself and them, without fear and without judging]. Because of that element of compassion, these abusive men finally got to the story of their own abused youth, and after a year or two of this work they could begin for the first time to feel guilt with respect to the person they had abused. In this way, they could get past it and could re-create wholeness and retrieve the parts of themselves that they had separated out.

I'm very much informed by the discoveries of self-psychology, as well as by psychoanalytic theory, having to do with the way in which selves have been separated and split off. To get to wholeness, one has to go back and retrieve the parts of oneself that have been left behind.

JONES: But what is the power factor that will bring about the effect of compassionate action? The effect of compassionate action is linked up here with the variable of what?

THANDEKA: The effect of compassion pertains to the way in which the human organism is a relational matrix. It has a multiplicity of events going on within it, so I cannot possibly use a mechanistic causal framework to describe this process!

MARJORIE BOWENS-WHEATLEY: My clarifying questions are these: How do you define racism, and how do you define white supremacy? Second, in your theology, is racism a sin? If not, how would you describe it in theological terms?

THANDEKA: There are two approaches to the human being: the subjective and the objective. The structural or objective side consists of power, privilege, and prestige. The subjective dimension has to do with the way in which oppressive behavior develops in the human organism and becomes part of the psychology of the self. The concept of the authoritarian self—which was developed by a number of psychiatrists and social psychologists after World War II to study what had happened in Germany—looked at the way in which the Germans were raised. These researchers found that the development of the authoritarian self could produce a separation of *affect* that would allow certain kinds of persons to be able to do certain kinds of acts. Thus, racism has an *objective* side and then a *subjective* side so that the self can participate in the demise of itself and others.

Racism as a sin: We must ask the question of who is broken. The definition of sin that I have is a *critical* definition of sin, in which whenever I see a brokenness in the psychological development of a person, I have to ask the question of human violence: *Who* broke this child up? Sin is the way in which traditions tend to break human organisms within an environment to perpetuate certain forms of abuse. If we want to focus on how European Americans are brought up to continue the culture of racism, look to the environment to see how it's doing that. Don't mystify the process by talking about demonic powers; this ignores the human tragedy that continues the abuse. Stay within the human environment; never go outside of human endeavor.

REBECCA PARKER: At the end of his life, William Ellery Channing became more outspoken against slavery. He risked and experienced a breach with the congregation to which he was fondly attached because it was the only way he could keep faith with his understanding of the self. For him, the self meant the abundant complexity of the powers of the soul, the full image of God unfolding as human destiny. The limitation of those powers, the breaking of the soul, is sin, a betrayal of God. So my question to you, Thandeka, is: What is useful in Channing, and what is not?

THANDEKA: What wasn't understood among the Transcendentalists after Channing was that the self in relationship (which they wanted to affirm) is the self *in community*. I'm interested in how community can be built so that the individual does not have to "keep faith with one's understanding of the self" alone, as Channing did. With the Enlightenment came the construction of the individual as totally isolated from the community and in direct relationship with God. I find Channing's sense of the self to be a continuation of the Calvinist tradition without the Calvinist doctrine of original sin.

Where we fall short is in our theological language for understanding the individual in relationship. Henry Nelson Weiman tries, but he has such a poor understanding about hierarchical structures of oppression.

PARKER: I think it is a misreading of Channing to think that he was a radical individualist. The same is true with regard to Emerson's

"Self-Reliance." The *loss of participation in the world* is what bothered Channing about slavery. And Emerson believed that the self rested in the Oversoul.

THANDEKA: When the basis of the argument is rationalism, then it sets aside affect and knows nature only through the mind. Emerson is an example: He had split off his affect and was depressed! So often the question is "What do I *do* about this?" That's why I set up the Theological Center for Community Values, where I am trying to organize small groups, and part of the requirement for participation is that these groups *must take action outside themselves.* This is the experiential basis for my theory.

Study Questions

1. What are you childhood memories about "race" and race relations? When did you first become aware of your race or ethnicity? How were you first made aware of others' race or ethnicity? What emotions do these memories evoke? How did these early experiences affect your understanding and your relationship to your caregivers, teachers, and others? If you are of Anglo-Saxon heritage, how does your youthful experience compare with Thandeka's description of the emotional child abuse involved in raising a child to be "white" and with her summary of "white" defense mechanisms around race?

2. What do you know about your family's racial, ethnic, religious, and national background? Did your ancestors experience pressure to "become white," or exclusion because they refused to do so? What impact has such family history had on your life?

3. Michael Lerner defines *surplus powerlessness* as the belief held by some people that they are "more powerless" than they really are; their actions then reflect and confirm this belief. The theory could also be stated in the reverse: Some people actually *have* more power to effect change in their lives and in society than they *feel* that they have. What advantages does this false sense of powerlessness offer those who believe in it? On the other hand, what disadvantages does "surplus powerlessness"

bring them? Consider your own life: What is *your* sense of your own power? How would you critique Lerner's theory?

4. Thandeka suggests that the theory of "surplus powerlessness" explains why people in the United States do not cross racial boundaries as allies to correct economic inequalities in this country. Does this explanation satisfy you? Why or why not? What other explanations would you offer?

5. Do you think that most Unitarian Universalists represent the middle-class poor or the working poor? What is the impact of such thinking on your understanding of economic and racial relations?

Toward a New Paradigm for Uncovering Neo-racism

WILLIAM R. JONES

ᗍ

Beyond my conception of ignorance and deliberate ill-will as causes of race prejudice, there must be other and stronger and more threatening forces forming the founding stones of race antagonisms, which we had only begun to attack or, perhaps in reality, had not attacked at all.

—W. E. B. DuBois

Where justice is denied, where poverty is enforced, where ignorance prevails, and where any one class is made to feel that society is an organized conspiracy to oppress . . . and degrade [it], neither persons nor property will ever be safe.

—Frederick Douglass

We live in a world, Frederick Douglass warns us, where "neither persons nor property are safe" and "no parity, no peace" is the order of the day. In other words, the fundamental cause of social conflict is uncorrected oppression. Social diagnosticians among us cite several causes for our predicament: the startling statistics of over- and under-representation with respect to specific groups in society who consistently get the "most of the worst" and the "least of the best"; the unsettled passionate debates about public policies such as environmental and social welfare, affirmative action, racial profiling, diversity, and multiculturalism. All these—and you can add your own causes to the list—are blamed for the expanding and exploding community conflict.[1]

But the preeminent cause of our predicament, about which Douglass counsels, is uncorrected oppression—a playing field without reparations in which groups that are allegedly superior use their surplus institutional power and privilege to maintain access to resources, thus assuring their survival and well-being. Douglass's warning is, in fact, a prediction about the causality of social conflict: If an unlevel playing field remains unleveled from generation to generation,[2] it will inevitably lead to the outcome that Douglass predicted, in which neither parity nor peace will exist, and "neither person nor property are safe."

Our nation and our faith community are mired in a fierce debate about the cause of and cure for this state of affairs. In the final analysis, this is a debate about whether racial discrimination is still present in our institutions and whether it continues to harm African Americans. Rival diagnoses of this nine-lived American dilemma compete for supremacy in public policy, forcing religious liberals—whether we want to or not—to "choose a side" and embrace one vision for the public domain.

The debate has been particularly intense in the legal and criminal justice systems. Examining the controversy there will instruct us on what is at stake for our faith community. One camp in the debate is committed to a social diagnosis that affirms "the declining influence of race" (see, for example, William Milbank's *The Myth of Racism in the Criminal Justice System*).[3] I label this the "demise" school of thought or the "demise hypothesis" because it acknowledges the presence of the cancer of racism in the past but postulates that it is now in remission. Accordingly, a remission diagnosis is advanced in response to today's allegations of racial discrimination.

Many of the policy decisions of federal and state courts—and, in particular, of the United States Supreme Court—embrace this hypothesis and its diagnosis. Predictably, as acceptance of this hypothesis expands, we encounter the charge of reverse discrimination, and we see this charge employed to overturn previous correctives for the acknowledged racism of the past.

Accounting for this policy reversal is not difficult. It follows predictably from the findings of the demise hypothesis. Our society's cancer of racial oppression is in remission; the melanoma has been isolated and appropriately treated. Happily, no malignant tumors of *institutional* racism still lurk in the bowels of the body politic. Once a remission diagnosis has been adopted, today's economic, social, and political inequalities are no longer visible because they are no longer connected causally or institutionally to past discrimination.

The social, legal, and educational remedies that follow from the remission diagnosis are easily predicted: The institutional policies and structures that were the vital organs of racial oppression are no longer targeted for radical or intensive therapy. Modifications in diet, less fat, and more bulk are now prescribed, which translates into "Abandon affirmative action and replace with diversity policies."

A remission diagnosis also leads to a policy of benign neglect with respect to the *effects* of prior institutional discrimination— that is, with respect to slavery's defects, deficits, disabilities, and disadvantages. They continue uncorrected, now protected by a new theory of social causation that blames the victim and erases the culpability of today's society lords. Indeed, such blame and such erasure support the economic, social, and political objectives of demise theory worshippers.

Because racism is no longer visible from the point of view of the demise hypothesis, the conclusion follows that it has been exterminated. Hail to the exterminator! To spot the error here, recall the Hubble telescope. This new telescope did not create the stars that it allowed us to see for the first time; they were there all along. The fact that something is invisible to us does not mean that it does not exist. Whether something is visible or invisible depends on the sophistication and accuracy of our viewing instruments, as well as on the point of view we choose.

I endorse and advance, as the foundation for Unitarian Universalism's anti-racist imperative, an opposing school of thought, the *disguise hypothesis,* which sees not racism's demise but its *disguise.* From this vantage point, institutional racism is not in remission or even declining, as is commonly believed; rather, it is mutating and reclaiming lost territory through ingenious disguises, conceptual camouflages, and hypocritical masks of moral invulnerability.

Our policy decisions fail to recognize that classical racism has not been dismantled; rather, it has evolved into neo-racism, and

Black preacher rhetoric; multiple charging; then ridicule; a rhetorical conclusion

apartheid into neo-apartheid. The mutant virus of racial oppression not only is immune to our updated economic, social, and political vaccines but feasts on them.

As we should have learned from our wrestling with AIDS, what chance we have of coping with a mutant virus depends on whether we have a precise understanding of its evolutionary history and its survival and maintenance needs, as well as its vulnerabilities. Thus, if Unitarian Universalists are to be part of the solution rather than the problem, we need more effective diagnostic tools to expose neo-racism's disguises, to make neo-racism visible, and to be aware of how we function as its carriers in the home, the workplace, and our faith communities. A distorted profile of oppression will lead us to conclude that racism is no longer present or prevalent, thus allowing it to continue its destructive work unseen and undetected. To effect the demise of racism, we must find a more sophisticated model, one that explains how our flawed understanding of the "what, how, and why" of *oppression* traps us in faulty social policies.

The need for this information dictates that we create a venue yet to be provided in our faith community: a space where we can conduct a radical "cuss and discuss" exercise, in which we examine competing models of social analysis and assess their comparative merit for helping us diagnose and reduce, if not eliminate, racism. This essay seeks to initiate such an exercise.

Here I will share some unpublished research, conducted over the past decade, on conflict reduction in South Africa.[4] In the fall of 1990, at the invitation of Edendale Lay Ecumenical Centre[5] in Plessislaer, Natal, I was invited as a scholar in residence. This invitation provided an attractive opportunity for a pilot study to test the validity of a new model of oppression theory that I was developing. The study was part of a program that brought theoreticians of conflict studies and practitioners of social change to South Africa during its fateful transitional periods. These individuals had developed, just as I had, innovative models of conflict resolution with respect to contexts similar to South Africa—places with heterogeneous populations and histories marked by gross economic, social, and political inequalities that had culminated in widespread demands for justice and equity. In all cases, such demands were no longer expressed exclusively or primarily in nonviolent tactics of social change.

The study addressed the following questions that are unique-ly relevant to the current contexts of the United States and the Unitarian Universalist Association:

Whither *post*-apartheid South Africa? Are we witnessing the miraculous birth of a new South Africa, the spawning of an authentic multiracial society from the ashes of apartheid's demise? Or is the wondrous vision of apartheid's timely death a mirage that gives the *appearance* of dismantling the old master-servant inequalities while actually preserving and perpetuating them in a new and disguised form of *neo*-apartheid?

Has South Africa abandoned its original *goal* of apartheid or just the *means*—a means that was no longer effective? Do the pro-posed policies for the new South Africa actually dismantle and disassemble apartheid? Or do they reassemble the disassembled essentials of apartheid—its surplus/deficit configuration of *power* and *privilege*—creating a more effective mechanism that will pre-serve apartheid's original goal and its power superstructure?

To answer these questions I drew upon an experimental model of social and theological analysis that is designed for policy decision-making in a context in which, as Frederick Douglass pro-jected, "neither persons nor property" are safe because of systemic oppression. At Florida State University, where I taught, the model is popularly known as JOG and JAM—acronyms for the Jones Oppression Grid (JOG), which is the core of the Jones Analytic Model (JAM). Capturing the distinctive spirit of jazz improvisa-tion, the model creates new and different angles of interpretation and a new experience of freedom and co-equality that equip us to "jog and jam" through the minefields of neo-oppression.

I will offer an unforgivably condensed overview of JOG and JAM. It is a cross-disciplinary pedagogy designed to teach specif-ic skills in sociocultural analysis and decision-making, blending key ingredients from oppression theory, liberation theology, and black religious humanism. It also draws upon research data from the civil rights and post–civil rights era in the United States that demonstrate that racism was not dismantled.

The JOG and JAM model aims to explain the context, content, format, and inner logic of racism. The model began by decipher-ing the persistence, prevalence, and power of oppression in human affairs and by locating "the founding stones of race antag-onisms, which we had only begun to attack, or perhaps in reality

Extremely + artificially precise analogies
As though it were describing some reality
Then grab one + plug it in: ↗ Proof!
Presto:

had not attacked at all."[6] This led me to explore the "not so odd couple" of religion and oppression, which in turn opened up the search for religion and oppression at the taproot of ontology and human culture. The final task was to reduce these findings to cultural universals—elemental human behaviors that inform all that we do and all that we make—as well as to categories of system analysis. The resulting JOG and JAM is a generic how-to kit that functions as a kind of policy Geiger counter to detect misguided diagnoses—specifically, those diagnoses that mistake the disguise of oppression for its demise. The JOG and JAM model provides a means of assessing rival policy positions and of successfully predicting the outcome of their policy recommendations.

JOG and JAM utilizes "the virus" as a master metaphor to describe its mission, which is to formulate an effective vaccine to neutralize the virus of oppression. Such a vaccine requires a precise design. To understand how to best utilize this design, you might picture yourself as someone in training to be a doctor. Such an objective demands that you master a specific kind of information as well as certain skills or technology. A doctor, for example, needs specific background knowledge about anatomy and the workings of the human body. A doctor must also understand systems of cause and effect, how the body's various organs and parts interact and how the body responds to particular stimuli. He or she must also augment this general knowledge with an understanding of the possibilities for contextual variation. The combination of generic and contextual knowledge allows a doctor to treat a generic problem in a specific context.

This analogy informs the way JOG and JAM uses "detect-and-destroy" technology in the training of "detect-and-destroy" technicians. The technology involves two phases. The first phase focuses exclusive attention on the virus—not on the anticipated vaccine, which is the focus of the second phase. Initially, the purpose is to provide profiles of the virus of oppression's survival mechanism, its maintenance needs, and especially its vulnerabilities from multiple perspectives. In short, the goal is to map the virus's genetic structure. These technical data are then used to customize a formula for an effective "vaccine."

At the heart of the JOG and JAM theoretical framework is the concept of structural oppression as expressed in institutional racism.[7] To bring institutional racism into focus, I suggest completing the following "list exercise":

1. List all the basic institutions in the United States that black Americans have created and/or controlled for four generations (about two hundred years).

2. List all the basic institutions in the United States that white Americans have created and/or controlled for six generations (about three hundred years).

3. List all the basic institutions in the United States that black Americans have created and controlled over the course of one generation (twenty-five years) *under which white Americans had to live.*

4. List all the basic institutions in the United States that white Americans have created and controlled for six generations (three hundred years) *under which black Americans had to live.*

When we answer these questions, we are invariably forced to conclude that African Americans have never created or controlled the basic institutions in America under which our two "separate and unequal" societies lived. This dialectic of causality and culpability indisputably assigns accountability and responsibility to those with surplus economic, social, and political power. In constructing public policy, the demise hypothesis is afflicted with historical amnesia and conveniently ignores this feature of institutional oppression; thus, it predictably blames the victim.

Another important dimension of institutional discrimination in the JOG and JAM model comes into view when we look at the startling statistics related to the life situations of African Americans in the United States. These data are startling because they confirm a striking disproportionality between the percentage of blacks in the general population and their representation in significant economic, social, and political indices such as children born out of wedlock, infant mortality rates, percentage of uncounted voting ballots, and disparities in sentencing and capital punishment. In the area of criminology, "there can be little doubt that blacks commit a disproportionate number of FBI Crime Index offenses and, in turn, are disproportionately victimized by crimes involving physical contact."[8] It does not matter which side of the fence one inspects—the victims or the victimizers, the oppressed or their oppressors—or which institutional unit we study—the family, crime, or players in the National Basketball Association. The startling statistics are always present. These statistics are another way of naming the societal inequalities, the omnipresent pattern of over- and under-representation, that we see whenever and wherever oppression occurs. The demise and disguise hypotheses fail to address the causality of and culpability for this state of affairs, as do almost all other discussions about blacks in America.

To clarify the claim that in recent years, classical racism has mutated into neo-racism, we must discuss further the causality/ culpability connection and its core principle: that diagnosis or determines the therapy (DDT). In the JOG and JAM model, the DDT principle is understood as a universal feature of human behavior and an ever-present consideration in policy decision making. DDT embraces the theory that each and every feature of the cosmos, natural and human, has a cause. We adopt this proposition as the foundation of human culture; that is, it relates to all that we do and all that we make. Causation analysis is the ultimate scaffolding for human and extra-human reality.

I would argue that diagnosis (identifying the controlling cause) is the first step in addressing any problem, be it an illness or a political, economic, educational, moral, or religious matter. It is generally accepted that our preferred way of coping with threats to our survival and well-being is to isolate the critical causal variable and manipulate it to our own benefit. This is the foundation for whatever therapy or prescription is recommended and whatever solution is advanced. Moreover, our deduction or conjecture about the causality of a situation regulates how we respond to it. The outcome will be the one that we expect if the controlling cause we have hypothesized is actually the dominant power at work. This supports the claim advanced in the following illustration:

I have a headache, so I go to a doctor who diagnoses why I have pain. The diagnosis, whatever it is, identifies a particular cause for my headache; the therapy, in turn, is linked to that causality. If, for instance, the diagnosis is constipation, one can predict the likely therapy: Ex-lax, more bulk, more water, and exercise. Suppose, however, that the diagnosis indicates a brain tumor. Same therapy? No. This diagnosis suggests a radically different therapy because it points to a different cause.

Similarly, attention must be given to the fact that diagnosis involves an inevitable process of picking and choosing, of selection and rejection, and this process predetermines the therapy. In other words, the choice of a particular cause, which leads to a diagnosis, is at the same time the choice of a correlative therapy. The choice of therapy, in turn, singles out a particular agent or agency as culpable. In essence, cause (or "blame") is an appropriate corollary.

Translated into policy and systems analysis, the DDT principle argues that successful social therapy requires an accurate diagnosis; that is to say, it requires a trustworthy account of the social causation as well as an accurate description of the causality/culpability connection. It must be remembered that the assignment of culpability has a power variable: Whoever has the economic, social, and political power to select the cause controls the definition of the social reality and the policy that it spawns.

The diagnosis-determines-therapy principle (DDT) also obliges us to incorporate the concept of "false" causality into our policy assessments. For example, a suburbanite on Long Island dug a huge hole in his backyard, ninety by ninety by ninety feet. An alarmed neighbor asked the "why" and "wherefore" of the gigantic crater and received this answer: "To keep the elephants away." The neighbor, now even more disturbed, retorted, "There aren't any elephants within ten thousand miles of this neck of the woods." And the hole-digging suburbanite came back with, "See how effective it is!"

This anecdote underscores the principle that at the heart of every policy recommendation is an implicit but seldom articulated argument about its particular diagnosis of the situation and its implicit causality. In other words, every policy recommendation is an endorsement that the causation specified is valid and accurate. Accordingly, the merit or demerit of any therapy, policy, or curriculum that is presented to us should be judged by its successful avoidance of false causality.

With this as background, let us return to the analysis of neo-racism. The prefix "neo-" indicates a specific relationship and resemblance between two items. It points to earlier and later "look-alikes" that share a common pattern but whose nuances and contextual differences rule out strict identity. For our purposes, it is important to highlight neo-racism's relationship to the earlier, "classical" form of racism.

When I speak of neo-racism, I am not talking about racism's classical mode, exemplified in the resurgence of the David Dukes of the world. (Actually, this is a revival of classical racism.) Rather, I have in mind the Reagan-Bush duo, Clinton, and ourselves—Unitarian Universalist and other liberal religionists. Our religious liberal lens does not bring into focus neo-racism's relationship with its classical pedigree. We fail to see that all of these are clones, institutionally engaged to keep alive the uneven playing field of white supremacy.

In general, classical racism is legally constituted racial oppression. Each form of racism embodies the same attribute of oppression—namely, the two-category division of the population into alleged superior and inferior groups, with the alleged superior group in possession of the gross surplus of economic, social, and political power and privilege while the allegedly inferior group remains in a deficit position. The critical difference between classical racism and neo-racism is one of means and method—not motivation, mission, objective, or moral principles.

A perceptive analysis by the Inter-Church Coalition on Africa almost a decade ago illustrates the point here:

> It is important to appreciate the nature of the choice offered the white electorate [in South Africa's recent referendum]. Both the "Yes" and the "No" camps were committed to the preservation of white power and privilege. They differed only on how to achieve the objective. The Conservative Party and its fascist allies retained an unbroken faith in the discredited precepts of apartheid. De Klerk, on the other hand, was discerning enough to recognize that apartheid was a failed god. His objection was not to the massive human misery it had occasioned or its immorality. It was simply that apartheid had proved unworkable. Internationally, it invited punitive sanctions; economically, it imposed a costly burden on the white taxpayer; and militarily it was ultimately unenforceable. Nor did de Klerk feel any compulsion to apologize to the victims. The forty years in the apartheid wilderness were the regrettable results of an honest error of judgment on the part of sincere men genuinely seeking a just solution to a real problem. That option having proved impracticable, de Klerk now offered worried whites a clever

alternative designed to achieve substantially the same result in a less overt and divisive way.[9]

To understand how neo-racism works, let us compare its DNA profile with classical racism. Neo-racism is often described as subtle. It is not, however, insubstantial or delicate but cunning, insidious, deceptive, ingenious, and indirect. Its subjugation style is a complex hall of mirrors, purporting to be what it is not. The decoy, the fake-out, the catch-22, and, especially, false causality are its primary tools. Neo-racism—and here it can be distinguished from classical racism—eschews the use of race or color to discriminate. It may even constitutionally outlaw discrimination based on race, and legalize colorblindness as a constitutional imperative. But this is its disguise mode of operation.

Classical racism is a form of oppression that operates through direct, institutionalized discrimination, resulting in the overt establishment of hierarchical domination. To sustain the hierarchy, it selects and *legalizes* one or more social variables (such as, race, gender, or class), which are then used as a yardstick of direct inclusion in or exclusion from the public arena. In this system, the *included* get the "most of the best" while the *excluded* get the "least of the worst."

In contrast, neo-racism operates through *in*direct institutional discrimination. Indirect institutional discrimination selects a social variable to sustain the hierarchy, but it also relies on a second set of variables—which result from the prior condition—as a yardstick for inclusion or exclusion.

For example, if race were the variable used to exclude African Americans from education under *direct* institutionalized discrimination, then *indirect* institutional discrimination will use a defect such as the inability to read or low GRE scores—whose *raison d'être* is poor education based on racial discrimination—as justification for exclusion.

South Africa learned from the United States how to dismantle slavery and segregation—yes, even constitutionally—and still retain the surplus-deficit pattern of power and privilege. Through neo-apartheid, a post-apartheid South Africa can be built where exclusion based on race is outlawed but blacks still get the "least of the best" and the "most of the worst." This masterful approach is defended as moral and just, thus allowing South Africa to declare the demise of apartheid and to announce to the world that it no longer discriminates and that a truly "color-blind" society is rising from the rubble of the discredited and dismantled apartheid system.

America's history and policy of discrimination in education illustrate how social deficits were intentionally created. The United States continues to follow this policy of deficit creation, and South Africa is replicating the same policy. It operates in the following way:

Step 1. Create deficits, defects, disadvantages, and disabilities—in other words, fundamental inequalities. The means are endless; examples include legal codes that make it illegal to teach slaves to read and write and inadequate prenatal care.

Step 2. Don't correct for the inequalities embodied in the deficits, defects, disadvantages, and disabilities. Legislate separate and unequal educational resources; provide for equal *access* but not equal *opportunity,* which would be the death knell for neo-racism; redefine correctives such as affirmative action and "reverse discrimination"; end proactive initiatives prematurely or replace them with diversity strategies; and convince the public that these measures are effective as correctives to past inequality.

Step 3. Repeat Step 2 for several generations.

Sept 4. This recipe of *government*-sponsored deficits and defects will predictably divide the society into two separate and unequal groups: the haves and the have-nots of social, economic, and political power and privilege; those with and those without a host of deficits, defects, disabilities, and disadvantages. Once these are in place (and it is easy to document this statistically), it is now easy for the advantaged group to maintain its surplus of power and privilege through rules and standards that discriminate against those with the uncorrected deficit *on the basis of that which has remained uncorrected.*

What is at work here is the fundamental principle of social causation, of institutional input (cause) and output (effect). Given this causality, the policy is unfortunately foolproof, the desired outcome guaranteed. Dismantling a social structure, even reducing it to rubble, does not obliterate its effects. Nor do diversity policies. Direct institutional discrimination produces predictable effects—a variety of social defects, deficits, disabilities, and disadvantages that can be manipulated indirectly to conserve and preserve historic oppression. This indirect connection between past and continuing discrimination is easily established by selecting a variable other than race that remains causally and institutionally linked to racism.

Clearly racial oppression has not died but has simply mutated. Although there has been a change in legal statutes and in governance, the essence of the system of racism in the United States and of the apartheid system in South Africa survives and thrives. Tragically, this confirms the JOG and JAM principle that we forget at our peril: Every correction is a change, but every change is not a correction. My fear is that the changes in social policies already accepted by black South Africans will make future corrections of neo-racism and neo-apartheid impossible, further confirming the JOG and JAM mantra: Neo-racism is predictable.

The heartrending lesson that we learn from history is that oppressors may tear down oppressive structures, but they never do so voluntarily. Perhaps Frederick Douglass best captured this idea when he said, "Power concedes to nothing without a demand. It never has, and it never will." Oppressors never demolish the *sine qua non*—that which upholds oppression: surplus power that ensures the master's entitlement, survival, and well-being. By virtue of their assumed role, the privileged define how resources are distributed and determine how responsibility and blame are assigned. The irreducible element of the master's power lies in his privilege to define social relationships and maintain hegemony over his subjects economically, politically, culturally, and intellectually.

To summarize, we return to our beginning. When the JOG and JAM grid was applied to South Africa, the strategy was clear and the outcome was predictable. The strategy was to dismantle racial oppression as claimed, but to make a sleight-of-hand maneuver from apartheid to neo-apartheid, based on the U.S. model of neo-racism adapted for South Africa's demographic peculiarities. Furthermore, if one applies the JOG and JAM lens to South

Africa's Truth and Reconciliation Commission, I argue that one will find a flawed understanding of reconciliation—a counterfeit claim, or what Dietrich Bonhoeffer called "cheap grace."

Finally, I suggest that the application of the JOG and JAM grid will bring invisible racism into clear view, forcing liberal religionists to raise fundamental questions about the very foundations of our faith community and government and, in particular, about our historic role and current function as agents of economic, social, and political oppression. Unpleasant though it may be, this is the task that confronts each of us now and tomorrow.

The Responses

Bill Jones opens the discussion of his essay with some thoughts about how this consultation might have been structured:

> I wish we had been asked to bring in a case study, take a theological apparatus, and apply it to the case study. When doing anti-racism and anti-oppression work, we are talking about concrete situations in real political, policy, and social settings, and we must have an apparatus for assessing them, such as a policy analysis, assessment, and articulation. That's one reason my essay draws on a case study from South Africa.

> We need to develop an approach to identifying oppression—and I prefer to talk about oppression, not racism. We have to start with a general understanding of the culture and the universals of human behavior, then demonstrate how a specific type of behavior is a case of oppression. Once we decide to do anti-racism or anti-oppression work, that choice commits us to a particular methodology because methodology follows from purpose. My method is one of internal criticism: We must validate things internally based on our own experience.

"The struggle against racism is both the practice of *revelation*—finding the ways and means to show racist oppression and white supremacy for what they are—and the work of *transformation*—searching for and holding a vision of Beloved Community," observes **Tracey Robinson-Harris**. "The theological capacity to sustain the struggle is rooted for me in the larger context of interdependence." She continues,

For me, our seventh Principle is the context for the other six, an antidote to the excessive individualism that our religious community can encourage and promote. Interdependence is where worth and dignity, justice, equity, and compassion, the democratic process, our searches for truth and acceptance and encouragement of one another in spiritual growth, and our vision of world community make embodied sense. Our principles have both strength and fragility woven into them. They are strong enough to survive despite all that we use to separate and divide ourselves from one another. And yet, for the same reason, they are fragile in the face of all that we use to separate and divide ourselves from one another.

The web of connection between and among us has two sides, one visible (the one we choose to see, our public face) and the other an underside, hidden as a result of systematic concealment and cultivated blindness. One theological task in the struggle against racism is to break through the concealment, to know the underside of interdependence, where the strands of racist oppression and white supremacy bind us. . . .

Bill Jones has said that you and I have only two choices: to continue and preserve or to correct and reform. What calls us—how can we call each other—to choose to correct and reform? Where do we find the strength for correction and reform when everything—systematic concealment, cultivated blindness, our defensiveness, the practice of labeling—reinforces the choice we make over and over to continue and preserve? For those who get more, or most, or sometimes even all of the "goodies" of the racist system, why bother? . . . Why should I, for example, choose anything other than to continue and preserve? Because as a white woman, my humanity is at stake in the struggle against racism—as is yours. We are interdependent. Our humanity depends on it. . . .

We Unitarian Universalists live our faith imperfectly, sometimes so imperfectly that it is right to ask ourselves if we are living it at all. And yet, we want to do the right thing. We hope to be better than we are. We long to live our values more fully, to embody the beloved community.

Applying the principle of DDT (diagnosis determines therapy) shows us the injustice, what it looks like, and how we can change. It teaches us to recognize, reorient, realize, rethink, and resist. And goddess knows we must! But this model alone is insufficient for me. I must *also* live in a spirit of longing so passionately for the beloved community that the work of the detection and destruction of racism is possible, bearable, doable, and survivable.

Bill, you have offered much to our religious community in the struggle against racism: analysis, challenge, and your continued presence and participation in honesty and truth. All that I have learned from you—may I use it in the service of our common struggle. And yet, it is but a prologue; it is not enough, or it is incomplete. It teaches me how to struggle, but my spirit longs for more, for something that touches the passion and the anger where my strength lies.

For **Dianne Arakawa**, Jones's essay must be placed in the context of the fruits and the failures of anti-racism work within Unitarian Universalism, past and present. She takes a deeper look at what remains invisible:

Like most of you, I can recount the tragedies of the past that still plague our Association: from the settler Indian wars of the seventeenth century in Massachusetts, Puritan policies related to slavery, the mixed Unitarian response to abolition, the unjust labor practices at the turn of the century, and the racist statements of our denominational presidents in the first half of the last century to the slowness to engage in the Civil Rights movement on the part of some of our congregations, the derailing of the Black Empowerment movement in the sixties, and the lack of support for congregations and clergy of color from Ethelred Brown's time to our present. . . .

I can also appreciate the fruits of initiatives set in motion over the last two decades by individuals; by our congregations, seminaries, and affiliate organizations; and by the Unitarian Universalist Association itself—initiatives such as the racial justice curriculum of the Religious Education Department; the *Singing the Living Tradition* hymnbook; and the Journey Toward Wholeness program. Being a religious person, I can hope—even hope beyond hope.

Still, I wonder if the kind of critical assessment of neo-racism that Bill Jones offers is enough. After all, it gets at only what is visible, behavioral, and quantifiable. What of the foundational, cultural, religious, and spiritual dimensions of racism that Jones seems to bypass? First, what about the internal geography of feeling: the pre-rational, the irrational, what is inside, deep down, real, painful, joyful, guilty, shameful, religious, spiritual, and full of life? Second, how does this internal terrain change; what is its *modus operandi*; what of transformation, faith, motivation, will, energy, and courage? And third, what of the context, the landscape surrounding the person, the support or antagonism—is it friendly out there, or is the map full of wild beasts, even wolves in sheep's clothing?

While Bill says that we have only two choices with this methodology—to continue and preserve or to correct and reform—I believe that the struggle against racism is much more wily and wicked. Given the variety of human personalities, possibilities for change, and situations in which people find themselves, I believe that a more multitextured and multivalent theological methodology of anti-racism can move us forward.

For these issues of feeling, faith, and community are what got me into ministry and hold me in it. It is the Spirit of God moving in, through, among, and beyond us. It is the reluctant but real recognition of the need for apology and forgiveness in order to break the chain of suffering. It is an intractable longing for understanding, compassion, peace, and justice. It is the ingenuity and courage to collaborate with others—or at times to go it alone, to say "No, no more!" and to turn the system upside down.

This does not essentially depend, I think, on whether our equipment for assessment is scientifically correct or technologically advanced, like the Hubble telescope. For is it not true that people are imperfect? Is it not true that life is messy? And is it not true that for some of us religion is more than one particular methodology of "detection and destruction," that it is even a commitment to live faith, which Paul reminds us deals with "things unseen"?

I am not against intellectual assessment that seeks to do institutional praxis. . . . Still, from where I stand, Bill's approach seems not to address the many layers of racism adequately. It fails to make room for an experiential, religious, and spiritual critique. Racism will not be dismantled by one rational methodology; rather, that will happen when human experience in all its myriad forms is invited into conversation and "conversion" at the table, or as Dorothy Day has pointed out, when will is stirred as by grace and when we as a community of faith exert our moral and ethical suasion for the Common Good. . . .

I want systemic change in our association, as well as the religious, spiritual, and theological empowerment of all our people. I want to hear stories of courage, strength, resilience, and dignity that got us through the storm, as the spiritual has it, and that helped others. In addition to the socioinstitutional analysis, we need to consider what is not readily visible, completely articulate, or easily quantifiable. . . . We need to consider what is salvific, redeems lives, and makes them as holy as the stars that are set in the heavens.

In this multifaceted, multivalent anti-racist theology, I need the stories of people of color—all colors—*and* those of whites. For example, I am interested in a Yankee parishioner who cherishes a teapot that, as the story goes, was given to her family by a runaway slave come back from Canada to thank the family for sheltering her on the Underground Railway. I am interested in a white laywoman who was the first to extend her hand in her town to an African American family who had just moved from inner-city Dorchester—a family with whom this woman still maintains an active mutual friendship forty years later. I am interested in a comfortable liberal church member who regularly contributes her money to anti-racist and multicultural causes. According to Bill's assessment, I am afraid that these women would become mere statistics. Their personal stories, feelings, religious motivations, and pastoral involvements would be considered nice but would count for naught.

Beyond the prolegomenon to anti-racism, I believe that we need to take seriously stories such as these. We need to look at and to lift up feeling, faith, and religious community.

The Dialogue

Individual experiences of invisibility, oppression, and "learning to be white" and different understandings of the place of the psychological and the spiritual inform participants' responses to Bill Jones's essay. The group struggles in this session with its own complex dynamics. The dialogue excerpted here witnesses to the group's efforts to work through tears and anger to deeper understandings.

PATRICIA JIMENEZ: I am reminded of the difficulty we have seeing who is in the room. Earlier in this consultation, Dianne asked James Cone to name a theological idea regarding non-black people of color that he had changed over the last thirty years. He didn't really answer the question. I am sitting here beginning to feel more and more invisible. And I am tired of being invisible. As in previous consultations in Chicago and Kansas City, all of the metaphors and symbols we are using are black and white, and people who are not African American or white are not in the picture. When are we going to see who is in the room? When are we going to develop a process that invites and encourages all of our stories to be heard? And I wonder not just about who is included in this room but also about who is in our pews—are we leaving them out?

JOSÉ BALLESTER: I want to say thank you, Bill. For so many years, you have been an inspiration. You have taught me and Dianne and a lot of us who have been doing this work many things, and you continue to inspire us. But I say to you, my brother, nothing has changed. It is *still killing us!* Because even though we have fought for some recognition, some dignity, and for being at the table, I am *still* invisible, and Dianne is *still* invisible. . . . I ask you, I beg you, help us! Because they [white people] don't see us—and they never have. This is oppression, Bill, it's oppression, and it's killing us.

PAUL RASOR: In Peter's response to my essay, he brought up this point, too, that the underlying assumption of race work is the black-white paradigm. I just want to acknowledge what he held up for me: that the dialogue partners for my paper are all black—and I should know better!

THANDEKA: I think if we had had an opening paper by someone who was not an African American or a European American and if the papers from the second half of the conference had been placed at the beginning[10]—in other words, if the structure had been rearranged—then this sense of not being heard and the problem of invisibility might not have occurred.

PETER MORALES: As long as we keep making race the focus of these discussions, we're going to stay stuck!

Pushed into inarticulate rage at the false realm of issues addressed Then called a racist for the courage to try to address the charm.

TOM SCHADE: There have been emotional moments in this discussion so far, and I do not believe that we have processed them properly. I believe that they expose what is going on in the room and that we need to confront that. The first moment occurred as Tracey was reading her response. Now I don't know Tracey and I don't know Bill, but having spent twelve years in a coercive organization, I know relationships of domination and subordination when I see them. . . . And I think that domination and subordination take the form of folks who are called white desperately, insanely, and maniacally needing the approval of African Americans. As a result of our desperate, maniacal, all-consuming need for the approval of African Americans, we will gladly invite any number of Chicanos, Asians, or Indians into the room—and then ignore them, because they are not important to us! Right now, our need is to recover our sense of humanity relative to African Americans. And the terms of the debate are such that we [whites] are told that it is impossible for us to "do the right thing"; therefore we are put in the position of willing ourselves outside of history, outside of our past, and this leaves us with just desperate longing. I think this reveals an ugly underside to what's going on in this room and in this consultation and in this Association.

JONES: I'd like to cuss and discuss that with you, Tom. I have some severe reservations about your analysis there, but to me this is the approach to take, to put out on the table the angle of perception that you see. The next thing to do is to try to validate it, not simply on the basis of your individual perspective but in terms of whether that's what's visible from other angles of analysis. Otherwise, we're in the situation where we give to you the dominant kind of position that you're attributing to *us*. And to me the principle should be one of co-equality, not this superior-inferior arrangement that informs your critique of the whole project.

JOELLEN WILLIS: Dianne's paper spoke to me, but I think that was partly because it was easier for me to hear. In my own response to Rosemary's essay, I too wrote about needing to hear stories, and I do think that's important, but I think we do a disservice if we think that that is all we need to be doing. I believe that listening to each other's stories and telling our stories and holding these stories in our heart can only bring us to the beginning. From there, we have to move on with the work.

We understand the language of individuals, and that's why stories have such power for us. They move us, they move our hearts, and at their best, they move us to action. But too often we believe that telling the story can be the sum total of our effort. We want to deny the truth that Bill brings to us, the bad news that regardless of the individual or individuals whom we may lift up— and perhaps *must* lift up—in stories, there is still a predictable pattern to the oppression that we face, some from one place and some from another. Regardless of what we tell ourselves, the oppression is out there, and it remains to be dealt with.

JOHN BUEHRENS: Bill, every time I come together with you I learn something new, and today a major lightbulb went off for me right in the middle of your summary about the need for case studies. Your methodological insights are always extraordinarily helpful. I think we need the kind of universal language analysis that you point us to, because it relates to all of creation and to how we behave in our common createdness. But then we also need case studies, because they show the redemptive possibilities within particular gathered bodies.

One of the difficulties of our discourse so far is the lack of focused attention on particularities. I've often complained that one of the most unexamined assumptions in our work has been your assumption that diagnosis determines therapy. It seems to me that we have tried to do a Unitarian Universalist–wide system analysis called anti-racism without *either* moving it to the more universal level that your anti-oppression grid suggests *or* fully explicating the need for the particularities of the excluded stories and the invisible groups that have been so poignantly alluded to here today. And I think the recognition of this complaint has been one of the biggest learnings and changes put in place by those who guide our anti-oppression initiatives.

I am the grandchild of peasant people who came over in steerage from Eastern Europe, and I sit here under Sam Eliot's portrait knowing that my whole life has been one of learning to be white and to take on forms of privilege. The major spiritual challenge for me now is to figure out how to use what privilege and power I've acquired to dismantle the structures of oppression I have been seduced into. That's a three-level analysis—like the personal, spiritual, and relational work that Tracey's powerful response evokes for me. I don't think we're ever going to do all the levels of work that we need to do if we talk past one another at these three different levels.

JONES: I think there has been a lack of cuss and discuss among the different models of doing anti-racism in our denomination. I think we made an error at the beginning by focusing primarily on one model and advancing that one rather than doing a number of individual pilot studies based on various models and then coming back later to synthesize what we'd learned.

As for some of the criticisms of my analysis that have been brought up in this discussion: Please understand that I am talking about oppression at the generic level. I don't care what kind of oppression you're talking about—sexism, racism, colorism (and I think we make a fundamental error in confusing racism and colorism; those are two different kinds of oppression)—there is a general, generic configuration for all of the different kinds of oppression. So if you understand that I am describing the generic level of oppression, you will begin to see that my system *does* address sexism, Chicano racism, and so on, in terms of their generic components. If you want to eradicate any of these oppressions, you've got to look at eradicating the generic components of oppression, not the particular species. Racism is a species of oppression; it is only one way to oppress a person.

My analysis rests on a quite different understanding of the ontological status of oppression than our denomination uses. I want to argue that oppression is the fundamental human behavior; all of us are oppressors in a certain context, and we are in denial about that oppression. I think this is true of most forms of life at the organic level. In order to survive, you have to feed on something other than yourself. Give me an exception to this rule! Oppression, then, is the response necessary for survival and well-being to a state of affairs that we human beings did not create. We were put into this reality where we have two and only two choices—to commit suicide or not. If I choose not to feed on something else, what's the effect? [A few say, "Suicide."] If I choose to feed on *myself*, the food supply is limited. Anybody who is alive demonstrates by the mere fact of being alive which one of these choices they have made; they have chosen to enhance their well-being and survival at the expense of whatever it is they consume. Everything that we do subsequently is simply a variation on that particular choice. We adopt a by-any-means-necessary value system in order to postpone when we become the eatee.

George Tinker: I want to pick up on the helpful move, Bill, that you have made away from the word *racism* to the word *oppression*. We have to remember that racism is simply a particular manifestation of oppression. But I am not buying this move *completely* because we need to link racism with all the other manifestations of oppression. We've got to understand that racism is part of a systemic whole that includes gender, class, colonialism, and globalization, which is a particularly nasty form of colonialism.

I'm also concerned that we not make the move too quickly toward an easy cultural hybridity and a new culture to be born out of anti-racist communities of resistance, as bell hooks has put it in *Killing Rage*.[11] That move steps around all the other oppressions in the world. I don't want to get rid of racism just for a while; *I want to change the world!* If we focus only on one issue, my fear is that it will come around and bite us in the tail again in a different way. So we've got to begin to see racism as part of a systemic whole and use some holistic strategy to deal with it.

There's one other thing I want to throw in here; it seems like kind of a wild card, but it's part of what I do for a living. There is a medicine man on my reservation who is incredibly wise. On my reservation, in particular, there are a lot of mixed bloods—I'm one of them. This medicine man has mixed-blood relatives and white relatives by marriage, and he loves all of us equally; he doesn't privilege full bloods over mixed bloods or Indian over white. But whenever he speaks publicly, at some point in his talk he will remind the audience, whether it's Indian or white or mixed: "Never ever forget that white people are liars, thieves, and murderers." And he is talking about people he loves.

This is part of that systemic whole, too, that we'd better pay attention to: that the European *experiment* in North America and in the Americas was built on a history of lying, thievery, and murder, and it hasn't gone away. Until we begin finally to deal with this reality with honest self-reflection and self-criticism, we're going to keep bombing the hell out of people like the Iraqis and saying,

"It's a right and just and godly thing to do." Just as, down the road here in 1620, William Bradford called the thievery of a year's supply of corn from an Indian village in Cape Cod "God's bountiful mercy." It started there, but it's still here!

I don't repeat what my brother Larry, the medicine man, says just to rile up white folk; I say it because it's something that white folk better pay attention to. And not only white folk but Indian folk better pay attention to it too because we're caught up in racism by wanting to be like our white brothers and sisters. In other words, we participate in lying, thievery, and murder so that we can be "real people" too.

BALLESTER: *Yo soy Newyorican, y yo soy Latino.* I am a Newyorican, I am a native of New York, and I am a Latino. With each step I take in naming my identities, I have to leave a certain part of me behind, to the point where when we start talking about "people of color," I have sacrificed way too much. In this room, we have used the term "people of color" and we have used the term "African Americans and people of color." My suggestion is to level the playing field here. If we're going to say anything—and if as a denomination, we can say "gay, lesbian, bisexual, and transgender"—then let us say "African American, Latino and Latina, Native American, and Asian American." I would like to open up even those categories, but I realize we are short on time, so I beg of you, at least try to call us by our names.

THANDEKA: Two points: First, I was surprised and relieved when I read all the essays, because I didn't expect there to be any internal criticism of the standard anti-racism program adopted at the Unitarian Universalist Association. And second, I want to encourage spiritual religious outbreaks like the one that Tom had, so that we have a way of spontaneously calling our attention to unsaid issues that shouldn't be left unattended.

ROBINSON-HARRIS [after the lunch break]: Tom and I have spoken briefly and agreed that we will speak again privately, but since the interaction took place in this public setting, it is important to me to bring it up again here.

I understand that a part of our task here is to bring our particularities to the table as we work on anti-racism. My immediate reaction to what you were saying, Tom, was that I understood your words and at the same time did not know what you were saying because *it wasn't about me.* What you were describing was not my experience. To me, your commentary seemed to replicate the kind of relationship of dominance and subordination that you were describing. In the moment, that was hard to take in. It felt to me as if something of obvious importance *to you* had been projected onto something that had happened between Bill Jones and myself. At lunch, I found myself in the hallway speaking with Bill about what had happened so that he and I could be clear about our understanding of the interaction. But then as I thought about that conversation with Bill, it felt to me as though he and I were in the hallway doing the "spiritual domestic work" of the group: A black man and a white woman were in the hall dealing with an issue that had been raised at this table by a white male minister.

MARJORIE BOWENS-WHEATLEY: All right, let's just sit with that, and there will be more. Thank you.

Study Questions

1. How does Jones distinguish between "classical racism" and "neo-racism"? What is the role of UUs in neo-racism?

2. Bill Jones writes, "The fact that something is invisible to us does not meant that it does not exist. Whether something is visible or invisible depends on the sophistication and accuracy of our viewing instruments, as well as on the point of view we choose. Thus, if Unitarian Universalists are to be part of the solution and not part of the problem, we need more effective diagnostic tools to expose neo-racism's disguises, to make neo-racism visible, and to be aware of how we function as its carriers in the home, the workplace, and our faith communities."

   What "diagnostic tools" and "viewing instruments" are available to you to make oppression visible and to raise our awareness of how we function as its carriers? What works against our awareness?

3. Do the list exercise on page 151. What do you understand differently as a result of this activity?

4. If diagnosis determines therapy (DDT), what is your diagnosis? What therapy do you propose? What are the implications of that therapy for your own life? To what extent does UUism "continue and preserve" and to what extent does it "correct and reform"?

5. Tracey Robinson-Harris writes, "I must also live in a spirit of longing so passionately for the Beloved Community." Diane Arakawa writes, "It is an intractable longing for understanding, compassion, peace, and justice." What do you long for? Have a passion for? What does our seventh Principle of interdependence mean to you in this context?

6. Do you agree with Jones that "all of us are oppressors in a certain context"? What are your stories of being oppressed? of being an oppressor? of fighting oppression?

7. What do you have faith in?

8. What is the place of personal psychology and personal experience in the work of anti-racism? Does it *have* a place?

Not Somewhere Else, But Here: The Struggle for Racial Justice as a Struggle to Inhabit My Country

REBECCA PARKER

A good deal of time and intelligence has been invested in the exposure of racism and the horrific results on its objects. . . . It seems both poignant and striking how avoided and unanalyzed is the effect of racist inflection on the subject. The scholarship that looks into the mind, imagination, and behavior of slaves is valuable. But equally valuable is a serious intellectual effort to see what racial ideology does to the mind, imagination, and behavior of masters.

—Toni Morrison

In 1976 I began a cross-country road trip, on my way to seminary. I traveled with a friend. We had time, so we decided to take back roads. One afternoon the road passed through rural western Pennsylvania. Late in the day, we came down through hill country into a valley. It had been raining hard, and as we neared a small town, we noticed blinking yellow lights warning of danger. We saw fields covered in standing water and passed several side roads blocked off with signs saying: Road Closed.

"Looks like they've had a flood here," we said.

Coming into town, we crossed a bridge over a wide river. The water was high, muddy, flowing fast. Sandbags lined the roadway.

"Gosh," we said, "They must have had quite a bit of high water to contend with here. Looks like it was a major flood!"

We headed out of town, following a winding country road, captivated by the evidence all around us that there had been a dramatic flood. Then we rounded a bend, and in front of us, a sheet of water covered the roadway. The water was rising fast, like a huge silver balloon being inflated before our eyes.

We stopped and started to turn the car around. The water was rising behind us as well. Suddenly we realized the flood hadn't happened yesterday or last week. It was happening *here and now.* Dry ground was disappearing fast. We hurriedly clambered out of the car and scrambled to higher ground. Soaked to the bone, we huddled under a fir tree. No longer were we lodged in our familiar vehicle; the cold water of the storm poured down on us, baptizing us into the present—a present from which we had been insulated by both our car and our misjudgments about the country we were traveling through.

This is what it is like to be white in America. It is to travel well ensconced in a secure vehicle; to see signs of what is happening in the world outside the compartment one is traveling in and not realize that these signs have any contemporary meaning. It is to be dislocated—to misjudge your location and to believe you are uninvolved and unaffected by what is happening in the world.

James Baldwin wrote, "This is the crime of which I accuse my countrymen, and for which I and history will never forgive them, that they have destroyed and are destroying hundreds and thousands of lives, and do not know it, and do not want to know it."[1] Reading Baldwin's *The Fire Next Time* has helped me recognize my experience. Born white in this country, I was gradually but decisively educated into an alienated state of mind. With this narrowing, my capacity for creative participation in my society was stunted, and I became compliant with social forms and patterns that failed to support the fullness of life for others or myself.

To come of age in America as a white person is to be educated into ignorance. It is to be culturally shaped to not know and not want to know the actual context in which you live.

I was born into the real world, in a small town at the edge of the rain forest, on the coast of Washington State. The world was a mixture of violence and beauty, human goodness and human greed, tender relationships and exploitation. But I learned to not see life whole. Our town was the white settlement. Up river was the Quinault Indian reservation. The two communities were separated by a stretch of forest, whose towering trees and thick undergrowth cloaked us from each other. Elton Bennet, an artist who lived in our town and went to our church, was one of a handful from our community who moved in both worlds. His silk screens depicted the land and its diverse people. "They Speak by Silence," he titled one of his silk screens, in which a small band of Quinault moved along the shore between the forest and the ocean. As a small child, I watched Bennet pull the stiff paper from the inked cloth that created the image. It took the alchemy of art for me to know that I had neighbors I did not know.

But in fact, the real world I was born into included richly diverse cultures and communities. In addition to the community I knew—the white settlement of people who logged the forests, fished the waters, and built wood frame houses warmed with steaming coffee—there were other communities. The Quinault, Makah, and Puyallup Indians lived throughout Southwest Washington, preserving tribal ways against all odds. Chinese American cultural organizations in Seattle nurtured Chinese traditions and institutions at the heart of the city. Japanese Americans established temples and churches, landscaped gardens, shaped architectural styles, farmed the land. Farm workers from Mexico harvested the apples in Yakima and Wenatchee and stayed to found Spanish-speaking towns. African Americans established churches, neighborhoods, clubs, and civic organizations.

By the time I came of age, neighborhood and church, economic patterns, cultural symbolism, theological doctrines, and public education had narrowed my awareness of the country I lived in to the point of ignorance. The Chinese, African, Latino/Latina, Japanese, and First Nations peoples had largely disappeared from my consciousness. Nor did I know the history of violence and exploitation that had occurred in my community. Two generations before I was born, Chinese workers on the Seattle waterfront went on strike for fairer wages; the white majority beat back the strikers with sticks and guns. Just before I was born, the strawberry farms of Japanese Americans living on the Puget Sound islands were seized on orders from General DeWitt. Their land confiscated by the U.S. government, the Japanese Americans were taken away to live in concentration camps, uprooted from their homesteads and communities. In our town, the Ku Klux Klan and the John Birch Society supported overt white supremacist agendas. The Birch Society's bright and large billboard on the highway into my childhood town broadcasted hate. And the First Nations people went to court over and over again, seeking to secure the fishing rights and land sovereignty that were theirs.

I inhabited a white enclave that did not know and did not want to know the complex, multicultural history of the land in which I lived. The white-washed world ignored the violence and exploitation in my country's history, as well as the resistance, creativity, and multiform beauty of my country's peoples. I was cut off from the reality of where I lived, whom I lived with, and what our history entailed of violence and of beauty.

There were moments of exception. During the Civil Rights struggle, our United Methodist congregation got involved. From the pulpit, my preacher father exposed the redlining practices that took place in our town. As a twelve-year-old, I went door to door, along with other members of our congregation, campaigning for open housing. Political involvement was exciting. I felt the importance of civic action.

But that same year, walking down the street holding hands with my best friend, Mary, we were passed by a car of hecklers who yelled profanities at us, words we didn't really know or understand. They turned the car around and drove by us again, calling us names, nearly hitting us as they sped by. Were they offended that we appeared as a black girl and a white girl together? Were they enraged that we were holding hands, laughing and embracing one another, as we walked along the road? I defended my friendship with Mary and stood by my love for her when other students and teachers communicated that there was something wrong with us. But I learned that such love was dangerous. Love became intertwined with fear.

Lillian Smith, probing the experience of being "cultured" into whiteness, describes growing up white in the South as an education into fragmentation and denial:

> They who so gravely taught me to split my body from my mind and both from my "soul" taught me also to split my conscience from my acts and Christianity from southern tradition. I learned

> [white racism] the way all of my southern people learn it: by
> closing door after door until one's mind and heart and con-
> science are blocked off from each other and from reality. Some
> learned to screen out all except the soft and the soothing; others
> denied even as they saw plainly, and heard.

The result of this closing-down process for whites, Smith says,
is that "we are blocked from sensible contact with the world we
live in."[2]

Smith describes racism as a fragmentation of knowledge—a
splitting of mind, body, and soul; neighbor from neighbor; disciplines of knowledge from disciplines of knowledge; and religion
from politics. This fragmentation results in apathy, passivity, and
compliance.

When I speak of the ignorance created by my education into
whiteness, I am speaking of a loss of wholeness within myself and
a concomitant segregation and fragmentation of culture that debil-
itates life for all of us. Who benefits from this fragmentation and
alienation? Does anyone? What I know is that I do not benefit from
this loss of my senses, this denial of what I have seen and felt, this
cultural erasure of my actual neighbors, this loss of my country. I
become, thus educated, less present to life, more cut-off, and less
creative and loving. Once I recognize it, this loss disturbs me
deeply. It is precisely this loss that makes me a suitable, passive
participant in social structures that I abhor.

Smith writes,

> Our big problem is not civil rights nor even a free Africa—urgent
> as these are—but how to make into a related whole the split
> pieces of the human experience, how to bridge mythic and
> rational mind, how to connect our childhood with the present
> and the past with the future, how to relate the differing realities
> of science and religion and politics and art to each other and to
> ourselves. Man is a broken creature, yes; it is his nature as a
> human being to be so; but it is also his nature to create relation-
> ships that can span the brokenness. This is his first responsibili-
> ty; when he fails, he is inevitably destroyed.[3]

I want to inhabit my country, not live as if we did not belong
to one another as surely as we belong to the land.

"Not somewhere else, but here" is a phrase from a love poem
by Adrienne Rich that invokes love's imperative. The lover is

drawn to what is present, to what is real, what is here, what is now, what is flesh. In its beauty and its tragedy, its burden of grief, and its full measure of joy, life is loved through presence, not absence; through connection, not alienation.

The moment my friend in Pennsylvania and I left our car and felt the rain falling on our bodies, soaking our skin, and had to exert ourselves to scramble to safety was a blessed moment—not because there is any virtue in danger, but because it was a moment when disoriented, alienated consciousness was interrupted. We became present to our environment. We ceased being passive observers or commentators. Our whole beings, bodies, minds, and senses became involved with the requirements of the situation. We arrived. We entered in. We left our compartment and inhabited the world. No longer tourists passing through the country, we became part of the place along with everyone else that day, in that corner of western Pennsylvania, in that storm.

I speak of this experience as a baptism because it was a conversion from distance to presence, from misconception to realization. It was an awakening to life, an advance into participation, and a birth into the world.

This is the conversion that is needed for those of us who are white Americans. We need to move from a place of passive, misconstrued observation about our country to a place of active, alert participation in our country. We need to recover our habitation and reconstruct our citizenship as surely, for example, as those of us who are women have had to learn to inhabit our own bodies and recover our agency when sexism has alienated us from ourselves.

How do those of us who are white come to inhabit our own country? Here are some of the steps in the conversion:

Theological reflection: To become an inhabitant of America, whites need to deconstruct the effect on our self-understanding of theological imagery that sanctions innocence and ignorance as holy states. This theological imagery is strong. For centuries, Christian theologians have told the story this way: Adam and Eve in the Garden were innocent of themselves and of the knowledge of good and evil. Within the safe confines of the Garden, all was provided for them. They were to ask no questions and be obedient to the rules outlined by God. In this state of primordial bliss,

Adam and Eve were compliant and dependent. They cooperated with the divine ruler and rules. This state was holy. The two were without sin, living in harmony with God.

This interpretation of the Garden of Eden story sanctions innocence, ignorance, and lack of self-consciousness. It teaches that a carefully contained life, walled in by a providential God whom one is never to question, is a good life. In the insular Garden, human beings are in right relationship to God.

This primordial state of innocence was disrupted by the serpent's temptation to Eve. The serpent enticed her with the desire to taste the forbidden fruit and gain knowledge of good and evil. To gain knowledge, however, was to defy God—to go against the will of the divine provisioner. The consequence was a punishing exile. Adam and Eve were sent away from the Garden, cast out from God's presence.

In this interpretation, to know the world, in its goodness and its evil, and to know ourselves capable of both *is to lose God.* To taste reality is to follow the devil. Such a theology is admirably suited to the preservation of compartmentalized, alienated states of mind. It teaches those who have absorbed its message that goodness is aligned with innocence and ignorance. To not know the world is to know God. To know the world is to lose God. Furthermore, it teaches that a social structure in which one is abundantly provided for is not to be questioned. Abundant provision is a gift of God. This image comforts whites who benefit from economic structures that assure their thriving. One is to accept privilege and never ask at what cost the walled-in garden is maintained.

When religion sanctions ignorance, it cultivates alienation from life. It blesses segregation and encourages people who are comfortably provided for to remain compliant with the created order.

As a white person, I have allowed this theological imagery to shape my self-understanding, even when I have consciously rejected this theology. In practice, I discover myself to be deeply attached to being "innocent," guilt-free, good. If I glimpse any blood on my hands, I will react defensively to preserve my identity and fend off the painful experience of shame that I associate with being exiled from the community that I depend on for my survival and affirmation. Or I may attack myself, viciously trying to deny or destroy that in myself that does not conform to an image of innocent goodness.

This piety of innocence preoccupies me and other whites. I strive to assure my goodness by assuring myself that I am all-good, "all-white," and blameless. Conversely, it makes me highly reactionary if I am blamed or confronted with complicity in violence—for my sense of goodness has been constructed on the suppression and exile of my capacity to do harm, as well as on the suppression of offending feelings of love and connection that, I learned early on, didn't belong in the garden.

One becomes "white," and this "whiteness" is a split in the psyche, a loss of consciousness, a numbing to the reality of what one has seen and felt and knows. This alienated state of mind is reinforced by religious imagery that sanctions "not knowing" and curses "knowing."

At the same time, part of us never forgets that we have achieved our goodness at a violent price. We have a guilty conscience. At some level, we know that our pristine garden has been created by what has been exiled and exploited. This primordial violence lies beneath our sense of privilege and security. We are fearful of this deeper violence being exposed. We feel helpless in the presence of our own violence.

But theology assists us, even here. The doctrine of the atonement valorizes violence as life-giving and redemptive. The interpretations of Jesus's death on the cross as a saving event speak of the violation that happened to Jesus as the will of God and the source of salvation. When this theological perspective prevails, either explicitly or buried within cultural patterns and norms, the violence and abuse that human beings experience or perpetuate becomes valorized as necessary and good for the salvation of the world. Victims of racial injustice, identifying with Jesus, may interpret their suffering as necessary, holy, and redemptive. Perpetrators of racial injustice, identifying with God, may interpret their violence as necessary, holy, and redemptive.

Most particularly, violating experiences that occur early in life in parent-child relationships can be misnamed as good. In *Learning to Be White*, Thandeka analyzes the violent shaming experiences that create white identity. Such shaming is theologically sanctioned as God's will. The suffering child is like the suffering Jesus, whose divinity is celebrated as his willingness to endure violation.

The violating parent is doing what must be done as the divine enforcer of the "orders of creation."

Thus, the doctrine of the atonement reinforces violating and shaming experiences. Through these experiences, the shamed child preserves his or her relationship to God and to goodness. I learn to interpret the violence that has formed my narrow, "white" identity as holy. If I begin to approach the underlying violence that creates white enclaves and white identity, theology will tell me that violence is holy. Instead of facing my participation in violence, I can feel the pathos of violence with pious gratitude. Thus anesthetized, I will not seek to end violence.

The sanctioning of violence as redemptive is at the center of William R. Jones's theological inquiry, *Is God a White Racist?*[4] He shows definitively that no formulation of redemptive suffering can succeed at ending violence. Such a theology will serve again and again, in its diverse forms, to sustain structures rooted in violence.

To recover and become an inhabitant of one's own life and one's own society, a different theology is needed. A new theology must begin here, a theology that assists in an internal healing of the fragmented self, that supports a new engagement with the realities of one's society, and that sanctions a remedial education into the actual history and present realities of one's country. Theology must direct us, like Eve, to taste the fruit of knowledge and gladly bear the cost of moving beyond the confines of the garden.

A different theology begins with the sanctification of knowledge and wisdom rather than the blessing of innocence and ignorance. The serpent can be re-imagined as a representation of a god who calls one beyond the circumscribed comforts of the garden. To long to know, to reach for wisdom, to taste and see the bitterness as well as the sweetness, to come to know good and evil—these movements can be embraced as movements of God's leading. Leaving the garden, one leaves the God who rules by rewards and punishments, and who offers security and comfort at the price of compliance to divine orders. Leaving the garden, one becomes a sojourner in the world, accompanied by the divine serpent who moves in the earth, sheds old skins and grows new ones as needed, slumbers long, and wakes to strike quickly.

Remedial education: The journey to the realm beyond the garden begins with claiming forbidden knowledge. Because my education cultivated in me and many others an ignorance rather than a knowledge of my country's history and its peoples, I can begin to change things when I accept my power and responsibility to re-educate myself. Resources for such restored knowledge abound. Reading Howard Zinn's *A People's History of the United States*[5] and Ronald Takaki's *A Different Mirror,*[6] I become acquainted with my actual country. Immersing myself in the primary texts of First Nation's writers, Asian American writers, African American writers, Latino and Latina writers, and more, I begin to be aware of the world beyond my isolated enclave. Multiple voices surround me. I enter a miraculous Pentecost that has been sounding from before I was born. Takaki writes,

> Throughout our past of oppressions and struggles for equality, Americans of different races and ethnicities have been "singing with open mouths their strong melodious songs" in the textile mills of Lowell, the cotton fields of Mississippi, on the Indian reservations of South Dakota, the railroad tracks high in the Sierras of California, in the garment factories on the Lower East Side, the canefields of Hawaii, and a thousand other places across the country. Our denied history "bursts with telling." As we hear America singing, we find ourselves invited to bring our rich cultural diversity on deck, to accept ourselves. "Of every hue and cast am I," sang Whitman. "I resist any thing better than my own diversity."[7]

Knowledge is never an individual achievement alone. It is constructed by communities of people, and its construction transforms communities. "Knowledge claims are secured by the social practices of a community of inquirers, rather than the purely mental activities of an individual subject."[8]

Ignorance is a precondition of violence. Once I as a "white" have been cultivated into ignorance of my society, its multiple cultures, their diverse gifts, and the history of cultural conflict and exploitation based on racial categorizations, then I am easily passive in the face of racism's re-creation. But my ignorance is not mine alone. It is the ignorance of my cultural enclave. Most of us do not know more than our community knows. Thus my search for remedial education, to come to know the larger reality of my country, is necessarily a struggle to transform my community's knowledge—not mine alone. As I gain more knowledge, I enter into a different community—a community of presence, awareness, responsibility, and consciousness.

I have learned that as a white American, I must face the conflict that erupts between whites when compulsory fragmentation of knowledge begins to break down because remedial education has taken place. This engagement among whites needs to take place with directness, wisdom, and a sustained commitment to build a new communion not dependent upon violence. It involves a spiritual practice of nonviolent resistance and non-avoidance of conflict.

Soul Work: To sustain the journey beyond the garden, those of us who are white must turn inward as well as outward. We must form a new relational capacity, less hindered by the fragmentation, silences, and splits in our souls. We must find the path that takes us beyond the narcissistic need to have people of color approve of us, tell us we are good, or be the prophetic and moral compass that is absent from ourselves.

The construction of white identity involves the suppression of aspects of the self as unacceptable and shameful. This internal violation of the wholeness of the self becomes, for many whites, symbolically represented as the internal suppression of that in oneself which is imagined as dark. This part of the self is the unjustly abused and despised aspect of the white person's own experience. At the same time, it is the suppression, often, of the white person's passionate feelings, sense of connection to others, ability to love, and ability to inhabit one's own body. Whites then project onto people of color the lost part of themselves: the silenced and abused "darkness," and the exiled and suppressed passion, emotion, and body. For whites, people of color come to represent the lost aspects of the self. Ambivalence and need emerge for whites who feel better about themselves if they have intimate association with people of color. But such intimacy may lack the quality of an authentic I-Thou relationship.

The inner journey for whites involves learning to withdraw our negative and positive projections from people of color. Whites must become relationally committed to meeting people of color *as themselves,* not as symbolic extensions of ourselves. To love more genuinely, whites need to do the internal work to recover and integrate the lost parts of ourselves—to find the silenced, suppressed, and fragmented aspects of our own being and to create internal hospitality to the fullness of our own lives. This work cannot be done by others for us. We must find an internal blessing, not seek a blessing from those we use to symbolize our loss and our shame.

Men who have projected their own exiled capacity to feel onto women need to recover the lost part of themselves rather than bond with women who will carry their emotional burdens for them. Likewise, whites need to accept the personal task of spiritual healing rather than project onto people of color our own loss of humanity, asking people of color to carry the burden of this loss. The soul work that whites need to do turns us to the sources of spiritual transformation that are transpersonal—to the presence of a deep reality of wholeness, connection, and grace that supports us beyond our brokenness and urges us toward a more daring communion.

Engaged presence: Racial injustice is perpetuated by the passive absence of whites who are numbly disengaged with the social realities of our time. Conversely, racial injustice will fail to thrive as more and more of us show up as present and engaged citizens.

Racism is a form of cultural and economic violence that isolates and fragments human beings. Engaged presence counters violence by resisting its primary effect. As a white, the cure for my education into ignorance is remedial education. The cure for my fragmentation of self is hospitality to myself. The cure for my cultivation into passivity is renewed activism. Social activism becomes a spiritual practice by which I reclaim my humanity, and refuse to accept my cultivation into numbness and disengagement.

The narcissistic preoccupation of whites in our present society is a symptom of how well established racism is. Hope lies in our ability to renew our citizenship through engaged action. Meaningful participation is advanced by specific concerns and sustained work. One does not have to take on the whole world at once. Racism takes specific forms in specific fields—education, health care, the justice system, economics, theology. Holistic engagement in any field offers significant opportunities for the sustained address and redress of racism. As a theological educator, I take heart from what is accomplished when students do field work in the community: working on environmental racism, homelessness, HIV/AIDS, cultural survival, youth at risk, the prison-industrial complex, public education, or economic justice. In this engaged work, I see our white students move beyond the limits of their enculturation into ignorance and passivity.

Congregational life can provide a similar base community for the restoration of humanity. In my childhood, the church was the primary institutional setting in which racism was publicly named and its effects actively resisted. When church members took to the streets, we changed an unjust practice in our community. We also changed ourselves. Social action is an incarnational event. It mends the split of mind from body, individual from community, neighbor from neighbor.

A person of faith, seeking out of love and desire for life to inhabit his or her country, needs to be engaged in incarnational social action. Activism returns one to the actual world as a participatory citizen and an agent of history. Through activism, compliant absence is transformed into engaged presence.

Conclusion: The struggle for racial justice in America is a struggle to inhabit my own country, a struggle to become a participant in the actual history and social reality of the land in which I have been born and to which I belong. The struggle for racial justice is a struggle to overcome the numbness, alienation, splitting, and absence of consciousness that characterize my life as a white and that enable me to unwittingly, even *against my will,* continue to replicate life-destroying activities of my society. It is a struggle to attain a different expression of human wholeness: one in which my inner life is grounded in a restored communion with the transpersonal source of grace and wholeness, and the primordial fact of the connectedness of all life.

The struggle is imperative. Racial injustice is not only a tragedy that happened yesterday, whose aftereffects can be safely viewed from behind the glass windows of one's high-powered vehicle; racial injustice is currently mutating and re-creating itself. Its dehumanizing effects are harming hundreds and thousands of lives.

Within the past seven years, we in California have dismantled affirmative action; pulled the plug on public funding for bilingual education in Spanish and English in a state that is more than 50 percent Hispanic, and passed "three strikes" legislation that has dramatically increased the number of people in jail, a disproportionate number of them people of color. New prisons are being built as a high-profit industry, and prisoners are being used to provide industrial labor at below minimum wage. We passed a referendum to restrict immigrants' access to education and health services, and last spring we passed a referendum extending "three strikes" legislation to teenagers. If you are fourteen and you steal a bike, the crime can be counted as a first strike against you. With this law in place, youth of color are most at risk of becoming slave laborers in the prison-industrial complex. Meanwhile, public high schools in the Bay Area show a marked difference in the kind of education they offer. Schools with a majority of students of color provide few college preparatory classes and only a small percentage of their graduates go to college. These statistics are reversed for the predominantly white high schools, where there are many college prep classes and a majority of graduates go on to college.

This is my country. Love calls me beyond denial and disassociation. It is not enough to think of racism as a problem of "human relations," to be cured by me and others like me treating everyone fairly, with respect and without prejudice. Racism is more: It is a problem of segregated knowledge, mystification of facts, anesthetization of feeling, exploitation of people, and violence against the communion/community of our humanity.

My commitment to racial justice is both on behalf of the other—my neighbor, whose well-being I desire—and for myself, to whom the gift of life has been given but not yet fully claimed. I struggle neither as a benevolent act of social concern nor as a repentant act of shame and guilt, but as an act of desire for life, of passion for life, of insistence on life—fueled by both love for life and anger in face of the violence that divides human flesh.

The habit of living somewhere else rather than here, in a constructed "reality" that minimizes my country's history of both violence and beauty and ignores the present facts, keeps me from effectively engaging in the actual world. I have the sensation of being a disembodied spectator as structures of racism are re-created before my eyes. But involvement in the steps of conversion—theological reflection, remedial education, soul work, and engaged action—moves me from enclosure to openness.

I step out of an insular shell and come into immediate contact with the full texture of our present reality. I feel the rain on my face and breathe the fresh air. I wade in the waters that spirit has troubled and stirred. The water drenching me baptizes me into a new life. I become a citizen *not of somewhere else,* but of here.

The struggle for racial justice in America calls those of us who are white to make this journey. Our presence is needed. We have been absent too long.

> If you are here unfaithfully with us,
> you're causing terrible damage.
> If you've opened your loving to God's love,
> you're helping people you don't know
> and have never seen.

> > —Rumi, "Say Yes Quickly,"
> > translated by A. J. Arberry and Coleman Barks

The Responses

Rebecca Parker's essay, she explains, "comes out of a practice that I've been trying to follow, which is to continually ask the question: What have I learned *as a woman* struggling to resist and recover from systemic constraints on the lives of women in our society that can inform and assist me in my commitment to anti-oppression work?"

Parker introduces her essay as follows:

> As a woman, I have come to understand that I live within a social context of institutional restraint on women's lives that has sometimes been experienced in my individual life as direct male violence against women. I have, as a human being, had to resist and recover from the effects of this systemic constraint on women's lives, and this resistance and recovery have involved for me both soul work—that is, an internal struggle to recover from the ways in which sexism has led to the loss of aspects of myself—and collaborative work with others for institutional structural change. I don't anticipate that this work will be finished in my lifetime.

> What I see is that there's a social context of institutionalized constraint on the lives of African Americans, Asian Americans, Latino and Latina Americans, and Native Americans in the country in which I live—as well as in the world. These constraints are specific and diverse; they are not the same in each

community, but they dehumanize and limit the lives of human beings. My question is: Where am I and where is my European American community within this social reality? By asking this question, then, I try to keep my commitment to anti-oppression work always closely motivated by and aligned with my own passionate desire *to live* and with my own internal revolutionary protest against that which constrains life. The European American communities in which I have lived for most of my life are places where I—and those in my community—have been cultivated into isolation and ignorance of the actual context in which we live. I believe that narcissistic self-concern and a loss of the public world are effects of the racist social structures in our society on the lives of whites. In fact, I think that the narcissistic self-concern and loss of the public world that are experienced by whites are primary *symptoms* of racism. I believe that my efforts to recover from and resist the ignorance into which I have been cultivated are some of the most important strategies I can adopt both for myself and for my community.

My community, in the largest sense, is my country, and I am try-ing to become a *citizen* of my country. I take my definition of *cit-izen* directly from John Dewey: To be a *citizen* is to experience with some measure of fullness the context in which one lives and to act in that context as a creative agent, a creative participant in a way that serves life. So I am interested in the achievement of citizenship, which is an arrival in my country. I don't believe that I have yet accomplished this, nor do I believe that European Americans are functioning here in the United States as citizens of our country. As a white, I have learned to live as if I did not live here, and this is a loss of body, of sense, of awareness, and of world. It is this loss of world that I am passionately seeking to recover from, and this recovery of presence in the world is one of the primary things I can do in my commitment to anti-oppression work.

The opening image in Parker's essay strikes a personal chord for respondent **Mel Hoover**, who comments,

I know what it feels like to be caught in a flood with the waters of racial oppression pouring down upon you, as do many Unitarian Universalists of color. You are just going along, trying to live your faith, when a remark or an action alerts you to the danger of racism. When it happens, we often are without a com-panion to share our danger. In our liberal Unitarian Universalist faith, it is hard to find the safety of high ground above the danger. . . .

Rebecca Parker uses a quotation from James Baldwin that has guided me: "This is the crime of which I accuse my countrymen, and for which I and history will never forgive them, that they have destroyed and are destroying hundreds and thousands of lives, and do not know it, and do not want to know it." I am not at the moment focusing on the "never forgiving" aspect, but on the destroying of others and on the not knowing of whiteness. This lack of knowing by white people places people of color in danger every day of our lives. Even when we are not in personal relationships with white people, we interact with institutions that historically were established by whites *for* whites to primarily serve *their* needs, not ours. This seems obvious to me, but apparently, it is not to many whites. . . .

Knowing how to see racial oppression and what strategies are available to endure or counter the violence of oppression is not an *option* for people of color but a *requirement*. To live in the American context, a person of color has to be skilled in what W. E. B. DuBois called "twoness"[9]—that is, knowing how to live in more than one world at the same time. For whites, this experience must be learned; it is part of the education needed to move beyond the "otherness" of most whites' interaction with peoples of color. . . .

One of the great challenges of anti-racism work within our faith is the belief among many whites that they know what they need to know with regard to history. Even when confronted with data to the contrary, they don't want to take responsibility for unlearning "that stuff"; they don't want to have the truth "pushed on them." . . . But if racial justice is to be made real, then pushing the truth is an essential spiritual task. . . . Our fourth Principle offers both a challenge and a resource for us here. It calls us to a responsible search for truth and meaning *wherever they are found*. Might there be truth among peoples of color? Might the experiences of people who are most victimized by racial oppression shed light on corrective actions?

I am not saying that the truth always lies in one place or that there is only one angle of analysis. We are all called to put our truths on the table and be open to the spirit of new insights and possibilities. If we are to move forward together as an anti-oppressive multicultural faith, then we must be able to "care-front" one another. Such "carefrontation" isn't about personal bashing or needing to control one another; it is about creating a justice table where people's gifts, histories, pain, and perspectives can be honestly shared. It is about creating new ways of seeing, hearing, and being with one another. . . .

The white piety of "innocence" and the lack of awareness on the part of many whites of the brokenness of body and soul among peoples of color leave little room for initiating authentic conversations and for developing strategies that alleviate the conditions of racial oppression. Such ignorance works against the building of trust and undermines the depth of relationship necessary to eliminate oppression. It is critical to our religious conversations that we all recognize that the loss of wholeness within ourselves is disorienting, fragmenting, and debilitating for everyone. Goodness and right are not the exclusive property of whites, and grace is available for all. I join Parker in believing that theological reflection, remedial education, soul work, and engaged action are necessary ingredients in reshaping ourselves and our faith. However, I also believe that we must intentionally and systematically dismantle the structures that create and maintain racist oppression. . . . We must have an angle of analysis that helps us to see and a faith that gives us the courage to do.

For **Susan Suchocki Brown,** Parker "is telling us that we must uncover, reveal, and name the sin of complicity and the implicit violence we engage in as we struggle with the issues of racism and oppression." She writes,

I believe that we must engage in this process as a prerequisite to attaining the beloved community—what Parker has called a "daring communion." It has been my experience that without the willingness to become vulnerable, open, and exposed to my lack of consciousness, my brokenness, and my alienation, I risk a spiritual incompleteness that leaves me, in Parker's words, "less present to life, more cut off, and less creative and loving." . . .

Human beings have an overwhelming drive to find that universal place called home. To many persons, safety, security, unquestioning love, and compassion define home. I assume that unquestioning love and compassion remain at least two of the foundational values for building and maintaining beloved community. Yet, we know that to become a beloved community—in fact, to become whole—we must sometimes take risks that *threaten* our security and safety. As Parker points out, to become whole, to break out of our isolated enclaves, to become able to be engaged in the struggle to transform our community's knowledge, we must become willing to engage in the spiritual practices of nonviolence and nonavoidance of conflict. I have learned that being engaged in this soul-transforming work also requires the need to be open to others' perspectives and the need to embrace and be willing to accept the possibility that I may be transformed while in the process of transforming. . . .

The Journey Toward Wholeness Transformation Committee has attempted to look at wholeness, beloved community, and dismantling racism through the lenses of diversity, justice, liberation, spirit, and faith. I recognize that a transformation has taken place when organizational structures, principles, policies, practices, programs, mission, and purpose encourage something new and perhaps unknown to come forth. When these structures foster and provide for authentic relationships of accountability, care, nurture, and sustenance of all, then we will be on the way to an anti-oppressive beloved community of justice grounded in the spiritual practices of presence, awareness, responsibility, and consciousness.

The Dialogue

Approaches to religious education, understandings of the self, and desires to "know about life" create a lively dialogue, as suggested by the following dialogue partners.

PETER MORALES: For the work of anti-racism, I love that image with which your paper begins, Rebecca, of being sealed off in the car and then getting out. This is an issue of religious education. I suspect too often we *tell* folks about what is outside the car, rather than helping them to *walk around* outside the car. I don't know how to help them do this, given the human and physical barriers in our churches, but I suspect that we have to help people get an *experience* of race to which to react. We have to *lure* them into new relationships. So I'd like to hear your thoughts on how we lure people "outside the car."

PARKER: Part of my proposal is for what I call the practice of engaged presence. This is an educational practice. It draws on the Freirian methodology,[10] and I think we ought to apply it at every level of educational practice in our churches. This educational practice begins with inquiry: OK, we notice that this thing is happening in our community and our world. For example, I live in Oakland, and it's possible to notice that in Oakland today, the injurious toxic waste sites are located in the poorest neighborhoods. So engaged presence through the church practice of education would mean first noticing that, and then asking: Why is this happening in our community? That initiates a learning process that requires direct investigation into one's neighborhood. An adequate direct investigation into what's happening in one's neighborhood will ultimately require a whole set of questions to be posed, especially if the aim of that investigation is to discover what would be the most appropriate and effective action or strategy that could be employed. So this educational practice begins with inquiry into what's happening in one's immediate neighborhood—which is always related to what's happening in the whole world—and then goes on to study and action in response to that. An ongoing cycle of this kind of engagement should be at the core of educational practice in our churches every year.

MARJORIE BOWENS-WHEATLEY: First of all, I want to thank you, Rebecca, for your paper; it really inspires me and gives us some helpful methodologies and approaches, which you call "steps in the conversation." One of those steps is remedial education, which I think is terribly important, and I find it a particularly challenging next step for people who are involved in this work. In working with our congregations, particularly those in isolated "bedroom communities," there is such an incredible ignorance of "the world"—of this country that we live in. We need approaches to help people understand that in spite of their graduate degrees and powerful positions and education, there is a whole area of life that they've lost. How do we help people, through religious education, to recapture part of that loss?

PARKER: I can tell you how I first got it that there were things that I didn't know. We were working on institutional change at Starr

King (School for the Ministry). We wanted the institution to become a more anti-oppressive, inclusive, just environment. In order to move forward on that hope, I invited to the school a group of people of color who had some relationship to the school, and I said, "Let's have a conversation about what you see could happen differently here." And Betty Freed Tuskine, who had been very active in the Black Empowerment movement in the 1960s, said, "If you want to work with us, you have to know our intellectual history." I knew *some* of that intellectual history, but I had had twenty years of formal education and no one had ever asked me to read a primary text from black intellectual history. No one had ever asked me to read a primary text from the Native American experience in the United States, the Asian American experience in the United States, the Latino or Latina experience in the United States. And I believed Betty when she said to me, "If you want to work with me"—and I did—"you have to know something about what *I* know so that we can work together." So that was the beginning of my remedial education—and by "remedial," I mean *remedying* education.

In some ways, there is nothing extraordinary about creating such remedial education; it's very straightforward. Unitarian Universalists, most of the ones I know in our churches, love to read. What if we created a fairly straightforward resource, a curriculum that I would propose we call *America*, which engages people in our congregations in reading Howard Zinn's *A People's History of the United States,* Ronald Takaki's *A Different Mirror,* and a selection of primary texts from African American intellectual history, from Latino and Latina experience, Hispanic experience, Native American experience, and Asian American experience? These should be texts that show a tremendous diversity of analysis of the U.S. context and a diversity of strategies about how to resist and survive in this culture. And they should not be just excerpts but *sustained* reading, in a setting where people can talk with each other about what comes up for them as they come to know this history. If we had such a curriculum, *in combination with* a church practice of engaged presence, I think it would create a synergy that would be transformative.

I also think that it would be very important that such study be conducted not in a context of "you stupid, ignorant people who do not know," but in a context of the idea that we inhabit a country, a land, in which if we are to live and grow fruitful, we have to continually deepen our world.

ELIZABETH ELLIS: My concern is about focusing on "your community" if your community is a place such as Lincoln or Concord or Lexington (Massachusetts). If you start by looking around at your community and getting to know the community, what do you find there that motivates you toward racial justice? After working with suburban churches for ten years or more, trying to engage them with urban issues, I'm very concerned about what motivation is really out there if your reality is this rich, comfortable suburb. What, then, is your motivation to be engaged in transforming yourself and the world?

PARKER: I do think our sense of neighborhood or community has to be large enough. I have to confess that throughout my life I have been terrified of the suburbs and have not been willing to live there. I think it would overwhelm me to be that isolated. So I don't know how people live there. As for ministers who are ministering there, I admire them and think they have a very difficult task.

What I hear in your question is this: How can we be motivated to work for racial justice if we can't *see* the suffering? I guess I'm trying to emphasize that those of us who are white need to ask ourselves: What is *our* life? What are *we* experiencing? I'm trying to speak of a dual motivation that is centered in a love for life, rather than just a compassionate concern for the suffering of others; it's a rebellious refusal to have your life constrained and destroyed. I'm trying to witness to the motivation that comes from the erotic lust for life. I think we have to find that *in ourselves,* rather than find it in the sufferer. So I think the spiritual task for those who are isolated is to find that *passion* for life, and I think churches are really important for creating a context for discovering or rediscovering that passion.

THANDEKA: My question focuses on the term *narcissism.* You suggest that European Americans have a problem with "narcissistic self-concern and with the loss of the public world." Mel asks: How can most whites not see? Now, there are two ways in which one can understand such a split in the psyche. One is Freudian, which is a very rationalistic psychology. In Mel Hoover's paper, we find the rationalistic response: There must be education; whites must act a certain way. So he leads with what *ought* to be done. But this way of understanding does not address the issue of what *can* be done.

The other standpoint is that of Wieman, the intersubjective perspective, which can be traced to the intersubjectivists in self-psychology. This standpoint begins with the understanding of the narcissistic injuries split within the self, "a walling up" so that the affect must be attended to, because the wall, while intact, can prevent the organism from stepping forward. I'm unclear in your language, Rebecca, as to whether you are taking the Freudian rationalist approach, or are you leaning to intersubjective post-Freudian analysis, recognizing narcissistic injuries as walled-off affect?

PARKER: I side with the intersubjective tradition! And to just say a little bit more about that, I do not regard what I was attempting to do in this paper as a baring of my sins, as Susan may have thought. I am not confessing sin here, nor am I saying that the ignorance that I observe in my life is a moral failing to be corrected by a moral commitment. The ignorance that I experienced is about a loss of soulfulness, and it includes not only a silencing of affect but a silencing of the senses.

What I mean by narcissism is the wound that happens when the community that reflects one back to oneself does not reflect back the wholeness of the self, and when one's desire for membership in community then leads one essentially to silence aspects of the self in order to maintain participation. This is not a "sin" but a fundamental life longing.

THANDEKA: I would encourage us Unitarian Universalists, when we do theology, to reflect on the psychological presuppositions that lie behind the analysis of the self. If we do not do this, we will end up with a rationalistic approach to a broken self that confounds our own thought.

ANITA FARBER-ROBERTSON: Mel talks about wholeness being lost. Susan talks about moving toward wholeness. Is wholeness something we begin with, and then it is dismantled and should be reconfigured? Or is wholeness part of a process toward which we grow? I'm not sure why this is important to me, but I think it is. Have we construed or misconstrued innocence as what wholeness looks like? When I think of how children develop their full humanity as they build relationships and as they understand—or don't—the world in which they move and select a place in it to grow, this suggests to me that wholeness is something we *grow into*, that it isn't fully there when we begin our life.

PARKER: One of my main points is that in white theology, we have misconstrued innocence as wholeness. The way the Garden story has been interpreted—or one of the ways—has contributed to that. My friend Rita Nakashima Brock says that in her experiences in Asian America, the innocence of children is respected but not admired, not aspired to; that the child's beginning place in the world is respected, but it doesn't become an image that adults aspire to. What adults aspire to is wisdom, which is an ability to be *aware* of the world.

Our capacity to be aware is constructed. So my concern is what kind of knowledge are we constructing, what kind of feeling are we constructing. I think our feelings are constructed; I think our sexuality is constructed; I think our ideas and even our imagination are constructed. So the educational task is always a question of how do we relate to one another in such a way that our constructions are serving life rather than constraining it? There are multiform ways that we can think and feel, and multiple cultures can serve life; there's not just one form of life-serving culture. There is space for creativity and for multiple cultural expressions. The critical question is what serves life, which means that to form an educational practice or a theology, we have to have wisdom about life itself—and by *life*, I really mean "living things," which means not only human beings but other living things.

KEN OLIFF: And that's a wonderful way to pose my question: I want to know about life! [The group laughs.] I'm really struck and encouraged by what you're saying about life. I think it's a central theological category in dealing with oppression. I like what you've done in connecting it to citizenship. In my opinion, citizenship is being present to and embracing the fullness of life in the place in which we live. But is life itself a constructed category? In the present reality, do we experience life directly?

PARKER: Yes, we are alive! [More laughter] We have constructed *theories* about life, but I would not say that *life* is constructed—not in the same way that I am using "constructed." I really want to respond to what you said about wanting to know about life, because that's exactly the want. My question is: How badly do you want it? [Laughter] I mean that! I want to know about life, and I want to live. And I want *you* to live. I think if we can stay with those elemental desires, not abandon them, and not let anybody take that desire away from us, then life will be served.

PATRICIA JIMENEZ: I'm fond of telling people that I have a particularly skewed view of the world because I see all the stabbings and the shootings and the heart attacks and the strokes and the neurological diseases and the aneurysms, and I see people struggling to live, *just to live,* and I see them struggling. So when you say, "We want to know life," I think, "That's it! That's the bottom line!" Thank you.

GEORGE TINKER: This question of whether we have a "loss of world" or are part of a process that is "growing toward wholeness" is already rooted in that systemic whole—that *language foundation*—that makes North American culture and society what they are today. It is based on a temporal view of the world; in fact, the European philosophical-social structure is *committed* to a temporal view of the world, and out of that view come the concepts of progress, of development—whether it's economic progress or moral progress—and the more dangerous side of that, I suspect, is to convert notions of economic progress into notions of moral progress.

I come from a world in which *spatiality* is much more important, *place* is important. In that context, we talk about reclaiming balance at any and every time in the existence of the people. In *this* moment in the world, in North America—but not just North America, it's now become a globalized reality—we're dealing with the destruction of balance, the consistent, persistent destruction of balance. This is our common history, whether we are oppressed, racialized "others" or those who are in the center of power, those who have been racialized as well, who have racialized *themselves* as "white."

Reclaiming balance is something we American Indians did with ceremony. We had specific ceremonies for re-establishing balance in the world. But our ceremonies were not prepared to deal with the advent of modernity and the beginning of the conquest, and now we're pretty far down the line with this destruction of balance. It's not a matter of growing toward wholeness; it's a matter of restoring balance for all of us in North America and in the world. We're clearer and clearer in the Indian world that we are responsible in one sense for our own well-being but we can't recover that until my mother's people, our white brothers and sisters, begin some serious engagement in a healing process that is focused on restoring balance.

PARKER: Though I have spoken about "loss of world," the underpinning of my thinking is a Whiteheadian metaphysic in which I understand *every* being to experience the whole of time and space every moment. When I say that we've lost the world, what I mean is we have disconnected from our experience. Just as Thich Nhat Hanh would say that it's possible to manifest enlightenment at this moment, the possibility of being with the wholeness of what we experience is present every moment. But I would not call that "wholeness," I would call that the fullness of life. The fullness of life is with us always; the question is: Are we with *it?*

Study Questions

1. Rebecca Parker vividly illustrates how she and others have been educated into denial and cultivated into ignorance about racism, resulting in "apathy, passivity, and compliance." Using "white theology" as an illustration, Parker argues that "goodness is aligned with innocence and ignorance" and that "we have misconstrued innocence as wholeness." Is the phenomenon that Parker describes familiar to you? If so, how have you seen it manifested?

2. After a brief period of reflection, discuss how compartmentalized thinking—"splitting of mind, body, and soul"—or any

kind of psychosocial alienation or fragmentation has affected your own experience of racism or the experience of someone you know.

3. Parker asserts that compartmentalized thinking "teaches that a social structure in which one is abundantly provided for is not to be questioned," that it is a "gift from God." Does this assessment ring true for you? To what extent do you think that classical theology—whether doctrinal teachings, biblical interpretation, or tradition—has shaped our cultural self-understanding with regard to racism and other forms of oppression? How does such thinking affect how we think about privilege and the relationship between race and class?

4. Starting with James Baldwin's accusation, Rebecca Parker asserts that many whites (Unitarian Universalist and others) "don't know and don't want to know" that they have been mis-educated about the history and culture of Native Americans, African Americans, Asian Americans, and Latinas/os, and have therefore been complicit in oppressing these groups. She considers such cultivation of ignorance a form of cultural violence. What remedies does Parker offer?

5. Parker contends that social patterns in the United States often lead to isolation, and that such isolation dulls our view of what it means to be a citizen. This pattern, she says, exonerates us from responsibility and may be a precondition for violence. From *your* perspective, what is the relationship between isolation and violence as it relates to racism? Does your neighborhood or community support getting to know people of a different racial/ethnic background or does it support isolation and ignorance of others? After reviewing what Parker means by *citizen* (and *citizenship*), consider the factors that are most critical in leading people to make different choices about building more diverse communities and more fully claiming citizenship in the country in which they live.

6. Parker outlines four spiritual disciplines that can lead us out of isolation and ignorance into deeper engagement of the context in which we live and with people who are different from ourselves. What are these disciplines? Have you engaged in any of these disciplines? If so, what differences have you

noticed in your own spiritual life? Have you witnessed change
or transformation in the lives of others?

7. Parker speaks of (and offers an example of) engaged presence
   as an educational practice. What would "engaged presence"
   look like in your church or community? Beyond a "compassionate concern for the suffering of others," how can we more
   fully embrace what Parker understands as the educational and
   spiritual tasks of embracing life more fully? Why does Parker
   believe that life and citizenship need to be claimed more fully?
   Why, in Parker's view, is having a passion for "life itself" or
   "an erotic lust for life" so important in the work of anti-
   racism? What can our congregations and our religious movement do to create such a context?

8. George Tinker says that our task is not so much "growing
   toward wholeness" but "restoring balance." What does restoring balance and wholeness have to do with racism? How does
   American Indian thought address this dilemma? How does
   the worldview of your family, culture, or community address
   the need to restore balance?

Conclusions

✍

The following briefly represents some of the observations from the participant-observers to the consultation.

- Robette Dias feels that it is important to acknowledge the centrality of worldview and the context for its development in human beings. She is disappointed that there was no articulation of how evil came into our world (in Unitarian Universalism and the larger world), specifically, the evil manifested as colonialism, racism, sexism, and heterosexism.

- Bill Gardiner says that in doing our theological work, it is important to have some understanding of the historical roots of our collusion with racism. He recommends two books that focus on the impact of our Puritan heritage: *The Name of War: King Phillip's War and the Origins of American Identity* by Jill Lepore and *Seeds of Racism in the Soul of America* by Paul Griffin.

- Susan Leslie observes that it is a continuing challenge to remain focused on theology versus sociology, and she appreciates that participants took "risks of faith" in looking at the theological implications of where oppression is located.

- Victor Lewis believes that the failure of empathy is intimately related to the question of self-understanding. "Perhaps we have no obligation to become experts in an oppression that is not our own," he says.

There were many recommendations for "next steps" in our anti-racism work, including multi-vocal calls to widen the horizon of participants in the conversation, and the following summary thoughts about the direction that future anti-racism work might take:

- We need to move in more than one direction to "stretch our collective souls." The systemic work of anti-racism is as important as "the personal work that has to do with healing." Our work needs to include both of these perspectives.

- We need to believe in the people in our pews, and that we are called to love them.

- We need more structured conversations among both clergy and laity, and creative ways to companion both clergy and laity. Specifically, the Unitarian Universalist Ministers Association should explore more deeply what forms ministry might take in engaging ministers and congregants in the work of anti-racism. And we need to hear the perspectives of youth, young adults, Diverse and Revolutionary Unitarian Universalist Multicultural Ministries, and Latina and Latino voices.

- Covenant groups are taking root in hundreds of our congregations. These groups are a natural way to link praxis and reflection.

- "There are some theological concepts that are absolutely essential" to inform our anti-racism work. In particular, we need to explore incarnational theologies (how we are relational), a theology of evil, and a theology of culture. The on-line *Journal of Liberal Religion* invites such exploration as a way to continue the work that has begun here.

- We need to encourage Unitarian Universalists to engage with whatever sources of community feed their souls.

- Beyond the bureaucracy of the UUA, we need a "stylistic change" that reflects "more openness and lightness" in the work.

- "The UUA should think less about training and more about educational practice."

- The UUA Religious Education Department (now Lifespan Faith Development) should develop more anti-racism resources for youth and more material to assist people in moving beyond their own contexts and worldviews. The UUA should also consider how to make study and resource materials "more God-friendly and Christian-friendly."

- Rebecca Parker's idea of a curriculum called *America* should be developed.

- We need to be informed by more people who are not part of our faith tradition, specifically to examine anti-racism programs "that are bottom-up."

- We need an internal critique of how an objective and rational approach to anti-racism work with Unitarian Universalism is perceived by the community at large.

- The consultation was referred to as "the justice table," but it needs to become more just with greater attention to language, to our various identities, and to "our inadvertent exclusions."

- The message of Universalism is central and life-giving for anti-racism work. "We need to see things in a truly universal perspective that has to do with all oppression."

- We might broaden our theological palate to include *womanist* perspectives as well as Native American, Asian, and other liberation theologies.

- Contextualizing the work through case studies might help us to focus our attention on what we are called to do.

- We need to read material that pushes us onward and helps us to break the silence.

- We need to listen more to the stories without sharing or responding.

- It would be a good idea to hold a consultation on models of the self.

- We should "ask congregations as well as associate and affiliate organizations that have not participated in anti-racism what would put anti-racism on their radar screens."

Creating Partnerships for Anti-racist Action

SUSAN LESLIE

As the preceding chapters have made clear, anti-racism work presents an opportunity for spiritual transformation powerful enough to eliminate the devastating violence and oppression of systems of domination based on race, ethnicity, and culture. Anti-racist partnerships offer a home base for this work—a spiritual and political foundation that provides opportunities for collaboration and accountability. Thus, creating partnerships can be a formative spiritual task. In addition to exerting greater influence on political issues and creating more equitable conditions in our communities, partnerships help to create new relationships. They require all parties to share and redistribute power within the alliance while simultaneously working for change on a broader scale.

Unitarian Universalists and other liberal religionists can do many things in the struggle against racism. We can

- work for reparations and affirmative action;
- work to reform the criminal justice system that maintains the oppression of impoverished people and communities of color;
- defend public education;
- support living wage campaigns;
- oppose toxic dump sites in oppressed communities;

- work to reduce infant mortality rates among those who have been historically marginalized because of race, ethnicity, or culture;

- promote greater learning about the history, experience, and perspectives of American Indians, Latinos/Latinas, African and Caribbean Americans, Pacific Islanders, and others; and

- transform our own congregations and institutions by applying an anti-racist lens to the structure and content of our worship services, religious education programs, membership process-es, leadership recruitment, social justice work, and how we spend our money.

To do this work most effectively, however, we need to work in partnership with people and communities of color and cultures that have historically been marginalized.

The transformative power of partnerships: As members of a large-ly European American (or white) denomination, Unitarian Univer-salists must reach across racial barriers to ensure an anti-oppressive multicultural approach to social change. To do otherwise increas-es the probability that we will participate in paternalistic service-oriented efforts—whites "helping the underprivileged" rather than creating self-determining alliances for systemic change in the relationship between privileged and marginalized groups. As we work for social change, partnerships require us to behave in anti-racist and anti-oppressive ways; and in this way, they keep all par-ties accountable. In faith terms, such partnerships are at the heart of creating a Beloved Community.

Creating anti-racist partnerships: How do we go about creating anti-racist and anti-oppressive partnerships? In much the same way that we go about developing any relationship: We move from identifying mutual interests and getting to know each other to developing trust and engagement with each other's lives. First we need to identify what relationship we wish to have with our com-munities. From whom are we divided? Whom would we like to get to know? Whose organizing efforts would we support? What are our mutual concerns? What alliances do we need? Once we have answered these questions, the next step is to initiate a conversation.

There is no limit to the ways partnerships can be structured or the number of parties in the partnership. Partnerships can be initiated between church or community organizations; between ministers; by social justice committees; through congregational visits; or in community meetings. They can be within the same community, between urban and suburban areas, regional or national. As in other relationships, attending to partners' needs—such as discussing the social context as well as more basic issues like food and day care—are helpful. Regardless of who the partners are, it is important to bring spirit to the gathering. Successful efforts have begun with theological or spiritual reflection, in which participants share their most heartfelt values and—through theological reflection—consider how these values translate into social change *as a statement of faith.* Many congregations and local grassroots organizations would welcome allies that can ultimately strengthen the potential for change.

Being good allies and knowing where we stand: Any alliance that reaches across race, class, and other boundaries must be critically aware of power and privilege. To be a strong ally is to be conscious of privilege and how it influences our worldview. Many of us make assumptions both about people and about systems— particularly about how change happens. Being a good ally means using one's privilege within the group—whether it is connections to the media, influence with legislatures, skills we possess, or other resources—to create access and opportunities for the collective interests of the partnership.

Too often we create our own projects based on what we think is needed rather than assessing what already exists, offering support, and entering into mutual work. Such collaborative work is an accountable and spiritual approach, and it can lead to deeper and more genuine relationships. Good partnership work means respecting the leadership of people of color and other disenfranchised groups. It means letting those who have been historically marginalized set the agenda. It means listening.

Confronting barriers to building community: As the anti-oppression movement expands and people begin to look at issues of power, privilege, and oppression, a community is emerging that has the potential to build bridges. Positive results can best be assured, however, through perseverance and training. Anti-oppressive partnerships allow people to discuss identity differences and to confront power differentials honestly and openly. In the past, coalitions have disintegrated over issues of racism, classism, homophobia, and sexism—largely because coalition partners were unwilling to explore these barriers. When conflict occurs in a partnership (as it inevitably will), developing strong conflict management skills will strengthen the alliance and create a learning environment. Conflict may focus on identity or cultural difference—for example, male/female, Latino/African American, straight/gay. Or it can manifest in other ways, such as acting without the group's authority, taking disproportionate "space" or "air time," expressing assumptions about others, harboring illusions about how systems operate, or resisting new solutions.

To build strong partnerships, leaders need to be sure all voices are heard and give particular attention and training to those who have not yet found their voice, as well as to those who have not yet learned the skill of active listening. Skilled facilitators are needed to build strong partnerships, and it may be necessary to introduce a behavior covenant at the beginning of a new initiative. Many organizations work on two tracks, wherein anti-racism and anti-oppression training is offered for middle-class white folks along with leadership training for people who have historically been marginalized. It may be useful to encourage or require participation in anti-racism and anti-oppression training as a prerequisite for partnerships.

Rapid response and long-term sustainability: Strong partnerships are able to swing into gear quickly around crisis issues such as hate crimes or police murder, when it is necessary to speak out and minister to victims, while working to change fundamental inequities. Building ongoing relationships rather than undertaking one-time projects is an important key to success and sustainability. These long-term relationships serve as a bulwark against attempts to divide communities from one another through fear tactics. Attempts to stereotype or falsely portray whole communities might be subverted.

Build community and social change will follow: When we develop intentional partnerships, we are well on the way to building community. Once relationship is established and mutual trust is developed, however, a variety of issues will emerge. With strong organizing, there is greater potential for both social change and a deeper sense of shared community. Being in partnership is about commitment—being in it together for the long haul, making mistakes, analyzing defeats, celebrating victories, and staying in relationship. A group might, for example, begin with a small educational forum and grow to the point where it can leverage change in town, state, and, eventually, national budgets for a more equitable allocation of resources. Thus, the group can influence public policy. It's about taking risks, and transforming ourselves as we work to change the world.

One congregation's story: After identifying racism as one of the most pressing issues, a group of members and friends of the UU Fellowship of Clemson, South Carolina, formed an Unlearning Racism Committee. In addition to exploring racism within the fellowship, steps were taken to move toward multiculturalism and greater involvement with the community. The Committee sponsored a project called "Approach to Strengthening Cross-Cultural Relationships." Their next step was to develop a partnership with a multicultural Baha'i Assembly congregation. The relationship began with small monthly meetings, alternately facilitated by each group, followed by two community-wide video screening and discussion projects: "The Color of Fear" and "The Way Home." Other topics were chosen to allow participants to learn something about each other's faiths. Joint events and celebrations were organized. Then a community project arose that included the production of what became a nationally acclaimed documentary of the untold experiences of people of color in World War II. Working together on these projects, the partnership then joined a statewide coalition and national campaign to remove the Confederate flag from the South Carolina State House.

Other anti-racist partnerships involving Unitarian Universalist congregations: Several UU congregations are working in partnership with other churches and community organizations through interfaith networks that organize in oppressed communities. Others are partnering with the NAACP, YMCAs, YWCAs, schools, and grassroots community groups. Some are participating in coalitions that advocate for affirmative action, gay marriage rights, affordable housing, and economic justice, including the living wage campaign.

The UU Church of Savannah, Georgia, for example, helped found the interracial Interfaith Community in 1993 following the Thomas Jefferson District's Dismantling Racism conference. In addition to bringing diverse communities of Savannah together, the coalition sponsored several community events on racism and introduced anti-racism curricula into the schools. One of their current projects involves working with local artists to install a statue of an enslaved family in the downtown riverside area (Savannah has no statues depicting people of color).

A few UU congregations are organizing against racial profiling— among them, First Unitarian Congregational Society in Brooklyn, New York; May Memorial UU Society in Syracuse, New York; and First UU Church of Houston, Texas (which also sponsored a service for reconciliation when James Byrd was murdered). The UU Church of Reading, Massachusetts, expanded its Racism Awareness Group to a town-wide organization after a police racial profiling incident. This group participated in the selection process for a new police chief and now meets monthly, sponsors community dialogue groups, and urges town employees to attend.

The What Color Is Community? Task Force of the UU Church of Bloomington in Indiana has been working on a joint study with the NAACP to document racial profiling in arrest and sentencing patterns in Monroe County, to publicize the findings, and to help create solutions to end this practice. The Task Force held its second annual Martin Luther King Day program at the Wabash Valley Correctional Facility, is sponsoring discussions on reparations for African Americans, and is studying *The Debt: What America Owes to Blacks* by Randall N. Robinson.

In Connecticut, an interfaith partnership emerged—Congregations United for Racial Equality and Justice. It includes several UU congregations, an African Methodist Episcopal church, and a Baptist church, which have come together to build community and address issues of racism together in the Greater Hartford area. In Norwich, a partnership formed by the UU congregation helped one of its members (an African American woman) get elected to the city council and—in order to support her—helped four of its members get elected to the town Democratic Committee. All five candidates ran on the anti-racist ticket!

In March of 2001, the Journey Toward Wholeness Transformation Committee (appointed by the Unitarian Universalist Association Board to monitor and guide our anti-oppression, anti-racist multicultural initiative) wrote to all UU congregations asking them to report on their anti-racism efforts and activities and to provide information on anti-racism/anti-oppression resources and their needs. Responses from over fifty congregations revealed a broad range of activities. Based on the responses, we learned that active engagement with the surrounding community, when undertaken in partnerships, involves the greatest degree of transformation. Some highlights follow.

The Anti-racism Working Group of First Unitarian Church of Wilmington, Delaware, was designated as an official committee of the church with line budget support to do strategic planning for participation in the Unitarian Universalist Association Journey Toward Wholeness initiative. Four anti-racism forums were held that reflected on what the church could do to address racism. The culminating event was a major forum with all seven African American state judges gathering (for the first time) to discuss racism in the criminal justice system. The sanctuary was overflowing; the event received wide press coverage and sparked much interest and debate. All the judges called for statewide review. The church is at the center of these efforts in partnership with Stand Up for What's Right and Just, a community group fighting crime, racial profiling, and mandatory minimum prison sentences.

Mountain Light Unitarian Universalist Church in Ellijay, Georgia, was welcomed into the Unitarian Universalist Association of Congregations in June of 2000. By August, this new congregation had held its first Journey Toward Wholeness Sunday and begun using the curriculum *Weaving the Fabric of Diversity* as a resource for interactive, intergenerational, lay-led worship services. Two public meetings were held featuring Native American elders who spoke on the theme "Healing the Family Circle." These events brought church members and Native American residents together, leading to both collaboration and accountability. Together, they have begun to actively support a local food pantry; sponsor a Parents, Families and Friends of Lesbians and Gays group; establish special parking for the differently-abled; and add pictures of people of color to the walls of their religious education space.

The Journey Toward Wholeness Committee of the UU Church of Cheyenne, Wyoming, partnered with Love and Charity, an African American women's service organization, and the school to offer anti-racism programming during Black History Month to fifty classes. Programs included videos and discussions on prejudice and racism, re-enactments of Martin Luther King's "I Have a Dream" speech, visits with Buffalo soldiers, African American art tours, talks on African American and Cheyenne history, and an opportunity to hear folktales and view African art. Teachers were given packets with follow-up discussion suggestions, interactive ideas, and bibliographies. The week of classes culminated in a community-wide gospel extravaganza on Friday night and an all-day Saturday celebration featuring African dance, art, history, food, and music. The trust and relationship that were developed among church members, Love and Charity, the teachers, the children, and the parents had a transforming effect in the work to dismantle racism. Future steps include a community-wide weekend workshop that will bring together people from the African American, Latino/Latina, Native American, and European American communities. "Miracle in Cheyenne" will be a General Assembly 2002 workshop, and a fuller account of this story will appear in the next issue of the UUMA News, the bi-annual newsletter of the Unitarian Universalist Ministers Association.

In Idaho, the Social Action Committee of the Boise Unitarian Universalist Fellowship is working with a large coalition to gain the minimum wage for farm workers—the majority of whom are Mexican American. In the course of this work, members of the congregation have struggled to learn about "the food on our tables," to fast in solidarity with the farm workers, and "to learn more about different people and the needs in our community."

In Ohio, members of Cincinnati's Northern Hills Fellowship and the First Unitarian Church of Cincinnati led their congregations' efforts in seeking reconciliation with the Carter family and the black community following the churches' exclusion of Rev. W. H. G. Carter, an African American Unitarian minister. Rev. Carter was pastor of the storefront Church of the Unitarian Brotherhood in Cincinnati from 1918 through the 1930s. A reconciliation weekend was held in January 2001 with area congregations. Since then, the two congregations have continued their partnership in addressing issues of racism in Cincinnati.

These reports demonstrate both commitment to and engagement with the Journey Toward Wholeness, as well as a variety of ways the program can include spiritual, political, social, and educational dimensions of congregational life. Other reported activities include the following:

- community organizing in coalitions around housing, education, poverty, and crime;

- community interfaith dialogue groups on racism and oppression, using videos such as "The Color of Fear" and other resources to explore barriers in deeply divided communities;

- co-sponsoring racism awareness programs in the schools;

- Martin Luther King Birthday Sunday Services and participation in Martin Luther King community events;

- active involvement in coalitions to abolish the death penalty;

- donations to community groups working to prevent racialized violence;

- money and volunteers for after-school programs; and

- integration of anti-oppression, anti-racism, and multiculturalism—especially the issue of unearned privilege—into social action and religious education programs and activities.

Many of the respondents reported using resources produced by the Unitarian Universalist Association, including curricula such as *Weaving the Fabric of Diversity* and *The Welcoming Congregation*. Others have attended Creating a Jubilee World workshops or sponsored a Journey Toward Wholeness Sunday to raise awareness and open a dialogue. Because of these and other initiatives, many reported increased attendance at anti-racist programming for both children and adults. Still other respondents reported using resources such as training by the People's Institute for Survival and Beyond (especially for teenagers); the National Coalition Building Institute; Visions, Inc.; and Teaching Tolerance. Journey Toward Wholeness committees and other lay leaders are organizing their own activities, including programs such as "Preparing for the Journey" seminars, "Creating an Inclusive Church Community," "How Racism Hurts White People," and "Open Hearts, Open Doors."

Respondents sent in wonderfully moving sermons, stories, and articles that involved personal, congregational, and community transformation on the journey. Reflecting a growing understanding of the linkages of oppression, some congregations reported that they have incorporated both anti-racism and anti-homophobia into their mission statements or in the welcome during Sunday worship services; others reported that they have begun to explore multicultural worship styles.

Finding partners: When you are ready, there are many potential anti-racist partner organizations, both Unitarian Universalist and community-based. For example, the UU Service Committee's Just Works program sponsors several urban community organizing projects as well as partnerships with indigenous people. The Unitarian Universalist Association's congregational services staffing group can recommend organizations and coalitions that UU congregations might work with throughout the United States. Grant-giving institutions such as the UU Funding Panel and the Unitarian Universalist Veatch Program can also recommend worthy organizations for potential anti-racist partnership initiatives. Churches, community organizations, health centers, and tenant groups may also offer partnership linkages. In many communities activists working on issues of racism often welcome the support and involvement of allies.

Resources
for Anti-racism
Work

Susan Leslie

⌒

The endnotes offer significant resources for those who would like to engage in additional reading and study. In addition, the following resources may be helpful in understanding the complexities explored within these pages.

Books

"Anti-racism as a Spiritual Practice," by Dorothy Emerson, in *Everyday Spiritual Practice*, Scott Alexander, ed. (Boston: Skinner House Books, 1999).

    A Unitarian Universalist minister invites readers to consider anti-racist engagement as a personal spiritual discipline and shares her personal experiences.

Bridging the Class Divide and Other Lessons for Grassroots Organizing by Linda Stout (Boston: Beacon Press, 1996).

    In clear, direct language, Linda Stout, founder of the Piedmont Peace Project, recounts the story and sums up the lessons of building an extraordinary alliance across racial and class lines that succeeded in bringing about major public policy changes in spite of opposition from entrenched politicians and terrorism from the Ku Klux Klan. This book is particularly helpful for white middle-class activists struggling to be good allies to low-income people and communities of color.

Why Are All the Black Kids Sitting Together in the Cafeteria? And Other Conversations About Race, by Beverly Daniel Tatum (New York: Basic Books, 1997).

This highly readable book begins with an examination of race by exploring the complexity of identity. This approach opens the door to how to *talk* about race. Tatum frames racism as a system of advantage based on race, a definition that she believes is more useful than "prejudice plus power" (commonly used by anti-racist trainers) because of the relative powerlessness that many white people feel. Nevertheless, Tatum insists that we must understand *institutional* racism. In addition to providing a cogent analysis, this book has a wonderful resource guide on getting started that is chock-full of annotated resources as well as a bibliography. For Unitarian Universalists, this book provides a bridge to some of the lively conversations within our movement around race and class, "the power analysis," and Thandeka's book *Learning to Be White: Money, Race, and God in America.*

Periodicals

ColorLines: Race, Culture, Action. This magazine regularly features stories of anti-racist partnerships and how they are working to dismantle racism in their communities. It also recommends resources and provides reflections on current racial issues. Published by the Applied Research Center. To subscribe, call 1-888-458-8588.

Faith in Action: News and Resources for Unitarian Universalists Working for Justice, vol. 4, nos. 1 and 2. These issues offer guidance on building partnerships, stories, and promising anti-racism practices from Unitarian Universalist congregations. Originally published by the Unitarian Universalist Association Faith in Action Department. For information on how to obtain this newsletter, contact the UUA Congregational Services Staffing Group at (617) 948-4265.

Journey Toward Wholeness News. A Unitarian Universalist Association cyber newsletter published every six weeks, this on-line publication features stories from Unitarian Universalist congregations and organizations about their efforts to build anti-oppressive justice-making congregations and communities. Also includes forthcoming workshops and other resources. To subscribe, send an e-mail to www.uua.org/mailman/listinfo/jtwnews.

The Latino/a Condition: A Critical Reader, ed. Richard Delgado and Jean Stefancic (New York: New York University Press, 1988)
In this anthology, a group of legal scholars, immigration lawyers, cultural critics, creative writers, and professionals respond to the void that exists when a group lacks the power of self-determination. The stories and essays gathered here—some legal and technical, some simple prose for lay readers—have in common an insistence on Latina and Latino self-definition. This collection is a basic primer of historical and sociocultural studies for Spanish-speaking people who come from the diverse culture of Latin America and the Caribbean. The book addresses questions about identity: whether *Latino* describes a race or an ethnicity; what the distinctions are between Latino, Hispanic, and Chicana/o. It also covers "the" Latina/o historical experience past and present, popular cultural stereotypes of "the silent minority"; the desirability and feasibility of Latino/a assimilation; conflict between Latinos/as and other cultural groups; and border theory and immigration—all within the context of language, power, and culture.

Other Resources

"From Exclusive to Inclusive: Signposts and Stages on the Continuum on Becoming an Anti-racist Multicultural Institution," by Jacqui James.
A typology and developmental tool that is useful in raising awareness and setting goals through which an institution can engage in the transformational process of becoming an anti-racist multicultural organization. Includes information about policies and practices of institutions at various stages of becoming anti-racist as well as attitudes and behaviors that inhibit or encourage an anti-racist stance and patterns of community involvement that range from *noblesse oblige* to restorative justice. Available from the Lifespan Faith Development staff group of the UUA. Call (617) 948-4361 to request a copy.

UUA Statements of Conscience and Resolutions on Race. *Social Justice Statements Handbook* available at www.uua.org, under the Commission on Social Witness link.

Anti-racism Inventory for UU Congregations and Organizations

Susan Leslie

∽

In addition to developing long-term anti-racist partnerships, ask yourselves the following questions:

- Are we engaging in socially responsible investing?

- Are we promoting affirmative action and diversity initiatives?

- Are we paying fair wages? Are we supporting the living wage campaign initiatives?

- Are we supporting efforts toward reconciliation and restorative justice?

- Have we reviewed all aspects of our congregational (or organizational) life with a view to noticing whether there are racial, institutional, or cultural barriers, or whether Eurocentric values or culture are dominant?

- Can people of color and Latinas/Latinos see their cultures reflected in the life of our congregation (or organization)?

- Does our congregation use its power to speak out against racism or to generate support for anti-racist initiatives?

- Has our congregation or organization noticed, documented, or opposed racial inequities in the criminal justice system and/or the application of the death penalty?

- Do we purchase from vendors who are engaged in equitable, anti-racist practices; for example, if we purchase coffee, is it from a farm cooperative or a member of Project Equality?

As we engage in building anti-racist partnerships, it is important to be intentional in building a strong sense of community, and to appreciate both the joy and complexity of new relationships. Theological reflection is important at every step. It may be as simple as asking questions like: How are we feeling? What are we learning? How are we changing? How can we go deeper, be more committed to transformative work? Alternatively, you might encourage your group to engage in a spiritual practice—such as journaling, meditation, or prayer—on an individual or collective basis. Blessings as you go about this sacred work.

Endnotes

〜

Introduction

1. The essay by William R. Jones included in this volume is not the same as the essay presented to participants prior to the consultation. However, the ideas presented are substantially the same and do not, in any significant way, affect the responses. Similarly, essays by George Tinker and Thandeka were edited substantially, but the changes do not significantly affect the responses.

2. Edward T. Hall, *The Silent Language* (New York: Anchor Press/Doubleday, 1973). Also see Edward T. Hall, *Beyond Culture* (New York: Anchor Press/Doubleday, 1977).

Theology's Great Sin: Silence in the Face of White Supremacy

1. Dietrich Bonhoeffer, *The Cost of Christian Discipleship* (New York: Macmillan, 1959), p. 79.

2. Cited in James H. Cone, *Martin and Malcolm and America: A Dream or a Nightmare* (Maryknoll, New York: Orbis Books, 1991), p. 315.

3. Cited in Peter Linebaugh and Marcus Rediker, *The Many-Headed Hydra: Sailors, Slaves, Commoners, and the Hidden History of the Revolutionary Atlantic* (Boston: Beacon Press, 2000), p. 17.

4. Eduardo Galeano, *Open Veins of Latin America: Five Centuries of the Pillage of a Continent* (London: Monthly Review Press, 1973), p. 50.

5. See Adam Hochschild, "Hearts of Darkness: Adventures of the Slave Trade," *San Francisco Examiner Magazine*, August 16, 1998, p. 13. This essay is an excerpt from his excellent book *King Leopold's Ghosts: A Story of Greed, Terror, and Heroism in Colonial*

Africa (New York: Houghton Mifflin, 1998). Louis Turner estimates that five to eight million were killed in the Congo. See his *Multinational Companies and the Third World* (New York: Hill and Wang, 1973), p. 27.

6. James Baldwin, *Nobody Knows My Name* (New York: Dell, 1967), p. 66.

7. Martin Luther King Jr., *Where Do We Go From Here: Chaos or Community?* (Boston: Beacon Press, 1967), p. 62.

8. "Conversation with Martin Luther King," *Conservative Judaism*, vol. 22, no. 3 (spring 1968), p. 8.

9. See the flyer *We Are Unitarian Universalists,* Unitarian Universalist Association, Boston, 1992; Suzanne Meyer, "The Curriculum of the Free Church," in *Unitarian Universalist Voice: An Independent Journal of News and Opinion* vol. 6, no. 3 (2000); "Racism: UUA Pounds Away at Structural Racism," *The World: The Journal of the Unitarian Universalist Association* vol. 14, no. 2 (March/April 2000).

10. Reinhold Niebuhr, *The Nature and Destiny of Man: A Christian Interpretation,* vol. 1 (New York: Charles Scribners, 1941), p. 282.

11. *Ibid.,* p. 226.

12. *Ibid.,* pp. 225–26.

13. Reinhold Niebuhr, "The Assurance of Grace," in *The Essential Reinhold Niebuhr: Selected Essays and Addresses,* ed. Robert M. Brown (New Haven: Yale, 1986), p. 65.

14. See *World,* op. cit. n. 9, p. 61.

15. Cited in Peter Goldman, "Malcolm X: Witness for the Prosecution," in John Hope Franklin and August Meier, eds., *Black Leaders of the Twentieth Century* (Urbana: University of Illinois Press, 1982), p. 315.

16. Malcolm X, "Unity Rally Speech," Harlem, NY, August 10, 1963.

17. See "Letters: Acts of Reparation" in *Christian Century,* December 6, 2000, p. 1283.

18. Excerpts from "Addresses at Lincoln Memorial During Capitol Civil Rights March," *The New York Times,* August 29, 1963.

19. The numbers regarding blacks teaching in divinity schools and at Union Seminary represent data as of January 2001.

20. Niebuhr, op. cit. n. 10, pp. 208, 209.

21. *The New York Times,* August 29, 1963.

22. See "Racism," op. cit., n. 9.

23. David Levering Lewis, *W. E. B. DuBois: The Fight for Equality and the American Century, 1919–1963* (New York: Henry Holt and Co., 2000), p. 43.

24. Dr. Delores S. Williams, a former student of Dr. Cone, is now Paul Tillich Professor of Theology and Culture and a professorial colleague of James Cone at Union Theological Seminary. She is the author of *Sisters in the Wilderness: The Challenges of Womanist God-Talk* (Maryknoll, NY: Orbis Books, 1993) and other scholarly works on womanist theology.

The Problem of Theology in the Work of Anti-racism: A Meditation

1. Reprinted in *A Testament of Hope: The Essential Writings and Speeches of Martin Luther King Jr.,* ed. James M. Washington (New York: HarperCollins, 1986, 1991).

2. Clayborne Carson, ed., *The Papers of Martin Luther King, Jr. vol. 1* (Berkeley, CA: University of California Press, 1992).

3. Charles Francis Potter. *Humanism: A New Religion* (New York: Simon and Schuster, 1930), p. 118.

4. Clarence Russell Skinner. *Worship and the Well Ordered Life* (Boston Universalist Historical Society, 1955).

5. Potter, p. 39.

6. Earl Morse Wilbur, *A History of Unitarianism: Socinianism and Its Antecedents* (Cambridge, MA: Harvard University Press, 1945), p. 208. It should be noted that in Wilbur's analysis, he relies on Theodore Parker's expression of what is essential in Unitarianism. However, Parker lists four elements: freedom, reason, tolerance, and action. See Henry H. Cheetham, *Unitarianism and Universalism* (Boston: Beacon Press, 1962), pp. 48–49.

7. César E. Chávez, *Education of the Heart: Quotes by César E. Chávez* (Keene, CA: César E. Chávez Foundation, 1995).

8. A. Powell Davies, *The Temptation to Be Good* (Washington, DC: All Souls Church Unitarian, 1952), p. 3.

Theology and Anti-racism: Latino and Latina Perspectives

1. Ismael Garcia quoted in Ada María Isasi-Díaz and Fernando F. Segovia, eds., *Hispanic/Latino Theology: Challenge and Promise* (Minneapolis, MN: Fortress Press, 1996), p. 304.

2. Renato Rosaldo, *Culture and Truth: The Remaking of Social Analysis* (Boston: Beacon Press, 1989), pp. 196–204.

3. William V. Flores and Rina Benmayor, *Latino Cultural Citizenship* (Boston: Beacon Press, 1997).

4. In Denis Lynn Daly Heyck, ed., *Barrios and Borderlands: Cultures of Latinos and Latinas in the United States* (New York: Routledge, 1994), p. 401.

5. This term is given to us by Cuban feminist theologian Ada María Isasi-Díaz, *Mujerista Theology* (Maryknoll, NY: Orbis Books, 1996), pp. 89, 103, n. 8.

6. If one assimilates culturally, then there is nothing of the original that remains. *Adaptation* suggests that an individual retains much of his or her own culture and is able to operate skillfully across cultures.

7. This element of Latino culture has no direct equivalent in the general culture of the United States. Combining stories, poems, songs, oral history, and allegories, it is similar to *heilsgeschichte* (biblical sacred history) and constantly evolves in the retelling. Each Latino nationality in the United States has their unique story, with a particular central theme (e.g., Mexicans—immigration; Puerto Ricans—statehood, independence, or commonwealth; Cubans—Castro and communism). See Heyck, *Barrios and Borderlands.*

The Other Side of Route Two: Some Autobiographical Struggles With Theology, Race, and Class

1. Audre Lorde, *The Black Unicorn* (New York: W. W. Norton, 1978).

2. "Stage Five" refers to institutions that are actively engaged in structural change. See Jacqui James, "From Exclusive to Inclusive: Signposts and Stages: Continuum on Becoming an Anti-Racist Multicultural Institution," available from the Lifespan Faith Devel-

opment staff group of the UUA. Call (617) 948-4361 to request a copy.

3. Rev. Joseph Tuckerman founded the Benevolent Fraternity of Unitarian Churches in 1826, now called the Unitarian Universalist Urban Ministry.

4. "E. B. White: Notes and Comments from His Down East Retreat," *New York Times,* July 11, 1969.

5. See Dalton Conley, *Being Black, Living in the Red: Race, Wealth, and Social Policy in America* (Berkeley, CA: University of California Press, 1999), and *Honky* (Berkeley, CA: University of California Press, 2000).

Racism and Anti-racism in a Culture of Violence: Dreaming a New Dream

1. In American Indian understandings of the world, the sacred always manifests itself as both male and female—in a variety of manifestations of the mysterious *one.*

2. Leslie Marmon Silko, *Ceremony* (New York: Penguin, 1977), p. 1.

3. David Wilkins and Vine Deloria Jr., *Tribes, Treaties and the U.S. Constitution* (Austin, TX: University of Texas Press, 2000).

4. Robert Williams. *The American Indian in Western Legal Thought: The Discourses of Conquest* (Oxford University Press, 1990), p. 1.

5. Jonathan Crush, in *Power of Development* (New York: Routledge, 1995), identifies the religious dimension of "development" language and draws a connection between development and redemption.

6. Felix S. Cohen, *Handbook of Federal Indian Law,* foreword by Harold L. Ickes; introduction by Nathan R. Margold (Washington, DC: U.S. Government Printing Office, 1942).

7. The situation in Canada is very similar. Note the recent news article "Native Suicides Hit High" *The Ottawa Sun,* November 21, 2000.

8. See Ward Churchill, *A Little Matter of Genocide: Holocaust and Denial in the Americas: 1492 to the Present* (San Francisco: City Lights, 1997).

9. Idealized and romanticized for contemporary Americans in the recent five-part PBS series *Lewis and Clark: The Journey of the Corps*

of Discovery, by Ken Burns (WETA, 1997). For an earlier critique of the use of media in this fashion to justify the colonial project that is America, see Elizabeth Cook-Lynn's essay "Why I Can't Read Wallace Stegner" in *Why I Can't Read Wallace Stegner and Other Essays: A Tribal Voice* (Madison: University of Wisconsin Press, 1996).

10. Neal Salisbury, *Manitou and Providence: Indians, Europeans, and the Making of New England* (New York: Oxford University Press, 1982), pp. 125–133.

11. Francis Jennings, *The Invasion of America: Indians, Colonialism, and the Cant of Conquest* (New York: Norton, 1975), pp. 202–227.

12. Michael Hardt and Antonio Negri, *Empire* (Cambridge: Harvard University Press, 2000), p. 46; Edward Auerbach, *Mimesis: The Representation of Reality in Western Literature,* trans. Willard Trask (Princeton, NJ: Princeton University Press, 1953).

13. Robert Warrior, "Canaanites, Cowboys and Indians: Deliverance, Conquest, and Liberation Theology Today," *Christianity and Crisis* 49 (1989): 261–265. See also the response to Warrior by William Baldridge in "Native American Theology: A Biblical Basis," *Christianity and Crisis* 50 (1990).

14. Albert Memmi, *The Colonizer and the Colonized* (Boston: Beacon Press, 1965), p. 89:

> In order for the colonizer to be a complete master, it is not enough for him to be so in actual fact, but he must also believe in its (the colonial system's) legitimacy. In order for that legitimacy to be complete, it is not enough for the colonized to be a slave, he must also accept his role. The bond between the colonizer and the colonized is thus destructive and creative. It destroys and recreates the two partners in colonization into the colonizer and the colonized. One is disfigured into the oppressor, a partial, unpatriotic and treacherous being, worrying about his privileges and their defense; the other into an oppressed creature, whose development is broken and who compromises by his defeat.

15. Bartolomé de las Casas, *History of the Indies* (New York: Harper and Row, 1971), vol. 3. Chapter 29 gives a vivid and devastating account of the massacre at Caonao.

16. Sherburne F. Cook and Woodrow Borah, *Essays in Population History* vol. 1, *Mexico and the Caribbean,* chapter 6 (Berkeley: University of California Press, 1971–79). It should be clearly noted,

upon reading Las Casas, that the Caribbean natives—the Arawak, Carib, and Tiano peoples—did not all die of diseases. Some of them died because of too high an iron concentration in their bellies—that is, on the point of a spear, or a sword, as Spanish soldiers bet with one another to see who could come closest to cutting a person in half with one swing of the sword. I apologize for the gory detail, but Las Casas is even more explicit and relates gory detail for hundreds of pages in his extensive writings.

17. George Tinker, "Columbus and Coyote: A Comparison of Culture Heroes in Paradox." *Apuntes* (1992): 78–88.

18 Nikhil Hemmedy has written a dissertation that argues for moving beyond a "preferential option for the poor" and toward a "preferential imperative" of the oppressed to take power into their own hands. For American Indians this might mean "acting" sovereign as opposed to merely asking for our sovereignty as nations to be recognized by an inherently racist U.S. government that dares not do so—because of the risk of great economic loss.

19. Ward Churchill has written a review of this movie, renaming it "Lawrence of South Dakota," in his *Fantasies of the Master Race: Literature, Cinema and the Colonization of American Indians,* rev. and expanded edition (San Francisco: City Lights, 1998), pp. 239–242.

20. George Tinker, *Missionary Conquest: The Gospel and Native American Genocide* (Minneapolis, MN: Fortress Press, 1993).

21. Michael Radu, "Ten Ways to Look at What Happened and What to Expect," Internet communication that was forwarded to me via e-mail, September 17, 2001. Radu's seventh point is: "Legislation has to be dramatically changed in Washington as well as Ottawa, Brussels, Strasbourg, and all the EU member states. If this war is to be won, the *European obsession with American death penalty legislation has to give way* to higher priorities, such as extraditing or putting down terrorists for good. The *politically correct campaign in Europe and the United States against "racial profiling" has to stop: after all, looking for tall, blond and blue-eyed persons in order to stop* Middle Eastern terrorism makes no sense" (emphasis added). Radu is a senior fellow at the Foreign Policy Research Institute, specializing in the study of revolutionary/terrorist groups worldwide.

22. Designed blindness is an action-science term first coined by Chris Argyris and Donald Schon in *Theory in Practice: Increasing Your Personal Effectiveness* (San Francisco: Jossey-Bass, 1974).

Action science was developed to understand how it is that skilled people, as they function in institutions and corporations, fail to learn from their errors. See also Anita Farber-Robertson, *Learning While Leading: Increasing Your Effectiveness in Ministry* (Bethesda, MD: Alban Institute, 2000).

23. "Just Works" is a program of the Unitarian Universalist Service Committee (UUSC).

24. Tinker, op. cit. n. 20.

Reclaiming Our Prophetic Voice: Liberal Theology and the Challenge of Racism

1. Cornel West, *Prophetic Fragments: Illuminations of the Crisis in American Religion and Culture* (Grand Rapids, MI: W. B. Eerdmann's, 1988), p. ix.

2. See Paul B. Rasor, "The Self in Contemporary Liberal Religion: A Constructive Critique," *Journal of Liberal Religion* 1, no. 1 (1999), especially part III. *The Journal of Liberal Religion* is published online by the Meadville Lombard Theological School, www.meadville.edu/jlr.

3. William R. Hutchison, *The Modernist Impulse in American Protestantism* (Cambridge: Harvard University Press, 1976), p. 2; H. Richard Niebuhr, *Christ and Culture* (New York: Harper and Row, 1951), chapter 3.

4. James Luther Adams, *On Being Human Religiously*, ed. Max Stackhouse (Boston: Beacon Press, 1976), p. 5.

5. See Paul Rasor, "The Christian Challenge to Unitarian Universalism," *The Unitarian Universalist Christian* 53 (1998): 13–23.

6. Niebuhr, op. cit. n. 3, p. 84.

7. West, op. cit. n. 1, p. ix.

8. See H. Richard Niebuhr, *The Social Sources of Denominationalism* (New York: Holt, 1929), esp. chapter four.

9. Parker J. Palmer, *The Promise of Paradox: A Celebration of Contradictions in the Christian Life* (Washington, DC: The Servant Leadership School, 1993), p. 26. See also Sharon Welch's analysis of the class ideology that lies at the root of what she calls the "cul-

tured despair of the middle class," in *A Feminist Ethic of Risk* (Minneapolis, MN: Fortress Press, 1990), p. 15.

10. Cook is speaking primarily of black-white race relations, but the larger issues he raises apply as well to all forms of race- and ethnicity-based oppression (as well as gender-based oppression) that constitute our colonial-patriarchal legacy: enslavement of Africans, genocide of aboriginal peoples, systematic disempowerment of Latinos/Latinas, conscription and internment of Asians, and more. We have a lot of unfinished business.

11. Anthony E. Cook, *The Least of These: Race, Law, and Religion in American Culture* (New York: Routledge, 1997), p. 161.

12. James H. Cone, *Martin and Malcolm and America: A Dream or a Nightmare* (Maryknoll, NY: Orbis Books, 1991), p. 233.

13. Robert L. Short, *The Gospel According to Peanuts* (Richmond, VA: John Knox, 1965), p. 122.

14. Cook, op. cit. n. 11, p.141.

15. I develop the idea of the social self and liberal religion's resistance to it in Rasor, op. cit. n. 2.

16. Bill Wylie-Kellermann, "Exorcising an American Demon," *Sojourners* (March–April 1998).

17. Walter Wink, *Unmasking the Powers: The Invisible Forces That Determine Human Existence* (Minneapolis, MN: Fortress Press, 1986), pp. 67–68.

18. Cook, op. cit. n. 11, p. 113, discussing King's conception of the Beloved Community.

19. Walter Wink, *Engaging the Powers: Discernment and Resistance in a World of Domination* (Minneapolis, MN: Fortress Press, 1992), p. 10.

20. See Francis Schüssler Fiorenza, "Theological Liberalism: An Unfinished Struggle," *Harvard Divinity Bulletin* 28, no. 1 (1998): 9.

21. See especially Tillich's sermon "You Are Accepted" in *The Shaking of the Foundations* (New York: Scribner, 1948), in which Tillich reflects on Paul's words in Romans 5:20: "But where sin abounded, grace did much more abound."

22. Robert Bellah, "Unitarian Universalism in Societal Perspective," address delivered to the General Assembly of the Unitarian

Universalist Association, Rochester, NY, 27 June 1998; available at http://www.uua.org/promise/handbook/bellah.html.

The Paradox of Racial Oppression

1. The best-seller by Richard J. Herrnstein and Charles Murray, *The Bell Curve: Intelligence and Class Structure in American Life* (New York: Simon and Schuster, 1996), is a classic example of such discourse.

2. Michel Foucault, "The Hermeneutics of the Self," in *Religion and Culture*, ed. Jeremy R. Carrette (New York: Routledge, 1999).

3. George Tinker, *Missionary Conquest: The Gospel and Native American Cultural Genocide* (Minneapolis, MN: Fortress Press, 1993).

4. Frantz Fanon, *Black Skin, White Masks* (New York: Grove Press, 1967).

5. Michael Lerner, *Surplus Powerlessness: The Psychodynamics of Everyday Life and the Psychology of Individual and Social Transformation* (Amherst, NY: Humanities Press International, 1986).

6. Martin Luther King Jr., *Where Do We Go from Here: Chaos or Community?* (Boston: Beacon Press, 1967).

7. "Citizens for Tax Justice," *New York Times*, February 11, 2001.

8. Thomas Byrne Edsall and Mary D. Edsall, *Chain Reaction: The Impact of Race, Rights, and Taxes on American Politics* (New York: W.W. Norton, 1991).

9. In identity theory, *encounter* is an early stage of self-awareness in relation to others. This initial encounter often leads to disequilibrium or resistance. See the following sources for further discussion: William E. Cross, Jr., Linda Clark, and Peony Fhagen-Smith, "African American Identity Development Across the Lifespan: Educational Implications" in Etta R. Hollins and Rosa Hernandez Sheets, eds., *Racial and Ethnic Identity in School Practices: Aspects of Human Development* (Mahwah, NJ: Lawrence Erlbaum Associates, Inc., 1999); Janet Helms, *Black and White Racial Identity: Theory, Research, Practice* (Westport, CT: Praeger, 1990); "Racial/Cultural Identity Development" in Gerald Wing Sue and David Sue, *Counseling the Culturally Different* (New York: John Wiley and Sons, 1990).

10. Peggy McIntosh, "White Privilege and Male Privilege: A Personal Account of Coming to See Correspondences Through Work in Women's Studies" (Wellesley, MA: Wellesley College Center for Research on Women, 1988).

Toward a New Paradigm for Uncovering Neo-racism

1. Given the view that uncorrected oppression is the preeminent cause of local and geopolitical unrest, I have predicted for almost four decades that conflict between oppressor and oppressed would enlarge, expand, and explode, and that *counter*-violence would be the response from the wretched of the earth to the *original* violence that established their wretchedness and to the institutionalized violence of government and the sanctioned oppression that maintains it.

2. To understand how equal opportunity differs from equal access, reflect on the image of a set of Olympic tracks and a team of runners. One track goes uphill, another downhill; one is strewn with glass, another with rocks; and the fifth is both level and free of debris. Each runner has equal access, in the sense that no one is excluded; each starts at the same time and runs the same distance. But do all runners have equal opportunity? No. Equal opportunity presupposes that a level playing field is already in place—not in the dream world of imagination, hope, or desire. Former president Lyndon Johnson, who instituted affirmative action programs in the United States, identified a second prerequisite for equal opportunity. Imagine a situation that satisfies the first prerequisite: The playing field is truly level for everyone. But before the race, you pick one runner and strap her leg below the knee to her thigh and make her live that way for a time. At the hour of the race, you remove the strap. By starting at the same time and running the same distance as everyone else the runner is guaranteed equal access but not equal opportunity, which requires—*before the race*—a correction for the deficits, defects, disadvantages, and disabilities created by the prior discrimination.

3. William Milbank, *The Myth of Racism in the Criminal Justice System* (Belmont, CA: Wadsworth, 1987).

4. I summarized my findings in an unpublished article, "Social Policy in the New South Africa: The Demise or Disguise of Apartheid?" which will appear in my forthcoming book, *Beyond the Religion of the Successful*. A later article, "Upon Closer Scrutiny: Assessing Moral Leadership in the Civil Rights Movement," edited by Rick Edmonds and published by the Florida Humanitarians Council Forum, treats this question in the context of one state's (Florida's) history.

5. The Edendale Lay Ecumenical Centre was the first of its kind to be initiated by black South Africans.

6. W. E. B. DuBois, *Dusk of Dawn* (New York: Harcourt and Brace, 1940).

7. The United States Civil Rights Commission also adopts structural oppression as its working hypothesis: "Discrimination against minorities and women must now be viewed as an interlocking process involving the attitudes and actions of individuals and the organization and social structures that guide individual behavior. That process, started by past events, now routinely bestows privileges, favors, and advantages on white males and imposes disadvantages and penalties on minorities and women. This process is also self-perpetuating. Historically, discrimination against minorities and women was not only accepted . . . it was also governmentally required. Overt racism and sexism as embodied in popular notions of white and male supremacy have been widely repudiated, but our history of discrimination based on race, sex, and national origin has not been readily put aside. The blatant racial and sexual discrimination that originated in our conveniently forgotten past, however, continues to manifest itself today in a complex interaction of attitudes and actions of individuals, organizations, and the network of social structures that make up our society. Past discrimination continues to have present effects. The task today is to identify these effects and the forms and dynamics of the discrimination that produced them."

8. Daniel Georges-Abeye, *The Criminal Justice System and Blacks* (New York: C. Broadan, 1984).

9. Douglas G. Anglin, in *South Africa Update*, Inter-Church Coalition on Africa, April 1992.

10. At the consultation the papers were presented in the following order: James Cone, Paul Rasor, Rosemary Bray McNatt, Bill Jones,

Patricia Jimenez, Tink Tinker, Gary Smith, Thandeka, Rebecca Parker.

11. bell hooks, *Killing Rage: Ending Racism* (New York: Henry Holt and Co., 1995).

Not Somewhere Else, But Here:
The Struggle for Racial Justice as a
Struggle to Inhabit My Country

1. James Baldwin, *The Fire Next Time* (New York: Dial Press, 1963).

2. Lillian Eugenia Smith, *Killers of the Dream* (New York: Norton, 1961), pp. 25–29.

3. Ibid., p. 21.

4. William R. Jones, *Is God a White Racist? A Preamble to Black Theology* (Boston: Beacon Press, 1998).

5. Howard Zinn, *A People's History of the United States, 1492–Present* (New York: HarperCollins, 1980).

6. Ronald Takaki, *A Different Mirror* (Boston: Little, Brown and Co., 1993), p. 428.

7. Ibid., p. 428.

8. Cornel West, *Prophesy Deliverance: An Afro-American Revolutionary Christianity* (Louisville, KY: Westminster John Knox Press, 2001), p. 21.

9. W. E. B. DuBois, *The Souls of Black Folk* (New York: W.W. Norton and Co., 1903).

10. Paulo Freire, *Pedagogy of the Oppressed* (New York: Sudbury Press/Continuum, 1970).

About the
Participants

〜

REV. DIANNE E. ARAKAWA is Interim Pastor at the Payson Park Church, UCC, in Belmont, Massachusetts. She has served Unitarian Universalist congregations in Westford, Massachusetts; Woodstock, Illinois; and New York City. Having served on the UUA Commission on Appraisal, she currently serves on the Ministerial Fellowship Committee. She holds degrees from the University of Chicago Divinity School, Harvard Divinity School, and Wheaton College in Massachusetts, and certificates from the Interim Ministry Network and other organizations. Born and raised in Honolulu, Hawaii, she resides with her husband, Rev. Stephen C. Washburn, and their son on the South Shore of Boston.

REV. WAYNE ARNASON is co-minister of the West Shore Unitarian Universalist Church in Cleveland, Ohio, and serves as a trustee-at-large and as secretary of the Unitarian Universalist Association. He is a Zen Buddhist student in the Soto tradition. His remarks, included as part of Rev. John Buehrens's response to Dr. James Cone's essay, were delivered at a worship service for the UUA Board of Trustees.*

REV. JOSÉ BALLESTER was born of Puerto Rican parents in New York City. In 1981 he left the Opera Company of Boston and entered Andover Newton Theological School. Ordained in 1984, he has served congregations in Malden, Braintree, Brockton, and Orange, Massachusetts, and Woonsocket, Rhode Island. From 1994 to 2001 he served as Associate Director of Member Action for the Unitarian Universalist Service Committee (UUSC), where he created the Just Works program. He is co-founder of the Latina/o Unitarian Universalist Networking Association (LUUNA).

234 SOUL WORK

REV. DR. GEORGE KIMMICH BEACH was ordained in 1961 and has served parish ministries in Massachusetts, Texas, and Virginia, where for eighteen years he was Senior Minister of the UU Church of Arlington. He also served a community ministry in Cleveland, Ohio, and interim ministries in Florida, New Jersey, and Virginia before retiring from full-time ministry. He is a graduate of Oberlin College and Harvard Divinity School and received a doctor of ministry degree from Wesley Theological School in Washington, D.C. He served as a member of the UUA Commission on Appraisal and edited three volumes of essays and addresses by James Luther Adams. His book on existential theology, *Questions for the Religious Journey,* will be reissued in 2002 by Skinner House Books. He was the 1999 Minns Lecturer speaking on the theme "The Parables of James Luther Adams," a synthesis of Adams's theological and ethical thought.

REV. MARJORIE BOWENS-WHEATLEY is the Adult Programs director for the Unitarian Universalist Association. She has served congregations in Austin, Texas, and in New York City; and as an anti-racism consultant and trainer in the UUA Metro New York District and for the Unitarian Universalist Association. She is a contributing author of three books: *Essex Conversations: Visions for Lifespan Religious Education; Interdependence: Renewing Congregational Polity* (the 1997 report of the Unitarian Universalist Association Commission on Appraisal); and *Weaving the Fabric of Diversity.* She holds degrees from American University and Wesley Theological Seminary. Bowens-Wheatley served as a member (and past chair) of the UUA Commission on Appraisal, and was a funding member of the African American Unitarian Universalist Ministry (AAUUM).

REV. SUSAN SUCHOCKI BROWN is a born Unitarian Universalist. She has been a parish minister in Leominster, Massachusetts, since 1992. Since 1997, she has chaired the Unitarian Universalist Association's Journey Toward Wholeness Transformation Committee. She has also served on the Unitarian Universalist Association Board of Trustees, was Massachusetts Bay District President, and served on the Ministerial Fellowship Committee. She holds a master of divinity degree and is a candidate for the doctor of ministry degree at Andover Newton Theological School.

She serves as chaplain to the Leominster Fire Department, the first female and the first Unitarian Universalist chaplain in the state of Massachusetts to do so.

REV. JOHN BUEHRENS served as president of the Unitarian Universalist Association from 1993 to 2001. A graduate of Harvard College and Harvard Divinity School, he currently serves as minister of First Parish in Needham, Massachusetts. He has served as a parish minister in Knoxville, Dallas, and New York City. He is currently Special Assistant to the Secretary General of the World Conference on Religion and Peace.

REV. DR. JAMES CONE is the Charles A. Briggs Distinguished professor of Systematic Theology at Union Theological Seminary in New York, where he has taught since 1969. He received a master's degree and a doctor of philosophy degree from Northwestern University in 1963 and 1965, respectively, and has been awarded eight honorary degrees, including doctor of laws, doctor of humanities, and doctor of divinity. He is an ordained minister in the African Methodist Episcopal Church. His research and teachings are in Christian theology, with special attention to black theology; the theologies of Africa, Asia, and Latin America; and twentieth-century European American theologies. He has published many books; the latest is *Risks of Faith: The Emergence of a Black Liberation Theology* (Beacon Press, 2000).

REV. DANIELLE DI BONA is a Unitarian Universalist community minister. Before coming to the Unitarian Universalist Association as program coordinator for anti-racism training, Rev. Di Bona served as Spiritual Care Coordinator for the Visiting Nurse Association Hospice of Cleveland, Ohio. She is the vice president of Diverse and Revolutionary Unitarian Universalist Multicultural Ministries (DRUMM) and is a convener of its Ministry Working Group. She lives with her husband, Larry Beck, in Onset, Massachusetts, where they enjoy the companionship of their three dogs and a cat.

ROBETTE DIAS is co-director of Crossroads Ministry and was formerly an anti-racism program and People of Color program manager for the Unitarian Universalist Association's Faith in Action

Department, providing training, technical support, and advocacy for the Journey Toward Wholeness initiative. She is a member of the Journey Toward Wholeness Transformation Committee. Robette is a founding member and past president of Diverse and Revolutionary Unitarian Universalist Multicultural Ministries (DRUUMM).**

REV. ELIZABETH ELLIS is the director of the Social Witness Program at Pendle Hill, a Quaker study and retreat center. She was a fellow with Harvard Divinity School's Urban Ministry Fellowship Program. She served as an associate minister and then senior minister-at-large and executive director of the Unitarian Universalist Urban Ministry in Boston, a UU presence in low-income communities since 1826. Under her leadership, the UU Urban Ministry established a shelter for battered women and their children and a program of alternatives to violence for youth gang members, ran a successful capital campaign to restore the First Church in Roxbury, organized a clergy coalition to address public policy issues concerning low-income children, and established programs for men coming out of prison. She is a former president of the Unitarian Universalist Christian Fellowship.

REV. DR. ANITA FARBER-ROBERTSON has been a parish minister since 1980 and has served UU congregations in Canton, Swampscott, and Rockport, Massachusetts. She also served as associate minister at Zion Baptist Church, in Lynn, Massachusetts. She serves as adjunct professor of communications at Andover Newton Theological School and is the author of *Learning While Leading: Increasing Your Effectiveness in Ministry* (Alban Institute, 2000). She is the daughter of an American mother of Jewish background and a German father of Lutheran background.

REV. DR. WILLIAM GARDINER serves as the director for anti-racism and social justice empowerment training programs at the Unitarian Universalist Association. He is a graduate of Crane Theological School at Tufts University and holds a doctor of ministry degree from Vanderbilt Divinity School. He has served as a parish minister in Washington, D.C.; Nashville, Tennessee; and Philadelphia, Pennsylvania.**

REV. MELVIN HOOVER served as co-minister (with his wife, Rose Edington) of the Unitarian Universalist Fellowship of the Kanawha Valley in Charleston, West Virginia, and as director of Interfaith Partnerships for the Unitarian Universalist Association. He is the former director of the Association's Department for Faith in Action of the Unitarian Universalist Association. In this capacity, he led the Association's faith-based justice-making efforts and coordinated its anti-oppression, anti-racist, and multicultural initiative. He serves on the Religious Leaders Roundtable for the National Conference for Community and Justice. He has three children—Leonard, James, and Melanie. Rev. Hoover is also involved in the business community in progressive economic development and sustainable economies.

REV. PATRICIA JIMENEZ is a Unitarian Universalist minister who currently serves as a hospital chaplain in Oakland, California. She has also served in a chaplaincy in Lansing, Michigan. Rev. Jimenez was born and grew up in New Mexico. She served on the steering committee of what was to become the Latino/a Unitarian Universalist Networking Association (LUUNA) and was elected its first chair. She also attended the first meetings of the group that would become Diverse and Revolutionary Unitarian Universalist Multicultural Ministries (DRUUMM), served on its steering committee, and helped it to begin the Multicultural Families group.

NANCY PALMER JONES graduated from Harvard Divinity School in June 2002 with a master of divinity degree. She hopes to build a parish ministry in which she and her congregants walk together in their commitment to anti-racism and anti-oppression work. Nancy did her field education work on white identity in the Unitarian Universalist Association's Faith in Action Department and served as liaison to the interdepartmental Youth Anti-Racism Working Group. Originally from Texas, she has lived in San Francisco and New York City.

REV. DR. WILLIAM R. JONES is professor emeritus at Florida State University and director of the Policy Institute for Conflict, Oppression, and Terrorism Studies (PICOTS), a new think tank at Tallahassee Community College that explores linkages among religion, oppression, and conflict. He received a bachelor degree from Howard University, a master of divinity degree from Harvard University, and doctor of philosophy degree in religious studies from Brown University. An internationally recognized scholar, he received the Unitarian Universalist Association's 2001 Distinguished Service Award.

SUSAN LESLIE holds a bachelor of arts degree in political science from the University of New Hampshire. She is the director of Congregational Advocacy and Witness for the Unitarian Universalist Association and has served as associate director for the Faith in Action Department. Prior to her service at the UUA, Susan worked in publishing at Harvard University Press and Banner Press. She has a long history of community organizing and has held staff positions with Volunteers in Service to America, the New Hampshire People's Alliance, the New England Municipal Center, and Refuse and Resist. Susan is the mother of a four-year-old named Kieran and the wife of Bruce Pritchard.**

VICTOR LEE LEWIS is founder and Director of the Center for Diversity Leadership (CDL), a human relations training and consulting firm. He specializes in teaching, inspiring, and supporting individuals and organizations of all sizes to create unified communities of commitment that can heal and dismantle racism, sexism, anti-Semitism, homophobia and the other "isms" that undermine people's ability to live, love, and work well together. Lewis is best known for his inspiring and catalytic leadership role as a prophetic voice of *The Color of Fear,* an unusually powerful film about racism which received the Golden Apple Award for "Best Social Studies Documentary" of 1995 from the National Educational Media Association. He holds a master's degree in Culture and Spirituality from Holy Names College and is a doctoral candidate at the University of Creation Spirituality.

REV. ROSEMARY BRAY MCNATT has been an author and editor for more than twenty years. She currently serves as minister at Fourth Universalist Church in New York City, and she has also served as consulting minister to the Skylands Unitarian Universalist Fellowship in Hackettstown, New Jersey. Rev. Bray McNatt holds a master of divinity degree from Drew University Theological School and a bachelor degree from Yale University. She is the author of several books, including *Unafraid of the Dark: A Memoir; Martin Luther King;* and *Beloved One: Prayers for Black Children.* McNatt writes the "Reverend Mother" column on parenting and spirituality for Beliefnet.com and is a contributing editor for the *UU World* magazine. She serves on the Board of Trustees at The Mountain, a Unitarian Universalist camp and conference center in North Carolina; is former chair of the Board of Trustees of Starr King School for the Ministry; and is co-chair of the Jessie Smith Noyes Foundation. She lives in New York City with her husband, Robert, and their two sons, Allen and Daniel.

REV. PETER MORALES was born and raised in San Antonio, Texas. He holds a master of divinity degree from Starr King School for the Ministry. Currently he serves as the director of District Services for the Unitarian Universalist Association. He was senior minister at Jefferson Unitarian Church in Golden, Colorado. He serves on the Unitarian Universalist Association Board of Trustees and on the Latina/o Unitarian Universalist Networking Association (LUUNA) steering committee. Prior to entering the ministry, he was an editor and publisher of community newspapers in Oregon.

REV. DR. FRED MUIR grew up in Oak Park, Illinois. He holds a master of divinity degree from Union Theological Seminary and a doctor of ministry degree from Wesley Theological Seminary. Since 1983, he has served as minister of the UU Church of Annapolis, Maryland. He is the author of three books: *A Reason for Hope: Liberation Theology Confronts a Liberal Faith; Heretics' Faith: A Vocabulary for Religious Liberals;* and *Maglipay Universalist: The Unitarian Universalist Church of the Philippines.* He has done extensive work for the Unitarian Universalist Association on sexual misconduct and safe congregations. He is a co-facilitator of the Empowerment Workshop for the Department of Faith in Action and serves on the UUA's Joseph Priestley District's anti-racism team and the Mid-Atlantic Regional Subcommittee on [Ministerial] Candidacy. He has been married to Karen for 28 years; they have two children.

REV. DR. KENNETH OLLIFF is currently a candidate for the doctor of theology degree at Harvard Divinity School. Ordained to the Unitarian Universalist ministry, he holds a doctor of ministry degree from Meadville Lombard Theological School. While at Meadville, he also served for five years as faculty administrator. He is editor of the *Journal of Liberal Religion* (www.meadville.edu/jlr.htm) and edited and introduced *Through the Rose Window: Art, Myth and the Religious Imagination* by John F. Hayward (Skinner House Books, 2002).

REV. DR. REBECCA PARKER is president and professor of theology at the Starr King School for the Ministry. She is an ordained United Methodist minister, with dual fellowship at the United Methodist Church and the Unitarian Universalist Association. She holds a doctor of ministry degree from the School of Theology at Claremont, California, and a bachelor's degree from the University of Puget Sound in Washington. Her latest book, co-authored with Rita Nakashima Brock, is *Proverbs of Ashes: Violence, Redemptive Suffering and the Search for What Saves Us* (Beacon Press, 2001). Parker is experienced as an educator, committed to social activism, practiced in the life of pastoral ministry, and dedicated to the discipline of theological thinking and writing. She participates regularly in academic conferences and meetings, where she presents papers and lectures on her special interests in feminist theology, religion and the arts, spirituality and sexuality, and process theology. She served on the United Methodist Study Committee on Homosexuality and on the Board of Directors of the Center for the Prevention of Sexual and Domestic Violence, a national educational center in Seattle.

REV. DR. PAUL RASOR is director of the Social Witness Program at Pendle Hill, the Quaker study center near Philadelphia. He has served as assistant minister at First Parish in Lexington, Massachusetts. With a doctor of philosophy degree in theology from Harvard University, Rasor has taught liberal theologies at Andover Newton Theological School. He has also been a law professor, a classical and jazz musician, a factory worker, a truck driver, a chess player, a Central American activist, and an actor.

Rev. Dr. Tracey Robinson-Harris serves as the director of Congregational Services for the Unitarian Universalist Association. Her portfolio includes anti-racism training, organizational and leadership development, growth and extension, work with field staff and volunteer leadership in the Unitarian Universalist Association's twenty-one districts, and urban ministries. Ordained in 1982, Tracey has served congregations in Virginia, Tennessee, Massachusetts, and New York.

Rev. Thomas R. Schade is Associate Minister at the First Unitarian Church in Worcester, Massachusetts. He holds a master of divinity degree from Perkins School of Theology at Southern Methodist University in Dallas, Texas. Schade has been married to Sue Schade since 1976. They parent two young women.

Rev. Gary E. Smith has been Senior Minister of the First Parish in Concord, Massachusetts, since 1988. He is past President of the Unitarian Universalist Ministers Association (1998–2001). Born and raised in Maine, he holds a master of divinity degree from the Divinity School at Vanderbilt University. Prior to accepting the call to serve as minister in Concord, he served the Unitarian Universalist Association staff as Director of the Visions for Growth capital campaign, Special Assistant to the President for Public Outreach, and Director for Public Relations. He and his wife, Elizabeth, have two adult children, Jonathan and Hannah.

Dr. Leon E. Spencer is Associate Professor of Psychology and Coordinator for the Community Counseling Graduate Program at Georgia Southern University. He holds master's and doctor of philosophy degrees in counseling psychology and specializes in family systems and cross-cultural counseling. Dr. Spencer has been a Unitarian Universalist for thirty-five years and currently serves as president of the Thomas Jefferson District of the Unitarian Universalist Association. He is a member of the Journey Toward Wholeness Transformation Committee and a former member of the Unitarian Universalist Association Board of Trustees. He is also President of the Research and Assessment Corporation for Counseling of the National Board for Certified Counselors.

REV. DR. THANDEKA is associate professor of theology and culture at Meadville Lombard Theological School in Chicago and affiliated minister at the Unitarian Universalist Church in Rockford, Illinois. She is author of *The Embodied Self: Friedrich Schleiermacher's Solution to Kant's Problem of the Empirical Self* (State University of New York Press, 1995) and *Learning to Be White: Money, Race and God in America* (Continuum, 1999). Before receiving her doctor of philosophy degree from Claremont Graduate School, Thandeka was an Emmy Award-winning television producer for sixteen years. She is currently at work on a book about systematic theology, the first volume of which will focus on the doctrine of human nature.

REV. DR. GEORGE "TINK" TINKER is Professor of American Indian Cultures and Religious Traditions at Iliff School of Theology in Denver. A faculty member there since 1985, Dr. Tinker teaches courses in American Indian culture, history, and religious traditions, cross-cultural and Third World theologies, and justice and peace studies. An ordained Lutheran pastor, Dr. Tinker continues to work in the Indian community as (nonstipendiary) director of the Four Winds American Indian Survival Project in Denver. He serves as "Honorary Advisor" to the International Movement Against all Forms of Discrimination and Racism (IMADR). He holds a doctorate of philosophy degree from the Graduate Theological Union, a master of divinity degree from Pacific Lutheran Theological Seminary, and a bachelor's degree from New Mexico Highlands University.

REV. JoELLEN WILLIS is a minister of the Unitarian Universalist Church of Little Rock. Before ordination, she directed religious education programs for congregations in Ridgewood and Montclair, New Jersey. She received her master of divinity degree from Drew University and was an interim minister in Westport, Connecticut, and Huntington, New York. Active in community and interfaith initiatives, she is vice president of the Arkansas Interfaith Conference. When tornadoes hit central Arkansas in 1997 and again in 1999, she worked with other members of the interfaith community to provide assistance in rebuilding homes destroyed by the storms. As a result of that involvement, she was a founding member and currently serves as president of the

Interfaith Disaster Recovery Team (IDRT), an organization that works with other nonprofit and governmental agencies to provide long-term support for rebuilding after disasters. Following the events of September 11, 2001, JoEllen was asked to participate in the Central Arkansas Interfaith Diversity Council, a coalition of faith and government leaders seeking to provide accurate information about all religious traditions.

*Did not attend the consultation
**Participant-observer

Acknowledgments

꧖

Organizing the work of twenty-seven writers and presenters was a challenging task. We wish to thank John Buehrens for his support of this project and Mel Hoover and Susan Leslie for not letting an idea die and for accepting the challenge of making this long-held vision a reality. We are grateful to colleagues—Danielle Di Bona, Judith Frediani, Pat Hoertdoerfer, Jacqui James, and Susan Leslie—for reviewing the manuscript and helping to formulate study questions. Thanks to Mary Benard and the UUA's Publications Office for their patience and guidance in making this book readable as well as for production and marketing. Thanks to Emily Mace, Jamain Persad, and Barbara Gifford for invaluable support in executing the many tasks for the consultation and for proofreading and reviewing the manuscript in its many stages. And finally, to all the participants and observers for their dedication and commitment to helping us to dig deeper in a subject of such vital import, and yet so often treated superficially.